BUDDHISM, KNOWLEDGE AND LIBERATION

Buddhism is essentially a teaching about liberation – from suffering, ignorance, selfishness and continued rebirth. Knowledge of 'the way things really are' is thought by many Buddhists to be vital in bringing about this emancipation. This book is a philosophical study of the notion of liberating knowledge as it occurs in a range of Buddhist sources.

Buddhism, Knowledge and Liberation assesses the common Buddhist idea that knowledge of the three characteristics of existence (impermanence, not-self and suffering) is the key to liberation. It argues that this claim must be seen in the context of the Buddhist path and training as a whole. Detailed attention is also given to anti-realist, sceptical and mystical strands within the Buddhist tradition, all of which make distinctive claims about liberating knowledge and the nature of reality. David Burton seeks to uncover various problematic assumptions which underpin the Buddhist worldview.

Sensitive to the wide diversity of philosophical perspectives and interpretations that Buddhism has engendered, this book makes a serious contribution to critical and philosophically aware engagement with Buddhist thought. Written in an accessible style, it will be of value to those interested in Buddhist Studies and broader issues in comparative philosophy and religion.

Ashgate World Philosophies Series

The Ashgate World Philosophies Series responds to the remarkable growth of interest among English-language readers in recent years in philosophical traditions outside those of 'the West'. The traditions of Indian, Chinese and Japanese thought, as well as those of the Islamic world, Latin America, Africa, Aboriginal Australian, Pacific and American Indian peoples, are all attracting lively attention from professional philosophers and students alike, and this new Ashgate series provides introductions to these traditions as well as in-depth research into central issues and themes within those traditions. The series is particularly designed for readers whose interests are not adequately addressed by general surveys of 'World Philosophy', and it includes accessible, yet research-led, texts for wider readership and upper-level student use, as well as research monographs. The series embraces a wide variety of titles ranging from introductions on particular world philosophies and informed surveys of the philosophical contributions of geographical regions, to in-depth discussion of a theme, topic, problem or movement and critical appraisals of individual thinkers or schools of thinkers.

Series Editors:
David E. Cooper, University of Durham, UK
Robert C. Solomon, University of Texas, Austin, USA
Kathleen M. Higgins, University of Texas, Austin, USA
Purushottama Bilimoria, Deakin University, Australia

Other titles in the series:

An Introduction to Yoga Philosophy
An Annotated Translation of the Yoga Sutras
Ashok Kumar Malhotra

Knowing Beyond Knowledge
Epistemologies of Religious Experience in Classical and Modern Advaita
Thomas A. Forsthoefel

Mencius, Hume and the Foundations of Ethics
Xiusheng Liu

Comparative Approaches to Chinese Philosophy
Edited by Bo Mou

Personal Identity and Buddhist Philosophy
Empty Persons
Mark Siderits

An Introduction to the Mādhva Vedānta
Deepak Sarma

Buddhism, Knowledge and Liberation

A Philosophical Study

DAVID BURTON
Mount Saint Vincent University, Canada

ASHGATE

Published by
Ashgate Publishing Limited
Gower House, Croft Road
Aldershot, Hants
GU11 3HR
England

Ashgate Publishing Company
Suite 420
101 Cherry Street
Burlington, VT 05401–4405
USA

Ashgate website: http://www.ashgatepublishing.com

British Library Cataloguing in Publication Data
Burton, David (David F.)
Buddhism, knowledge and liberation : a philosophical study.
– (Ashgate world philosophies series)
1. Enlightenment (Buddhism) 2. Suffering–Religious aspects
–Buddhism
I. Title
294.3'442

US Library of Congress Cataloging-in-Publication Data
Burton, David, 1966–
Buddhism, knowledge and liberation : a philosophical analysis of suffering / David Burton.
p. cm. – (Ashgate world philosophies series)
Includes bibliographical references and index (alk. paper).
1. Suffering–Religious aspects–Buddhism. 2. Buddhism–Doctrines. 3. Knowledge, Theory of (Buddhism). I. Title. II. Series.

BQ4235.B87 2004
294.3'42118–dc21

2003048197

ISBN 0 7546 0436 5 (Pbk)
ISBN 0 7546 0435 7 (Hbk)

This book is printed on acid-free paper

Typeset in Times Roman by N²productions
Printed by MPG Books Ltd, Bodmin, Cornwall.

Contents

Preface

I am indebted to Keble College and the Faculty of Theology of the University of Oxford where I was the Gordon Milburn Junior Research Fellow from 1998 to 2001. Much of the research for this book was completed during this period. Further work has been done while I have been a member of the Department of Philosophy/Religious Studies at Mount Saint Vincent University in Halifax, Nova Scotia. Thanks are due to the University for providing an internal research grant to assist with the cost of preparing the manuscript.

I would also like to thank Michael McGhee, Elizabeth English, Jonardon Ganeri, Paul Williams, John Schellenberg, Dan Satterthwaite, Franky Henley and Robert Morrison for comments and/or discussions which have influenced the content of this book. I am very grateful to Sarah Lloyd and everyone at Ashgate Publishing Limited for including this work in their 'World Philosophies' series. Finally, I would like to express my heartfelt gratitude to Franky Henley (Vajrashraddha) for her love, understanding, constant friendship and enthusiastic appreciation of life.

Buddhist thought has been expressed in many Oriental languages. In this book I have chosen to give technical terms in the Sanskrit unless the context demands the Pāli or Tibetan. In the interests of readability and accessibility to non-specialists, translations of texts are given in English, without the Pāli, Sanskrit or Tibetan originals. Unless otherwise indicated, translations are my own.

CHAPTER ONE

First Thoughts on Knowledge and Liberation

Religious traditions commonly offer an account of what they consider to be the human spiritual predicament. Buddhism is no exception. It generally says that the root difficulty faced by human beings is suffering (*duḥkha*) which is caused by the appropriative, selfish desire of craving (*tṛṣṇā*). And Buddhists often say that craving is itself rooted in ignorance (*avidyā*). Our craving is fuelled by lack of understanding. This is not any ignorance, however. Craving is not caused by unawareness that Little Rock is the capital city of Arkansas or of how to make soufflés, for instance. On the contrary, it is ignorance of 'how things really are' that is thought to produce craving and hence suffering.

Like many other religions, Buddhism not only gives an analysis of the human spiritual predicament but also offers a solution. Indeed, the principal concern of Buddhism is to provide an answer to the problem of suffering. Buddhist texts often describe the Buddha metaphorically as the 'Great Physician'. Buddhism is fundamentally about providing a cure for a disease. However, the disease of suffering is not an ordinary, physical sickness and the cure is not potions or ointments. As suffering is thought to be caused by ignorance of 'how things really are', the cure for suffering is said to be the removal of this cause. Buddhism is thus intensely engaged with eradicating this ignorance which, it thinks, lies at the heart of our spiritual malady.

The opposite of ignorance is knowledge or understanding. Ignorance is not knowing or not understanding. For instance, if I do not know or understand that Julius Caesar was a Roman emperor then I am ignorant about this fact. My ignorance is dispelled when I achieve knowledge or understanding that Julius Caesar was a Roman emperor. Similarly, the ignorance of 'how things really are' is eradicated by knowledge or understanding of the true nature of things.

Buddhism often maintains, therefore, that the cessation of suffering requires knowledge (*jñāna*) or understanding (*prajñā*, sometimes translated as 'insight' or even 'wisdom') of 'how things really are'. The Buddhist claim is that liberating knowledge has the true nature of things as its special content. This knowledge is considered to be the cure that will cut off suffering. Hence, the people who have transcended craving and suffering are said to have achieved Awakening (*bodhi*) and are Awakened (*buddha*), indicating that they have 'woken up' to the true nature of reality. Buddhism is thus, in many of its forms, a gnostic soteriology in so far as it identifies knowledge, or gnosis, as a necessary condition for liberation.

This is a characteristic which it shares with a variety of other Indian philosophical and religious traditions, such as Advaita Vedānta, Sāṃkhya, Nyāya-Vaiśeṣika, Jainism and others. However, there is an important difference. These non-Buddhist systems claim that liberation (*mokṣa*) results from insight into an eternal essence, soul or abiding self, variously called the *ātman*, *puruṣa* or *jīva*. For instance, Advaita Vedānta says that people attain liberation when they achieve the understanding that the essential, eternal self (*ātman*) is identical with the one, non-dual Absolute reality (*brahman*). Sāṃkhya describes liberation as occurring when individual, eternal consciousnesses (*puruṣa*) achieve isolation or separation (*kaivalya*) from the material world (*prakṛti*) by means of insight into their real nature. Nyāya-Vaiśeṣika agrees that the individual souls or essential selves (*ātman*) can break free from the material world by means of such knowledge. Jains also speak of the need to understand that the individual and eternal soul (*jīva*) is distinct from the material world, including the body, by which it is trapped. The belief in such an eternal, spiritual essence of the person has been a feature of much popular Indian religiosity.

By contrast, we will see that the Buddhist liberating knowledge does not involve insight into the true nature of the eternal soul or self, but rather the understanding that no such entity exists. The insight into not-self (*anātman*) is basic to Buddhist soteriology. A prevalent Buddhist formulation of 'how things really are' declares that all conditioned things are (1) impermanent, (2) suffering and (3) devoid of self. These are called the 'three characteristics of existence'. The Awakened Buddhists are those who stop craving because they understand that everything is impermanent, that no thing has an eternal essence, and that suffering occurs because we crave for and get attached to such impermanent, essenceless phenomena. This book is a philosophical exploration of this Buddhist liberating knowledge of 'how things really are'.

A brief synopsis

Chapter 2 examines in detail these three characteristics of existence. In addition, the chapter explores the nature of craving and why it is thought to cause suffering. Also, it discusses the Buddhist idea that one's craving is rooted in ignorance of the three characteristics and that the solution to the problem of craving, and hence suffering, involves knowledge of impermanence, suffering and not-self. The chapter also uncovers a number of debatable philosophical claims that underlie the Buddhist analysis.

Chapter 3 discusses the apparent conundrum that many people seem to understand the three characteristics and yet still crave and suffer. If this knowledge is supposed to be liberating, how is it that such people have not put an end to their craving and suffering? Various solutions to this problem are critically examined, all of which distinguish Unawakened people's *deficient* understanding of the three characteristics from the Awakened people's *thorough* knowledge of them. According to Buddhism, only the thorough knowledge is sufficient to remove craving and suffering.

For instance, the Awakened people's knowledge might be depicted as knowledge by acquaintance, whereas Unawakened people have a merely propositional knowledge or knowledge by description. Or else Unawakened people, though in some cases apparently believing that things are impermanent, selfless and cause suffering when craved, might be said to have an unconscious belief to the contrary. Finally, the Awakened people's knowledge of the three characteristics might be characterized by meditative reflection and constant attentiveness, which is absent from the Unawakened people's more distracted and reflectively shallow understanding.

Chapter 4 evaluates two ideas that seem to underpin the Buddhist account of liberating knowledge. First, there is the moral belief that suffering ought to be overcome. Buddhism appears to claim that thorough knowledge of the three characteristics entails the moral judgement that one should not crave impermanent, selfless things because this craving will cause suffering. The way the world is has implications for how we should act. In short, Buddhism seems to derive an 'ought' from an 'is' in a way that is problematic from the perspective of a moral relativist. That is, Buddhism seems not to make a fact-value distinction, regarding 'the way things really are' as including what might be called 'moral facts'. Second, the Buddhist account of liberating knowledge appears sometimes to imply that knowledge alone can compel one to change one's behaviour. If one has the thorough knowledge that one ought not to crave, then one gives up craving once and for all. Is it really the case, however, that knowledge alone, even thorough knowledge, will necessarily stop one from doing what one knows one ought not to do and not doing what one knows one should do?

In reply to this question, I argue that for many Buddhists it is not in fact the case that knowledge by itself brings about liberation. While Buddhists do contend that craving is rooted in ignorance they also say that ignorance is sustained by craving. They are mutually supporting phenomena. It is thus inaccurate to see Buddhism as only concerned with replacing ignorance with knowledge. On the contrary, liberating knowledge needs to be viewed in the context of the Buddhist path as a whole, which emphasizes the cultivation of one's entire character, which includes correct behavioural habits and emotional attitudes as much as the intellect. The cognitive and non-cognitive aspects of the practitioner's personality are to be developed in tandem. Liberating knowledge is the outcome of a comprehensive training that stresses not only development of one's understanding but also diligence in moral observance. One stops craving and becomes unselfish and non-appropriative because of ethical endeavour in conjunction with knowledge.

In Chapter 5, the focus is on a variety of 'anti-realist' Buddhist understandings of the not-self idea, according to which having no self means not just that entities are dependently originating and have no permanent essence but also that these entities are unreal or fabricated. Particular attention is given to the Madhyamaka notion of emptiness (*śūnyatā*), which can be interpreted to mean that all things are conceptual constructions. Other forms of Buddhist anti-realism, found in the Sautrāntika, Sarvāstivāda and Yogācāra traditions, are also discussed. I consider the Buddhist anti-realists' claim that liberating knowledge includes the perception of the merely fabricated nature of things. However, I argue that there are some serious philosophical problems with Buddhist anti-realism, especially in its Madhyamaka form where it seems particularly extreme.

Chapter 6 considers the very different interpretation that Buddhism is a form of scepticism, and that, far from seeking knowledge of 'how things really are', some Buddhist texts seem to encourage the practitioner to realize that such knowledge is impossible, and that hankering after it is a form of craving. The unfabricated 'things in themselves' are always hidden from view. They are unknowable, being veiled by the interpretive activity of the mind. Entities *as experienced* are fabricated by the mind, which always construes them in terms of its own concepts of space, time, causality and so forth.

Special consideration is given to a reading of Madhyamaka Buddhism – different from the anti-realist interpretation presented in Chapter 5 – according to which the Mādhyamikas are advocating such a sceptical variety of Buddhism. It is also possible, I suggest, to construe the early Buddhism of the Theravāda scriptures as promoting a sceptical soteriology. I argue that it is a debatable point whether these Buddhists, understood as sceptics, are right to be so pessimistic about the prospects for knowledge. I propose an alternative and more optimistic Buddhist theory of knowledge that is a type of moderate epistemological realism.

Buddhist sources not uncommonly refer to the true nature of things as ineffable. Chapter 7 is a critical study of this idea and identifies a variety of ways in which it might be understood. I focus particularly on the idea of the inexpressible knowledge of an ineffable reality as it occurs in some Yogācāra and Madhyamaka sources. I consider the possibility that these philosophies might be best construed as forms of 'mystical scepticism', where the ineffable 'things in themselves' are unknowable only for Unawakened people. By contrast, the Awakened people can strip away the veil of fabrications which conceals reality and attain an inexpressible insight into these 'things in themselves'. The common Buddhist notion that *nirvāṇa* and the Awakened person's knowledge of it are ineffable is also explored. I suggest that for many Buddhists liberating knowledge is not only of the three characteristics of existence, but also of a sacred reality which transcends words and the spatio-temporal world of impermanent, dependently originating things. In addition, some important philosophical objections to the Buddhist idea of such a mystical gnosis are considered.

In the conclusion, Chapter 8, I discuss the relationship between liberating knowledge and two other key Buddhist virtues, namely, compassion and faith. Furthermore, I consider the possibility that most human beings are unlikely, even with considerable effort, to transcend completely their moral and cognitive imperfections. They are not able entirely to cut off behavioural and intellectual faults and I argue that Buddhism has often accepted this to be the case. Buddhist liberation or spiritual awakening, understood as the transcendence of all craving and ignorance about 'how things really are', might thus be considered a virtually unattainable 'regulative ideal' that teaches and reminds Buddhists that values such as wisdom, compassion and non-attachment are to be cherished and cultivated even if they cannot usually be perfected.

The diversity of Buddhism

Buddhism is a vast and multi-faceted phenomenon. Damien Keown (1996, pp. 1–3) uses the famous Indian story, related by the Buddha at *Udāna* 69 f., of the elephant and the blind men to explain the dangers of partial understanding of Buddhism. According to this tale, a king divides his blind subjects into groups and they are taken to an elephant and asked to feel it. Each group of blind men grasps only one part of the animal – the trunk, the tail, the head, the foot and so on – and take this to be the character of the entire elephant. Similarly, Keown says, there has been a tendency to grasp one aspect of Buddhism and incorrectly take it to be the whole. Thus, one needs to be aware not only of misapprehensions but also of partial characterizations.

In addition, it should not be assumed that there is one fundamental 'Buddhism' that underlies all of the manifestations. Instead, some scholars have suggested that we might take Buddhism to be an 'umbrella concept' that refers to a family of distinct though interrelated religious phenomena. Buddhism might not be simply *one* animal after all. It might be argued that to seek to identify some essence shared by all or, at least, most forms of Buddhism is thus misguided.

Whether or not there is a common core to the various forms of Buddhism is a moot point and a debate which I do not wish to explore further here. However, it seems fair to say that these diverse Buddhisms, with or without a shared essence, often have strong conceptual connections with and resemblances to one another. They are not utterly distinct and often have overlapping terminology, values and assumptions.

One basic assumption shared by many, though certainly not all, forms of Buddhism is that knowledge of the true nature of things is vital for achieving liberation from suffering. However, as this study will show, it is not necessarily the case that the various forms of Buddhism which make this assumption agree about the precise content or nature of this knowledge. Many Buddhists would contend that knowledge of 'how things really are' is required for liberation, but there is considerable divergence about how this knowledge is to be characterized. One of the tasks of this book will be to demonstrate some of this diversity.

I will not endeavour to investigate Buddhism as a whole, which is surely a nearly impossible task. On the contrary, I will be highly selective. This is due in part to the limitations of my knowledge and partly a result of my specific interests. My hope is that the ideas expressed in this volume will provide some basis for further creative philosophizing by thinkers whose understanding of Buddhism and philosophical acumen complement and/or exceed my own. My ideas rely heavily on early Buddhism, as recorded in the Theravāda scriptures, on certain philosophical developments within Indian non-Mahāyāna and Mahāyāna Buddhism as well as on some Tibetan Buddhist notions. My emphasis is on Indian, Tibetan and Theravāda Buddhism, with only occasional references to the East Asian traditions and some developments in contemporary Buddhism.

Admittedly, there are types of Buddhism – for example, its Pure Land and Vajrayāna forms – in which devotion to a salvific Buddha or Bodhisattva, rather than liberating knowledge, has a primary role. My concern here, however, is with types of Buddhism that stress knowledge and liberation rather than devotion and salvation in the quest to transcend suffering. This is certainly not to imply that the forms of Buddhism that stress salvific devotion are less authentic, inferior or less worthy of study than the gnostic Buddhism on which I concentrate.

Nor is it to suggest that the gnostic Buddhist's liberating strategy is exclusively concerned with knowledge. Far from it, the Buddhist liberating knowledge is often presented as an outcome of a 'path' that includes ethical conduct, faith and meditation as essential components. It will be one of my contentions in the present study, especially in Chapter 4, that the liberating knowledge that eradicates suffering cannot be understood in isolation from the entire Buddhist training which is its context and of which it is the fruition.

The philosophical study of Buddhism

The approach taken in this book will perhaps be frustrating to the historically or anthropologically minded reader, interested mainly in the detailed social and intellectual context of Buddhist ideas to which I refer, and to the philologist intent on unravelling the linguistic complexities of ancient Buddhist texts. Though I make substantial use of such texts, and am not oblivious to their historical and social context, my primary aim is to engage in philosophical reflection upon the Buddhist soteriology. Buddhist ideas as expressed in the various traditions thus function as a touchstone for philosophizing. By 'philosophizing' here I mean thinking in a critically aware manner about fundamental issues and concepts in Buddhist thought such as the nature of reality and the knowledge of it, why knowledge of reality is thought to lead to liberation, how one ought to conduct one's life and so forth. My intention is not to stick slavishly to the reports of Buddhists writings about these matters but rather to offer a creative continuation of Buddhist philosophy, exploring possible meanings and implications of the texts. And one of the principal themes of this study will be that Buddhist written sources often contain a measure – sometimes a considerable amount – of ambiguity, so that a range of interpretations is often possible.

I am not here functioning as a mere expositor of traditional Buddhism, still less as an apologist. My intention in part is to uncover apparently questionable assumptions underlying the Buddhist worldview. However, my statement that they are 'questionable' is not meant to imply that they are necessarily wrong. Rather, my claim, somewhat more modest and less contentious, is that they are not necessarily right. There are various ways in which these Buddhist ideas can be reasonably challenged and their veracity doubted.

My assessment of Buddhist thoughts about knowledge and liberation does not, of course, take place from a neutral standpoint. One must take seriously the insight of thinkers such as Hans Georg Gadamer (1975) that there is no completely objective, detached observer and that all thinking takes place within a tradition and from a cultural and historical vantage point. There are thus no definitive interpretations. Perhaps the best one can do is to become as self-conscious as possible about the prejudices and biases that inform one's understandings and readings, recognizing that human beings cannot have a 'view from nowhere' or a God's-eye view.

I write as a Western academic who has familiarity with both Eastern and Western religious and philosophical traditions. My position is that cross-cultural understanding is possible, and that attempts at such understanding are not simply a belligerent imposition of one's own cultural norms and standards of rationality. Understanding of other cultures is no doubt difficult and fraught with pitfalls, but they are not hermetically sealed monads.

This is, of course, a debatable point, and no doubt my attempts to assess philosophically, sometimes with fairly critical results, Buddhist ideas about knowledge and liberation might be taken as a 'colonial' attempt to impose Western values and ideas of reason on a tradition that has different but equally valid standards. Is not such an endeavour yet another arrogant Eurocentric attempt to subjugate another culture by claiming that its religions and philosophies are inferior and that its deficient rationality needs to be corrected by the superior Western mind?

Perhaps this is a valid criticism. However, my intention is not to be destructive, condescending or dismissive. On the contrary, I have the utmost admiration for, and often sympathy with, Buddhism and its attempts to find solutions to the problem of suffering. Indeed, I consider my attempts to engage in a critically reflective manner with Buddhist ideas as a sign of respect. A very good way to take such ideas seriously, I suggest, is to probe them, considering their strengths and weaknesses as best one can. That such an assessment will itself inevitably involve a degree of interpretation and also misunderstanding seems to be no reason to stop making the effort.

Such a project must, of course, be undertaken with a spirit of humility, acknowledging that one's assessments will have their own weaknesses, some of them no doubt serious. But this book is, I trust, a contribution to an ongoing cross-cultural philosophical conversation. Hopefully readers can take the conversation further, perhaps showing, among other things, where I have gone wrong and how my cultural bias has led to confusions. My assessments and criticisms undoubtedly often display my lack of comprehension. But such errors are perhaps not to be feared. They can provide a starting point for fruitful discussion and clarification. Any criticisms I make are not, I hope, displays of arrogance but rather attempts, successful or unsuccessful, to understand more clearly.

I also have a background as a 'Western' Buddhist practitioner, but one who has endeavoured to be critically aware of the philosophical assumptions undergirding his religious or spiritual tradition. I suppose, then, that to some extent I am an 'insider' but I do not think that this necessarily invalidates my attempts to offer a rigorous assessment of the religious tradition to which I have been aligned. A collection of essays by a variety of Buddhist practitioners has called this sort of critical endeavour by those who have or have had some form of religious commitment to Buddhism 'Buddhist theology' (Jackson and Makransky, 2000). The application of the term 'theology' in this context is possibly problematic, given that theology literally means 'study of God or the gods' and is widely associated with the confessional reflection on Christian doctrines about the divine. However, whatever the nomenclature, I believe that the project of critical reflection on Buddhist thought by those who are or have been practising Buddhists can only be an enriching contribution both to academic discussion and the tradition's self-awareness.

I readily admit that my approach here has the limitations that a historian, anthropologist or philologist might find irksome. However, I also think that it has a significant strength, in that I attempt to do some serious critical thinking about key issues of meaning in Buddhist thought. Historians, anthropologists and philologists have, of course, enormous amounts to offer in understanding the nature of Buddhism. If I am an apologist, it is as a defender of the legitimacy of this sort of philosophical reflection about Buddhism. Such ruminations, I contend, have a place in academic discourse alongside historical, anthropological and philological methods.

Though this book is an academic study, it deals with issues that are, I would suggest, of significance to any individual who reflects on the human situation and the purpose or meaning of life. The topics of suffering, its transcendence, the nature of reality, and whether and how we can know it are paramount human concerns and Buddhism has extremely interesting things to say about them. Etymologically, of course, philosophy is 'love of wisdom' and philosophers of this type, in search of wisdom about the human condition, will surely find Buddhism a rich vein of ideas and insights to mine. Whether one agrees or disagrees with what Buddhism says – and I suggest various possible points of disagreement – the study of Buddhism's treatment of suffering and liberation is bound to be fruitful. It is a complex and intelligent attempt to understand and offer solutions to human suffering and to comprehend the nature of reality. A serious consideration of what Buddhism has to say is bound, I think, to stimulate serious reflections of one's own, whether one finds oneself concurring with or diverging from the Buddhist analysis.

A critic might object that the highly philosophical and idealized Buddhism I describe and investigate here has a rather weak relationship to Buddhism as it occurs 'on the ground', so to speak. Indeed, my study gives primary attention to Buddhism as found in the textual tradition, which was accessible only to privileged intellectuals and probably practised meticulously by relatively few. Though it is true that Buddhism, as expressed 'doctrinally' in many texts, is fundamentally focused on liberation by means of knowledge of 'things as they really are', it would be a serious misconception to think that the majority of Buddhists are primarily concerned with developing such liberating knowledge.

In a sense this criticism is quite fair. The quest for liberating knowledge is and has been a dominant interest for only a small minority of Buddhists. Traditionally they have usually been members of the monastic elite, whose established function is, by contrast with the laity, to strive to achieve liberation. The laity generally has practised a form of Buddhism that aims mainly at materially supporting the monastic community and leading a virtuous life, thereby gaining good future rebirths. Indeed, it seems clear that in actuality even most monks and nuns have had and have this more modest aim, regarding the goal of liberation as a lofty aim achievable only by a spiritually advanced few and only under very supportive conditions. In this study, I am thus not purporting to represent the social and historical reality of Buddhism as it would be found to exist by the anthropologist or historian.

Nevertheless, the rather rarefied Buddhism that I am concentrating on is not entirely divorced from what actually happens on the ground. There are, after all, Buddhists who do strive, and there have been Buddhists in past times who have strived, for the liberating knowledge that is purported to eradicate suffering. And, I contend, even if no Buddhists were in fact trying, or ever have tried or will try, to achieve the liberating knowledge described in this book and referred to in many Buddhist texts, it would nevertheless be a worthy object of philosophical enquiry and scrutiny. The Buddhist texts contain many remarkable ideas about liberating knowledge that I want to examine. The number or percentage of Buddhists who have tried, are trying, and will try to embody them is not my main concern. Let us begin, then, this philosophical study of Buddhism, knowledge and liberation.

CHAPTER TWO

Impermanence, Not-self and Suffering

As we have seen, Buddhist sources claim that Awakened people achieve knowledge of the three characteristics (Sanskrit: *trilakṣaṇa*, Pāli: *tilakkhaṇa*) of existence and thus put an end to their craving and suffering. These three characteristics are impermanence (Sanskrit: *anityā*, Pāli: *anicca*), suffering (Sanskrit: *duḥkha*, Pāli: *dukkha*), and not-self (Sanskrit: *anātman*, Pāli: *anattā*). Awakened individuals have woken up to or fully understood these truths. As the *Aṅguttara Nikāya* 3, 134 (trans. Nyanaponika and Bodhi, 1999, p. 77) declares, a *tathāgata* – that is, a Buddha – 'fully awakens' to and 'penetrates' the facts of impermanence, suffering and not-self. And the *Dhammapada* 20, 5–7 says that discerning the three characteristics is 'the path to purity'. Thera Nārada's commentary (1978, p. 224) on these verses explains that 'impermanence (*anicca*), sorrow (*dukkha*) and no-soul (*anattā*) are the three characteristics of all things conditioned by causes. It is by contemplating them that one realizes Nibbāna.'

This brief account raises some important questions. First, what exactly and in more detail are these three characteristics? Second, what precisely is craving and why do Buddhists think that it causes suffering? Third, why is it thought that knowledge of the three characteristics will eradicate craving and hence suffering? It is these three questions that the present chapter will address. I will then make some observations and critical remarks concerning the Buddhist analysis.

What are the three characteristics?

For the sake of explanatory convenience, I will treat impermanence and not-self, often listed as the first and third characteristics, together. This will be followed by an examination of the second characteristic, that is, suffering.

Impermanence and not-self

Buddhism envisages the world to be a vast complex of transient events. It can thus be viewed as a form of process philosophy which depicts the universe in terms of becoming and transformation rather than stasis. The truth about entities is that they do not stay the same and they must eventually cease to exist. Things come into being, undergo many alterations and inevitably pass away. All phenomena are subject to this law of impermanence. Each and every thing is born and dies.

Rita Gross (1998, p. 143) claims that this 'Buddhist insight into all pervasive impermanence' is 'the fulcrum point of all Buddhist teaching'. She cites the influential modern Zen teacher Shunryu Suzuki (1970, pp. 102–3), who writes that:

> The basic teaching of Buddhism is the teaching of transiency, or change. That everything changes is the basic truth for each existence. No one can deny this truth, and all the teachings of Buddhism is condensed within it. This is the teaching for all of us. Wherever we go, this teaching is true.

There is a strong connection between this first characteristic, impermanence, and the third characteristic, not-self (*anātman*). In so far as they are impermanent, things have no abiding, unchanging essence and in this sense are without a self. As Shunryu Suzuki (1970, p. 103) comments:

> This teaching [of impermanence] is also understood as the teaching of selflessness. Because each existence is in constant change, there is no abiding self. In fact, the self-nature of each existence is nothing but change, the self-nature of all existence.

Buddhism often claims that all things are analysable without remainder into the five bundles or aggregates (*skandha*), namely, material form (*rūpa*), sensations or feelings (*vedanā*), perceptions and discrimination of ideas (*saṃjñā*), volitions and dispositions (*saṃskāra*), and states of consciousness (*vijñāna*). Inanimate things, such as rocks and tables, are simply analysable into form alone. Human beings (and animals too) have material form or bodies but they also have a mental life, described by the four remaining *skandha*s. Forms, sensations or feelings, perceptions and discrimination of ideas, volitions and dispositions as well as states of consciousness are ephemeral. This impermanence of the aggregates, coupled with the Buddhist contention that things are reducible to these aggregates, means that no thing has a permanent, abiding essence. It is not surprising, therefore, that *Majjhima Nikāya* 3, 115 (trans. Ñāṇamoli and Bodhi, 1995, p. 975) states that a monk who contemplates the rise and fall, the transitoriness, of the aggregates abandons the conceit 'I am'. The 'I' and 'me' are simply names or conventional designations for what is actually an ever-changing stream of mental and physical events. There is no reality to which the label 'self' refers other than the five *skandha*s.

However, the Buddhist teaching of not-self is not simply that things have no permanent, abiding essence. It also means that each and every thing relies upon causal factors for its existence. Not-self has as its corollary the central Buddhist teaching of dependent origination (*pratītyasamutpāda*). No thing exists autonomously. There is no independent, self-standing entity. Every thing that exists does so in dependence on causal conditions.

Some of these causal conditions are external to the entities themselves. The existence of a tree, for example, depends upon various extrinsic causal conditions, such as the earth in which it is rooted, rain, sunshine, the seed from which it grew and so on. Without these causal conditions, the tree would not exist. But entities also depend for their existence upon intrinsic factors, namely, the various necessary parts which make up the entity. The tree cannot exist without its essential constituents, such as the roots, the trunk, the branches and so forth. So, the tree does not have an autonomous existence. It does not and cannot stand alone in the world, as it were, unsupported by other entities and independent of its indispensable parts.

And what is true of the tree in this respect is equally the case, according to the Buddhists, for other things. This can be most potently realized in the case of one's own existence. One's being is clearly dependent on numerous causal factors both external and internal. It relies, for instance, on the benign environmental conditions in which one lives – that there is enough oxygen to breathe, and that the sun has heated the world to a temperature which makes human life possible, that one lives in a peaceful society and one without epidemics and so on. Further, one's existence depends on the continued functioning of one's various parts; one would cease to exist if one's essential parts such as one's heart, lungs or brain stopped working. According to the traditional Buddhist categories, one's existence depends on the intrinsic factors which are the five constituent aggregates (*skandha*). The person I am is constituted by my body, my sensations or feelings, my ability to discriminate ideas or perceive objects, my volitions or dispositions, and my consciousness. If these change, then the person I am changes too. If they cease to exist, then I cease to exist as well.

In addition, the principle of dependent origination is thought to explain the process of rebirth without positing an unchanging substratum. For the Buddhists, the ever-changing process of mental and physical events which constitutes the person in this life continues on into the next life and has continued on from past lives. There is a continuum, a series of causally linked events. The good or bad actions (*karman*) performed in this life are causally connected with the sentient being that arises in the future life, influencing its personality and circumstances, just as good or bad actions in past lives influence one's present personality and circumstances. Thus, the present always-changing sentient being is neither identical nor entirely unconnected with the sentient being of the past lives and of future lives, just as my middle-aged self is neither identical with nor entirely different from myself as a young child or an old man.

Of course, this explanation of the rebirth process is, and is intended to be, in direct opposition to the account given by many other forms of Indian philosophy and religion, such as Vedānta in its various forms, Jainism and popular Hindu spirituality in general, all of which claim that there is a permanent, unchanging self or soul which is thought to underlie the empirical individual and to persist and get reincarnated when the current body disintegrates. The Buddhist idea of not-self and dependent origination is a complete rejection of such a reincarnating permanent essence. Rebirth is about process and a continuing stream of events rather than an eternal soul which takes on new bodies.

Furthermore, the Buddhists think that not-self and dependent origination explain the possibility of spiritual transformation from an Unawakened to an Awakened state. The absence of a permanent, fixed self means that human beings can change and, the Buddhists think, this change can be for the better. The Buddhists are optimistic in this respect. They often think that a total transformation is eventually possible, replacing ignorance with knowledge, selfishness with altruism and suffering with genuine happiness. The Buddhist contention is that this is achievable by following the Buddhist training, as set out, for instance, in the Eightfold Path (see Chapter 4). Following the instructions set out by Buddhism will cause, it is thought, the eradication of ignorance, craving and suffering. In other words, in dependence upon the Buddhist discipline arises Awakening. By setting up the appropriate causal factors as explained by the Buddhist training, the human individual can attain liberation.

Suffering

Buddhist teaching says that human beings are afflicted by *duḥkha*, a term that I translate as 'suffering', but which is also sometimes rendered into English as 'anguish', 'pain', 'sorrow' and 'unsatisfactoriness'. The variety of translations indicates that *duḥkha* does not correspond entirely to any single English word. It refers to a variety of unpleasant experiences of varying strength. The stock Theravāda explanation of *dukkha* is that:

> Birth is *dukkha*, and old age is *dukkha* and disease is *dukkha* and dying is *dukkha*, association with what is not dear is *dukkha*, separation from what is dear is *dukkha*, not getting what one wants is *dukkha*, in short the five groups of grasping are *dukkha*. (*Mahāvagga* 1, 19 of the *Vinaya*, trans. Horner, 1971, p. 16, slightly modified)

The Tibetan Buddhist philosopher Tsong kha pa (1357–1419) explains, in the *Lam Rim Chen Mo* (trans. Cutler and Newland, 2000, pp. 265–80), that these are the eight types of suffering. That is, the suffering of birth, old age, illness, death, encountering what is unpleasant, separation from what is pleasant, not getting what you want and, finally, the five groups of grasping.

Suffering here refers to actual physical pain of differing intensity, such as that experienced when one suffers an illness, is born and dies. No doubt one might add other purely physical forms of discomfort, such as being hit, hunger and tiredness. But it also means the psychological suffering caused by loss of or not getting pleasant things as well as the enforced connection with unpleasant things. Sometimes we do not get what we want and we get what we do not want. This is distressing to varying degrees. Included also is the mental anguish which arises when one worries about the prospect of losing pleasant things or of acquiring something unpleasant.

Given the Buddhist teaching that everything in the world is impermanent, whatever pleasant things one experiences are transitory. They will pass away. Thus, while Buddhism certainly does not teach the pessimistic view that life is simply miserable, it does point out that life is a mixture of pleasure and pain, happiness, and sorrow, and that even the pleasant, happy experiences in life – and there may be many of them for some people – will inevitably end. They are unreliable and they are always of limited intensity. They do not yield ultimate fulfilment. So, even pleasant things are causes of suffering.

Thus, there is nothing in life which does not produce suffering. This is why the passage above declares that 'all five groups of grasping' are *dukkha*. The five groups of grasping are the *khandha*s, the Pāli form of the Sanskrit word '*skandha*s', and together they include everything in the conditioned world. Whatever one might grasp – be it a physical object, a feeling or sensation, a perception or idea, a habitual state of mind, or one's continuing consciousness – it will be unreliable, cannot remain forever in one's possession and is thus not ultimately satisfactory.

The *Lam Rim Chen Mo* (trans. Cutler and Newland, 2000, pp. 281–7) gives a further sixfold classification of suffering. First, there is the suffering of uncertainty. Nothing can be trusted because things change, nothing stays the same. There is thus fear for what the unpredictable future will bring. Second, the suffering of insatiability. No matter how much worldly pleasure one gets, one's appetite is never satisfied. We might say, then, that worldly pleasures are rather like addictions in this respect. Third, the suffering of casting off bodies repeatedly. Given the Buddhist belief in beginningless rebirths, all beings have had to and will have to (short of Awakening) face the horror of death countless times. Fourth, the suffering of repeated rebirth. Presumably this refers both to the pain involved in the physical act of being born (and, we might add, giving birth!) over and over again and to the various difficulties and sorrows which occur subsequently in the course of life. Fifth, the suffering of repeatedly descending from high to low. According to Buddhist cosmology, there are extremely unpleasant lower realms of existence, including various hells, into which sentient beings descend as a result of their bad *karma*. The belief is that, since the cycle of rebirths is beginningless and (unless one achieves Awakening) is without end, sentient beings have had and will have to endure the pain of falling into lower realms of existence on numerous occasions. Sixth, there is the suffering of having no companions. This refers to the fact that one's suffering must be experienced by oneself single-handedly. No one else can really share that burden with us. This sense of 'existential aloneness' in the face of our suffering is a cause of distress.

Theravāda Buddhist texts distinguish between three basic forms of *dukkha*: ordinary suffering (*dukkhadukkha*), suffering that arises through change (*vipariṇāmadukkha*) and the suffering which is inherent in conditioned existence (*saṃkhāradukkha*) (see, for example, *Dīgha Nikāya*, 3, 216, trans. Walshe, 1987, p. 484). *Dukkhadukkha* is the straightforward suffering involved in physical pain, disease and so forth. *Vipariṇāmadukkha* is the suffering caused by impermanence. That is, when things we like pass away or are taken from us, we suffer. *Saṃkhāradukkha* refers to the fact that, as all things in this world are conditioned – that is, they are transitory, dependently originating phenomena – they can provide no genuine refuge from suffering. All conditioned things are finite and are thus incapable of providing real satisfaction.

What is craving and why does it cause suffering?

A successful remedy for an illness depends on a correct diagnosis of the cause of the ailment. Analogously, the Buddha is said to have identified the cause of suffering so that he might apply an appropriate cure. Buddhism says that suffering is caused by craving (*tṛṣṇā*), a form of desire that leads to attachment (*upādāna*), attachment being the natural consequence of the acquisition of the object that one craves.

Craving and attachment take many forms. There is craving for one's own continued existence and attachment to one's own personality. And there is also craving for and attachment to various other internal and external entities. One can be attached to one's opinions and views, one can crave and be attached to particular emotions or mental states, fame, success, wealth, one's car, tasty foods, one's family and friends and so forth. Buddhism even warns against craving for and attachment to its own rituals and rules of conduct, states of meditative absorption (*dhyāna*) and *nirvāṇa* itself.

Traditional Buddhist analyses of craving – such as those found at *Mahāvagga* 1, 20 of the *Vinaya* (trans. Horner, 1971, p. 16) and *Dīgha Nikāya* 3, 216 (trans. Walshe, 1987, p. 483) – say that three of its principal forms are craving for sense pleasure (*kāmataṇhā*), for existence (*bhavataṇhā*) and for non-existence (*vibhavataṇhā*). Sense pleasures are obviously objects of craving and attachment. In this case, the craving is for pleasant, enjoyable visual, oral, aural, tactile, olfactory and mental experiences (the mind being a sense organ for Buddhism) of one form or another. I might, for instance, crave the pleasant taste of chocolate, the delightful sound of my lover's voice, the mental experience of meditative absorption or a happy memory. Craving for existence is most fundamentally the craving for one's continued being. It is the desire for immortality. More broadly, it might be construed as the craving for the acquisition or continuation of an experience. Enjoying my lover's company, for example, I might crave for her to visit or for her to remain with me. Craving for non-existence is at root the craving no longer to exist, that is, to be utterly annihilated. It is the sort of craving which, in its most extreme form, leads to self-harming and suicide. More broadly, it might be understood as the craving for an unpleasant experience to end or the destruction of something that stands in the way of the acquisition of an object of craving and attachment. I might crave, for instance, the end of an illness or prisoners might crave the destruction of the bars and walls that keep them from their friends, family and freedom.

Karl Werner (1997, p. 127) notes an alternative translation of *vibhava* is 'prosperity' or 'wealth' leading him to suggest that 'craving for prosperity' is an alternative reading of *vibhavataṇhā*. In this case, Werner says, it refers to 'the desire to prosper by expansion; by creating a family, building an empire or enhancing the sense and size of one's self-importance in another way.'

There is an intimate relation between craving and other mental states – traditionally classified as 'bad', 'unskilful' or 'unwholesome' (*akuśala*) because they lead to suffering – such as hatred, jealousy, boredom and so forth. Buddhism has a long tradition, thoroughly systematized in the Abhidharma literature, of identifying many unskilful mental states that practitioners are exhorted to identify and eradicate from their minds. Hatred can be said to arise when one is frustrated in one's attempts to get what one craves, or when someone or something takes away someone or something to whom or to which one is attached. Jealousy occurs when someone else has something which one craves and when one is prevented from having it. And it seems reasonable to suggest that the mental state of boredom, a restless disengagement from life, is rooted in the craving for non-existence. So, it is plausible that unskilful mental states of various types can be traced back to and are founded in craving. Craving is, we might reason, the root unskilful mental state from which the others stem.

The Buddhists seek to eliminate suffering by cutting off craving, and the resulting attachment, in all its manifold forms. This is expressed in the second Noble Truth: 'And this, monks, is the ariyan truth of the stopping of *dukkha*: the utter and passionless stopping of that very craving, its renunciation, surrender, release, the lack of pleasure in it' (*Mahāvagga* 1, 21 of the *Vinaya*, trans. Horner, 1971, p. 15, slightly modified).

Why, though, do the Buddhists think that craving causes suffering? Let me suggest an answer to this question. Craving is essentially a desire rooted in possessiveness and clinging. When one craves one sticks, so to speak, to entities and does not face up to the reality of change. Under the sway of craving, one attempts to make the coveted entity one's own, and one is unwilling to let go of the thing once it is in one's possession. Furthermore, one is unable to accept undesirable changes in the entity. For instance, influenced by craving and attachment, I want my beloved to be mine, to remain mine, to never leave me and never to change in ways that I would find unpleasant.

So, craving is bound to lead to frustration, as the entity that one craves and to which one gets attached will eventually no longer be one's own, either because it will pass away or because it – given the changing circumstances of life – will fall out of one's possession. And even before the entity passes away, and even if one does not lose possession of it in some other way, one has to suffer often disagreeable alterations in its state. When the object of craving and attachment changes in an unpleasant fashion, falls out of one's possession or passes away, then one is disappointed and dissatisfied: one suffers. The extent of one's suffering will depend on the intensity of the craving and attachment.

Rita Gross claims that, according to Buddhism, we suffer because we fail to accept the truth of impermanence. By 'acceptance' here Gross means an affective accommodation of transitoriness, and not simply an intellectual assent to its truth. We suffer because we have not come to terms with the reality of impermanence, and we are emotionally unable to 'let go' of transient phenomena. The person afflicted by craving cannot acknowledge emotionally that, as the *Udānavarga* 1, 20 says, 'the end of every hoarding is spending, of every rising falling, of every meeting parting and of all living dying' (trans. Guenther, 2001, p. 42).

So, for example, my youthful, healthy, beautiful beloved, whom I crave and to whom I am attached, will eventually die. Or else my beloved may well stop being my beloved when her affections change and she no longer cares for me. And even before her death, and even if she remains my beloved until her demise, she will be ill, will grow old; she will lose her youth, her health and her beauty. All of these events will cause me suffering, attached as I am to my beloved, and attached as I am to her as youthful, healthy and beautiful. I cannot accept emotionally that these events must occur, that they are 'the way things really are'.

The Buddhists might claim that if the world were static and unchanging, then there would be no harm in one's craving for and attachment to entities for they would then not be subject to alteration and dissolution, and one would not have to suffer their unpleasant changes and their loss. But this is of course, the Buddhists say, not 'the way things really are', and thus craving and attachment must bring suffering.

It might be objected that, even if one eradicated one's craving for and attachment to entities, one would still be subject to the various types of suffering to which the body is susceptible due to accident, disease and old age. In fact, many Buddhists would accept this point, as is clear, for example, from the account in the Theravāda scriptures of the historical Buddha's final months before his decease, during which he evidently experienced much bodily pain, though clearly bearing it with mental equanimity (see *Dīgha Nikāya* 2, 72–168, trans. Walshe, 1987, pp. 231–77).

However, the Buddhists would claim that, though one might continue to suffer bodily pain even if one eradicates one's craving, one would at least no longer be subject to the distress which often plagues those who cannot accept emotionally the fact that their impermanent body is no longer functioning properly. The Buddha might have suffered the pain of disease, old age, and the dying process, but he did not suffer the anguish of resenting this pain or yearning for good health, youth and continued life.

Furthermore, Buddhism shares with many forms of Indian religion and philosophy the admittedly contentious assumption that sentient beings are subject to rebirth and that craving fuels the rebirth process. When craving ends so too does rebirth. In which case, according to the Buddhists, people who have extinguished craving do eradicate – after the present life is finished, at any rate – even the pain involved in having a body. Thus, it is only with the achievement of the final *nirvāṇa* – sometimes referred to as the *nirvāṇa* without remainder (*nirupadhiśeṣanirvāṇa*) – which occurs at the end of a Buddha or an Awakened person's life, that the complete cessation of all suffering is said to occur.

Why does knowledge of the three characteristics eradicate craving?

As we have seen, Buddhism seeks to show people how to overcome craving and to accept emotionally the reality of impermanence. The eradication of craving is the achievement of *nirvāṇa*, which is often defined as the cessation of suffering. Having cut off their craving, Awakened people have let go of their grasping for impermanent, selfless things. As the *Sutta Nipāta* 805 and 811 says:

> People grieve for the things they are attached to as 'mine', but there is no enduring object of grasping ... As a drop of water does not stick to a lotus leaf or as a lotus flower is untainted by the water, so the sage does not cling to anything, seen, heard or thought. (trans. Saddhatissa, 1985, pp. 95–6)

Awakened people no longer rail against the unalterable transitory nature of things but rather align themselves emotionally with this reality. Impermanence no longer causes mental pain and distress. Indeed, such an emotional acceptance of impermanence and selflessness is thought to bring a sense of freedom and peace, as one no longer protests against the inevitable and no longer resists the unchangeable truth of change. As Shunryu Suzuki (1970, p. 103) says: 'This [selflessness and impermanence] is also called the teaching of Nirvana. When we realize the everlasting truth of "everything changes" and find our composure in it, we find ourselves in Nirvana.'

How precisely is this 'composure' in impermanence, which may be equated with the eradication of craving, to be achieved? How is the ordinary, Unawakened person's emotional resistance to transitoriness to be transformed into the peace and freedom of complete acceptance? How is suffering to be overcome and liberation achieved?

To answer these questions, we need to enquire into the cause of craving itself. If craving for and attachment to impermanent, selfless things must cause suffering, why do people still crave and get attached? In other words, why is it that people fail to accept emotionally the way things really are? Why do they remain in turmoil and longing rather than achieving the affective 'letting go' which occurs when one no longer seeks to appropriate things which are and always will be transitory?

The common Buddhist answer to these questions is that craving is rooted in a cognitive weakness. That is, people fail to understand fully the impermanence and selflessness of things, and thus, in the desire to be happy, they mistakenly seek happiness by appropriating transitory objects. Having failed to see that things are impermanent and selfless, they fail to comprehend that such changing, essenceless entities will cause suffering if clung to. This misunderstanding, insofar as it produces craving, leads to misery. Thus, at *Bodhicāryavatāra*, 1, 28, Śāntideva (seventh century CE) makes the following observation about people who have not achieved Awakening: 'Hoping to escape from suffering, it is to suffering that they run. In the desire for happiness, out of delusion, they destroy their own happiness, like an enemy' (trans. Crosby and Skilton, 1996, p. 7).

Here craving is seen not as an autonomous entity, a brute instinct that is quite independent of one's intellect. On the contrary, it is thought that craving is rooted in one's failure to understand the true nature of the object of craving. Craving occurs for a reason, and the reason that it occurs is that the object of craving is considered to be worth possessing. One considers the object of craving to be worth possessing because, failing to understand its impermanence and selflessness, one does not understand that one will eventually have to suffer the pain of disagreeable changes in and the loss of the coveted object. With respect to the type of desire that is craving, the Buddhists would, it seems, agree with the moral philosopher John Finnis (1983, p. 35) who writes:

> The desirable figures in my practical thinking not as whatever I happen to have a feeling for, or an 'independent desire' for. Rather it is that which, *qua* possible action or possible object of action, appears to me in a favourable light, i.e., as

> having a point, i.e. as somehow good to be getting, doing, having, being. ... This conception of something as desirable provides, typically, sufficient motivation to act.

Craving is a desire that is rooted in a belief, and that belief is that the object of craving is worth appropriating. The object of craving is desirable. But this is, according to Buddhism, a misguided belief or misconception. In fact, if one understood that the object of craving, as impermanent, is not worth appropriating it would lose its attraction; it would no longer be desirable. Craving is caused by a particular (and erroneous) way of cognizing rather than being a free-floating and blind impulse. In which case, craving is to be overcome by properly cognizing 'how things really are'. That is, the stopping of appropriative desire is achieved by knowledge of the three characteristics of existence.

Craving and other desires

Craving might in this respect be contrasted with what might be called instinctual desires, which are in no way tied to the failure to understand impermanence, not-self and suffering. I have in mind here such bodily needs as the desire to eat when one's body requires nourishment, the desire to sleep when one's body needs rest, the desire to keep warm when one's body is too cold and so forth. I suspect that Buddhists have no objection to these instinctual desires; they might accept them as an inevitable and necessary feature of having a body. Even an Awakened person would have them.

Arguably Buddhism might also permit an unselfish desire, that is, an aspiration, for *nirvāṇa*. As Steven Collins (1998, p. 186) remarks, the question of whether one should desire *nirvāṇa* 'crops up standardly in introductory classes or discussions of Buddhism' yet it is not a question which any Buddhist text, to his knowledge, has ever posed. However, it seems plausible that Buddhism could admit that it is permissible to desire, but not to crave, the irreversible ending of craving and attachment. Craving *nirvāṇa* would by definition stop one attaining it. But desiring it in a non-appropriative way might not be a hindrance. Indeed, it is quite possible that such desire is necessary in order to motivate the practitioners in their efforts to achieve the complete eradication of craving and attachment. Furthermore, Buddhist traditions generally value non-possessive, altruistic emotions such as friendliness (*maitrī*) and compassion (*karuṇa*), emotions that are rooted in the desire for the welfare of other sentient beings. These other-regarding desires are perfected rather than given up by the Awakened person.

Thus, it is not surprising to find that, in an important Theravāda Abhidhamma text, the *Abhidhammatthasaṅgaha* (trans. Bodhi and Nārada, 1993, pp. 82–3), the author Anuruddha distinguishes desire (*chanda*) from greed (*lobha*) and lust (*rāga*). Unlike greed and lust, which are always unskilful, desire is said to be ethically variable. It can be unskilful, skilful or neutral. The desire for *nirvāṇa* or to help someone who is suffering is presumably skilful. The desire to kill someone or to possess their property is clearly unskilful. Perhaps the desire to eat when the body requires sustenance or to sleep when one is genuinely tired is ethically neutral (though one might argue that it is skilful, in so far as one is acting with kindness and consideration towards one's body). Collins (1998, p. 187) notes that almost all words denoting emotions and intentions in Pāli can be described as either with corruptions (*sāsava*) or without corruptions (*anāsava*). Desires such as the aspiration for *nirvāṇa* and the unselfish wish to assist someone in need would, I think, fall into the latter category, whereas the desire which is appropriative craving belongs in the former category. It is apparent, then, that the enemy to be defeated for Buddhism is craving rather than desire in general. And this enemy, which causes suffering, is to be overcome by coming to understand fully the three characteristics of existence.

Some critical reflections

This, then, is the Buddhist explanation of the three characteristics, the nature of craving, and how knowledge of impermanence, not-self and suffering can eradicate craving and hence suffering. It seems difficult to deny that it has a remarkable elegance and an internally consistent logic. However, in the remainder of this chapter, I will embark on some critical analysis, identifying some of the fracture points where the Buddhist explanation is most questionable.

Are all things impermanent?

To begin with, the claim that all things are impermanent is clearly controversial. Though the Buddhist contention seems to be supported by empirical evidence, it is still possible that there are things that Buddhists have not experienced – for example, souls and God – that are permanent. Indeed, there are many religious people who would claim to have faith in and even some experience of a permanent soul and/or God. Buddhism, in many of its forms at any rate, would say that such religious doctrines are a denial of reality, a desperate flight from the truth of transitoriness. But this Buddhist position, though not necessarily wrong, is surely contestable.

It is difficult to see how this dispute could ever be resolved. On the one hand, it does not seem likely that there would be any evidence that would be admissible in order to prove publicly and conclusively the existence of such permanent entities as the soul and God, for it is likely (barring an open, general revelation by the divine being) that experiences of such things are always private in nature, and it is hard to know how much credence to give them. On the other hand, the Buddhists' claim that no thing is permanent is always open to the charge that there may be things such as souls and God that exist, are not transitory and are beyond the Buddhists' limited experience. The Buddhists are here confronted by the problem of induction. That is to say, they seek to establish a general law on the basis of limited evidence. It is always possible that there is data, to which they have not had access, which contradicts the conclusion they have reached.

Furthermore, the Buddhists must, I think, accept that there is a logical problem with the truth claim that 'all things are, always have been and always will be impermanent' because this truth must itself be permanent. It is always and everywhere the truth. In which case, if it is true that everything is impermanent, then it is false that everything is impermanent. The Buddhists must surely make an exception here, and say that 'all things are impermanent, excluding the truth that all things are impermanent'.

It might also be objected that Buddhism often claims that *nirvāṇa* is not impermanent. Now, the precise nature of the Buddhist *nirvāṇa* is disputed and open to interpretation. For instance, is it simply the permanent absence of greed, hatred and delusion attained by Awakened people and the permanent truth, realized by Awakened people, that all things possess the three characteristics? Or is it something more than this – a timeless ontological realm and sacred reality that somehow transcends or stands behind the mundane world of impermanent phenomena? This issue will be discussed in more detail in Chapter 7. What is clear is that Buddhists commonly claim that *nirvāṇa*, whatever else it might be, is not transitory. So, the Buddhists except *nirvāṇa* from the general rule that everything is impermanent. Thus, they often say that everything conditioned (*saṃskṛta*) is impermanent, and *nirvāṇa* is unconditioned (*asaṃskṛta*).

Some Buddhists contend that space (*ākāśa*) is permanent as well. As Y. Karunadasa (1967, pp. 92–4) notes, the Vaibhāṣika tradition, for instance, claims that space is an unconditioned phenomenon (*asaṃskṛtadharma*) which is omnipresent (*sarvagata*) and eternal (*nitya*). It is also said to be non-obstructive (*anāvaraṇa*) in the sense that it does not impede the movement of matter through it. But perhaps further exceptions are also required. The Buddhists say that things are impermanent, but can this include, for instance, the moral law of *karma*, which is traditionally said by Buddhists to govern the universe? And does it include the moral principle that compassion is good, that hatred is bad, that craving can be eradicated by following the Buddhist path and so forth? Are not these thought by the Buddhists to be permanent features of the universe, as it were? And finally, one might object that various mathematical and logical truths as well as scientific laws are permanent. The truths that $2 + 2 = 4$ or that if all xs are ps and all *p*s are *z*s, then all *x*s are *z*s, that every event has a cause and that $e = mc^2$ seem to be truths that pertain permanently.

So, it seems that, faced with these objections, the Buddhists should maintain a mitigated version of their claim that all things are impermanent. Nevertheless, they might with considerable plausibility still claim that most things are transitory. Furthermore, many of the things which are arguably permanent – such as the truth of impermanence and scientific and mathematical laws – are not ordinarily the types of things that human beings tend to crave and get attached to. So, the Buddhists might contend that there may be some exceptions to the law of impermanence, but it remains true that human beings' craving for and attachment to impermanent things is the cause of suffering.

A query about suffering and craving

It seems difficult to deny the Buddhist claim that suffering results from craving and attachment to impermanent things. In a sense this position is uncontroversial. It would be foolish to argue otherwise. Nevertheless, it might be objected that the happiness caused by craving and attachment can in some cases outweigh the suffering, and thus it is at least sometimes best to continue to crave and get attached. For instance, I might decide that craving and being attached to my beloved brings me much happiness, even though it does and will cause me suffering too. I might judge that the happiness is so intense that it more than offsets the suffering. Might it not be better, then, to continue craving and to reap its bittersweet rewards? Suffering and happiness appear to be highly subjective experiences, and it is quite possible that the balance of suffering and happiness derived from craving and attachment might vary from person to person. In this case, the supposed universal truth that craving and attachment cause more suffering than happiness would actually be contingent, dependent on the individual's own psychological propensities.

It seems to me that there are two types of response that Buddhism might have to this objection. Both replies are perhaps reasonable enough, but, as I will show, rely on beliefs or assumptions which would not convince a sceptic.

First, Buddhists might concede that the happiness resulting from craving for and attachment to impermanent entities might sometimes outweigh the actual suffering entailed. However, they might continue, it is nevertheless the case that the happiness is finite and thus not fully satisfying. It always comes to an end, is of limited intensity and always involves a degree of imperfection. In this sense, even such happiness is *duḥkha*.

Now, it seems that the Buddhists must be right to claim that the happiness derived from impermanent phenomena is limited. It is difficult to see how unlimited happiness, whatever that might be, could be derived from any finite thing. However, the problem with the Buddhists' position here is that it is hard to see why one ought to give up this admittedly limited happiness. If it were the case that the actual suffering caused by craving and attachment invariably outweighed any happiness derived from them, then one might have a strong argument for giving up craving and attachment. But if it is the case that craving and attachment can lead to limited, imperfect happiness, which nevertheless outweighs any suffering involved, then why give it up? Surely the person who has no craving and attachment might be in a less happy state than the person who chooses the finite happiness which can result from craving and attachment? Imperfect happiness, with a degree of suffering, might be better than the alternative, which is the mere absence of suffering.

An answer to this objection is that the Buddhist Awakening, which occurs with the cessation of craving and attachment, is not simply an absence of suffering. In addition, the Buddhists consider it to be a fully satisfying, blissful state. It is perfect happiness. Thus, the Buddhists might argue that the limited happiness achieved by craving and attachment should be relinquished because it stands in the way of the fully satisfying happiness which is the craving and attachment-free Awakening.

Of course, this reasoning relies on the debatable claim that there is a state of fully satisfying happiness devoid of all craving and attachment. The sceptic might argue that such a craving and attachment-free state is, far from being perfect happiness, dull and unattractive, even barely distinguishable from death. To be alive fully is to be a craving, attached human being. Craving functions as a basic life-force, perhaps akin to Nietzsche's 'will to power', that motivates us, driving us to self-preservation and self-enhancement. In this case, the only fulfilment that one might have is the limited happiness achieved by one's attachments to the things of this world. The pursuit of a higher happiness, which supposedly arises when one is free from craving and attachment, is the pursuit of a fantasy. So, the Buddhists might believe in a fully satisfying happiness which results from giving up one's cravings and attachments, but sceptics might doubt that such a state really exists.

The Buddhists can, of course, appeal to their own experience, pointing out that when craving and attachment are reduced, they have had glimpses (or more) of this higher happiness. Perhaps. But such subjective evidence will not convince sceptics who might say that when they have experienced times with diminished craving and attachment there has been no adumbration of a higher happiness for them, but just a sense of emotionally dull disengagement from life.

Second, Buddhists might bite the bullet and take the position that the suffering caused by craving for and attachment to impermanent entities eventually exceeds whatever happiness they might provide. Thus, it is never worthwhile to crave and get attached. They might argue that people who think that craving for and attachment to impermanent entities can cause more happiness than suffering can only do so because they have not considered the consequences of such craving and suffering in future lives. It is pertinent here that many Buddhist sources place great importance on the Buddha's extraordinary perception of sentient beings being reborn and dying in good or bad circumstances in dependence on their past actions, skilful or unskilful. This is said to arise just prior to or as a preliminary stage of the Awakening experience.

There is a stock account of this knowledge given in the Theravāda scriptures, in which the Buddha describes how on the night of his Awakening he perceives in detail his manifold past lives 'in the first watch of the night'. This is called 'the first true knowledge'. And he recounts that in the 'second watch of the night' that 'the second true knowledge' arose. This is the 'divine eye' which sees other sentient beings both coming into existence in fortunate or unfortunate circumstances and also passing away in dependence upon their past actions. These two knowledges are a prerequisite, it seems, for the attainment of Awakening. They give the Buddha-to-be direct perception of the consequences of past actions, and thus complete confidence that the results of actions based on craving and attachment are various future sufferings that certainly do outweigh any brief happiness that such craving and attachment might bring. As the *Majjhima Nikāya* 1, 22–3 says:

> With the divine eye which is purified and surpasses the human, I [the Buddha-to-be] saw beings passing away and reappearing, inferior and superior, fair and ugly, fortunate and unfortunate. I understood how beings pass on according to their actions thus: 'These worthy beings who were ill-conducted in body, speech, and mind, revilers of noble ones, wrong in their views, giving effect to wrong view in their actions, on the dissolution of the body, after death, have reappeared in a state of deprivation, in a bad destination, in perdition, even in hell.' (trans. Ñāṇamoli and Bodhi, 1995, p. 106)

Thus, the knowledge of suffering that an Awakened person possesses is no ordinary understanding. It is a perception of the moral law of *karma* in its detailed workings. This perception proves that, given the long-term implications of craving and attachment, there is no case for arguing that any happiness accrued by craving and attachment might be greater than the suffering they cause. The truth that craving and attachment result in more suffering than happiness is not a contingent phenomenon, dependent on an individual's psychology. It is an inescapable fact and part of the fabric of the universe, as it were. In this case, the Buddhist claim is firmly rooted in the notion of extraordinary and wide-ranging perception of the cosmos. This perception demonstrates that there is more suffering than happiness as the eventual effect of all craving and attachment. In relation to the great sufferings in lower realms of existence, such as the hells, that result from craving and attachment, any happiness they bring in this life is negligible.

However, the obvious difficulty with this position is that it makes the claim that craving and attachment cause more suffering than happiness impossible to validate unless one has the requisite direct perception. Without having had the extraordinary vision of sentient beings being reborn over countless lives in accordance with their actions, it is impossible to know whether the Buddhist claim is correct (and even if one had it, one might still doubt its veracity). One can at best remain agnostic or else take the Buddhist claim as an article of faith, trusting the recorded testimony of the Buddha as the grounds for one's belief. For the sceptic, for whom the declarations of the Buddha or other supposedly Awakened individuals are not authoritative, the Buddhist contention that craving and attachment lead to more suffering than happiness thus rests on an unjustified belief, which might or might not be true, in the moral law of *karma* functioning over many lifetimes. The sceptic might suggest, then, that the Buddhist teaching about craving and attachment as the cause of more suffering than happiness rests on shaky foundations.

Craving and enjoyment

Within the Indian philosophical tradition the position that the happiness outweighs the suffering caused by craving and attachment was held by the Cārvākas, who were materialists and hedonists. They denied the existence of rebirth and any reality other than this world, and advocated, not unlike the Epicureans of classical western philosophy, that the pursuit of worldly enjoyment is the highest aim. As Richard King (1999a, p. 18) remarks:

> The [Cārvāka] emphasis on happiness (*sukha*) can be seen perhaps as a direct affront to the emphasis placed upon suffering (*duḥkha*) by the other [Indian] schools of thought. Life may contain a great deal of pain but it also contains much in the way of pleasure and who in their right mind would 'throw away the grain because of the husk'. (*Sarvadarśanasaṃgraha*, Ch. 1)

It is also noteworthy that many religious traditions would support the belief that this world is to be enjoyed, even though the satisfaction to be gained is finite and is bound up with a degree of suffering. Mainstream Judaism and Islam, for instance, far from advocating that the things of this world are to be renounced, consider that, as this world is the creation of God, it is quite appropriate to enjoy its pleasures (within the constraints of the moral laws of the respective traditions, of course). Thus marriage, family life, sexual activity, the generation of wealth and so forth are positively valued over against asceticism, which is not generally approved of. It might be argued, then, that the Buddhist vision, with its emphasis on the eradication of craving and attachment for impermanent things, is different in that it sees enjoyment of things of this world as an obstacle to the eventual attainment of real happiness.

However, maybe the Buddhist position is more subtle than this analysis suggests. Although Buddhism clearly rejects craving for and attachment to impermanent entities, it need not necessarily devalue all enjoyment of transitory things. It is arguable that the Buddhist rejection of craving and attachment need not be incompatible with the acceptance of a non-possessive appreciation of impermanent entities. The Buddhists might argue that human psychology is so constituted that it is possible to appreciate entities without craving for and getting attached to them. In so far as people do not try to hold on to the appreciated entities, they will not suffer when the entities change disagreeably, fall out of their possession or pass away. Many things in this world have positive qualities or characteristics that, it might be contended, one can enjoy without descending into covetousness. Thus, natural and artistic beauty might be appreciated, and the virtuous attributes of people – for instance, their kindness, compassion and wisdom – might be savoured without jealousy, attachment and so forth. And it might be argued that an awareness of the transitory nature of phenomena in fact can increase one's aesthetic appreciation of them, as one delights in the fleeting, fragile beauty, fully aware of the futility of trying to grasp or hold on to it.

Indeed, there is evidence that the appreciation of impermanent things is recognized as valuable by the Buddhist tradition, or some aspects of it. Peter Harvey (2000, pp. 154–5) points to various passages in the Theravāda scriptures in which Awakened disciples of the Buddha, such as Mahā-Kassapa and Sāriputta, express a delight in natural phenomena such as forests, rocks, streams, elephants, flowers and peacocks. These passages indicate, Harvey contends, that 'the Awakened appreciate nature in a non-attached way'. In recent times various Buddhist groups have been active in environmental movements in Thailand, Sri Lanka, and so forth (see Harvey, 2000, pp. 177–85), an activity that also shows a valuing of the natural world, clearly thought to be compatible with the eradication of craving and attachment. Indeed, such environmental appreciation is often thought to be possible only with the weakening of craving and attachment, for only with the diminishing and eventual overcoming of selfish desires can individuals truly regard and act towards the world in a non-exploitative way.

Martin Boord (2001, pp. 291–2) notes that, for Buddhists from all time periods, natural places – the sun, the moon, the planets, rivers, rock, mountains, and so forth – are the homes of deities and spirits which are to be respected rather than despised. Offerings are made to the earth-dwelling *nāga*s before building commences. The earth itself is considered sacred and is personified as the golden goddess who bears witness to the defeat of Māra on the eve of the Buddha's final Awakening. Far from devaluing the world of impermanent phenomena, the Buddhist attitude here would seem to be one of respect and interest.

No doubt the notion that the Buddha-nature is immanent in the entire animate and inanimate world, an idea that became influential especially in Chinese and Japanese Buddhism, might also lead to an enjoyment of the natural world. Zen Buddhism, for instance, is well known for its artistic and poetic achievements, which often draw out the exquisite if transitory beauty of natural phenomena. The Middle Way between asceticism and hedonism might also be construed as implying that one ought to appreciate the beauty in the world of impermanent phenomena, without falling into the extremes which are aversion and greed. Such evidence indicates that the Buddhist liberation need not be life denying or world negating. It might in fact lead to a non-appropriative receptivity and openness to the beauties of the fleeting, ephemeral things of this world.

That being said, there is clearly a considerable amount of evidence in some Buddhist sources that points in the opposite direction, suggesting that the world of impermanent things is to be renounced and is of no value whatsoever. The world of rebirths and nature (*saṃsāra*) is to be left behind and is of no intrinsic worth. Texts suggest that though we think there is beauty in the world, in fact there is only ugliness. For instance, at *Sutta Nipāta* 192–206, the practitioner is encouraged to reflect on the body as unattractive and repulsive (trans. Norman, 1984, pp. 32–3), a reflection which has become a common meditation technique. And a famous list says that there are four basic distortions of perception and views. These occur when one takes conditioned things to be (1) permanent when they are actually all impermanent, (2) causes of happiness when they all really result in suffering, (3) endowed with self when they are in fact all devoid of self and (4) beautiful when in reality they are all foul (see, for example, *Aṅguttara Nikāya* 4, 49, trans. Nyanaponika and Bodhi, 1999, p. 91). There seems here to be no admission that the world of impermanent things might be an object of legitimate aesthetic appreciation. And the monks' and nuns' renunciation of family life and sexuality, so central to much Buddhism, might itself be taken as indicative of an essentially negative attitude to the transitory world and nature. Perhaps it is not surprising, then, that Tsong kha pa encourages, in the *Lam Rim Chen Mo* (trans. Cutler and Newland, 2000, p. 266), the practitioner to develop disgust with cyclic existence (*saṃsāra*). There is in these cases arguably little room for a non-appropriative appreciation of impermanent things.

Maybe, however, the Buddhist disdain for the world evinced here is to be understood simply as therapeutic. It is strong medicine to enable those overcome by craving to be rid of it by generating a repulsion for the things they crave. The cultivation of disdain is just a means to an end. When craving has been eradicated the disdain would fall away too, as it is no longer necessary. The Awakened individuals would thus be receptive to and appreciative of impermanent things in a way that they could not be when they were still battling against craving and attachment.

This is certainly a possibility, but it also seems highly plausible that, while some Buddhists have considered the eradication of craving and attachment to be compatible with a life-affirming non-covetous appreciation of impermanent things, others have felt that eradication of craving and attachment requires a total and permanent renunciation of and disinterest in the beauty of transitory things. Buddhism not uncommonly seems to be concerned with escaping from *saṃsāra* to *nirvāṇa* as quickly as possible, leaving behind and devaluing the things of this world, rather than coming to appreciate this-worldly entities and activities in an non-covetous and non-attached manner. Perhaps such Buddhists would think that human psychology is such that it is impossible, and never will be possible, to enjoy impermanent entities without falling into craving and attachment, even if in very subtle forms. The legitimate Middle Way between greed and aversion might be indifference rather than appreciation.

So, whether the Buddhists can countenance a non-appropriative enjoyment of impermanent things is a moot point, and, unsurprisingly, the Buddhist tradition does not seem to give a single, unequivocal answer. What seems clear is that both an appreciative regard, devoid of craving and attachment, for the transitory world and also thorough disinterest in it are alternatives that are both logically compatible with the Buddhist quest for release from craving and attachment. We have here two important Buddhist conceptions of the nature of liberation: one seeking beauty in the ephemeral, the other seeing the impermanent world as a mire of suffering to be escaped.

CHAPTER THREE

Thorough Knowledge Versus Deficient Understanding

As we have seen, Buddhism often identifies knowledge of the three characteristics as vital to liberation. It is thought to bring an end to craving and hence suffering. However, it can be objected that people often understand that entities are impermanent, have no fixed essence and cause suffering when craved and yet this understanding does not result in the cessation of their craving and attachment. Admittedly, some Unawakened people do think that some things are permanent. For example, there is a common religious belief in a permanent soul and an eternal God. However, many Unawakened people, especially those without such religious convictions, seem to have no such belief in permanent entities. On the contrary, they would claim to believe that things are impermanent. Furthermore, they would also apparently accept that craving for such transitory phenomena causes suffering. For instance, I do not seem to be ignorant about the impermanence of entities. I appear to understand that entities have no fixed essence and that they often change in disagreeable ways. I seem to understand that what I possess will fall out of my possession. I apparently accept that all entities must pass away. And I seem to acknowledge that my craving causes suffering. Yet I am certainly not free from craving and attachment. Buddhism, according to the explanation that I have given, appears to say that my understanding of the three characteristics should liberate me. But the reality is that I continue to crave and suffer. How, then, might one preserve the common Buddhist claim that knowledge of the three characteristics of existence results in liberation in the face of this objection? This is the question that the present chapter will address.

Buddhist sources themselves seem to recognize this issue. There are various texts in which it is lamented that people, though apparently understanding that things are transitory, nevertheless do not cut off their craving and attachment. For instance, Nāgārjuna's *Yuktiṣaṣṭikākārikā* 41 says: 'Those people are disgraceful who say, adhering to the Buddha's path, that all is impermanent and yet remain attached to entities through their disputes.' Presumably the idea here is that these people, though seemingly recognizing the truth of transitoriness, quarrel over the impermanent things which they covet. And the *Theragāthā* 187–8 declares:

> I have seen lay-followers, experts in the doctrine, saying 'Sensual pleasures are impermanent'... Truly they do not know the doctrine as it really is, even though

> they say 'Sensual pleasures are impermanent'. They have no power to cut their desire; therefore they are attached to children, wives, and wealth. (trans. Norman, 1997b, p. 25)

There is clearly here a distinction being made between Unawakened people's assent to the truth of impermanence and the full-blown liberating knowledge possessed by the Awakened people. Unawakened people's understanding is somehow lacking and superficial. Though it is the case that many Unawakened people in a sense understand all three characteristics of existence, there is nevertheless still some deficiency in their knowledge. It is this deficiency that results in the continuation of craving and attachment. If their knowledge of the three characteristics were perfected, if the deficiency were overcome, then the craving for and attachment to entities would be eradicated. Thus, liberation from craving and suffering is not achieved simply by an understanding of the three characteristics. It requires a thorough, complete knowledge.

But what precisely is the difference between a thorough knowledge of the three characteristics that is the prerequisite for liberation and the deficient understanding that many Unawakened people possess? In this chapter I will reflect on and critically analyse two ways, not necessarily mutually incompatible, in which Buddhism might depict the difference. I will argue that the ordinary, deficient understanding of the three characteristics might be characterized as: (1) knowledge by description rather than knowledge by acquaintance, where only knowledge by acquaintance will bring about liberation, and (2) undermined by unconscious beliefs which continue to cause craving and suffering. By contrast, Awakened people's knowledge has neither of these deficiencies.

Knowledge by description rather than knowledge by acquaintance

Modern epistemology commonly makes a distinction between knowledge by acquaintance and knowledge by description. The verb 'to know' has two senses. First, one can know *x*, where *x* stands for any entity or group of entities. I can know the lake in Hyde Park, for example. Second, one can know that *p*, where *p* stands for any proposition. For instance, I can know that 'there is a lake in Hyde Park'. As David Cooper (1999, p. 232) has commented, the English language employs the single verb 'know' in both of these circumstances, whereas the French and German languages each have two verbs, one (*connaître* and *kennen* respectively) for knowing *x* and the other (*savoir* and *wissen* respectively) for knowing that *p*. The English verb 'to know' does double-duty, as it were.

To know *x* is to have a direct acquaintance with *x*. It is knowledge by means of perception. I know the lake in Hyde Park because I have perceived it or I know the large lake in Hyde Park because I have perceived the lake in Hyde Park, including its largeness. By contrast, to know that *p* does not require direct acquaintance. It is knowledge by description or propositional knowledge. I might know that 'there is a lake in Hyde Park' or that 'the lake in Hyde Park is large' without ever having had perceptions of the lake in Hyde Park or its largeness. The knowledge might, for example, be a result of the descriptions provided by a trustworthy friend or an authoritative travel book. I may have this propositional knowledge while never having been to Hyde Park to see the lake for myself. I have a true belief, justified by a means – for example, reliable testimony – other than my perception.

Furthermore, if I know the lake in Hyde Park – that is, if I have knowledge by acquaintance of it – I am able to describe the lake to others who have not perceived it, thus giving them knowledge by description. These people may impart their knowledge that 'there is a lake in Hyde Park' to yet other people, thus creating a chain of propositional knowledge that 'there is a lake in Hyde Park', which can be ultimately traced back to my acquaintance with the lake in Hyde Park.

According to this account, knowledge by acquaintance has epistemic primacy because it is a foundational form of knowledge upon which a string of knowledge by description can be established. Thus, Harry might have knowledge that 'there is *x*' or that '*x* is *y*' without knowing *x* or the *y*-ness of *x*, and Harry might have gained this knowledge by description from Nancy who has knowledge that 'there is *x*' or that '*x* is *y*' without knowing *x* or its *y*-ness. And so on. But at the beginning of this series, there is a person or people, say Chris, who knows *x* or the *y*-ness of *x* and not just that 'there is *x*' or '*x* is *y*'.

Of course, often people have both knowledge by acquaintance and knowledge by description of the same thing. I have both perceived the lake in Hyde Park and know that 'there is a lake in Hyde Park'. In other words, knowing *x* often means that one will know some facts about *x*. However, it is also possible to have knowledge by acquaintance without knowledge by description. A dog or a young child, for example, might perceive the lake in Hyde Park, but be quite unable to formulate the proposition that 'there is a lake in Hyde Park'. Furthermore, it may be that in some cases there can be knowledge by description of an entity or entities which no one has ever known by acquaintance. For instance, in the case of subatomic particles, no one has ever perceived these entities, but scientists infer their existence as the best explanation of observable phenomena. Here they have propositional knowledge that 'there are subatomic particles' without knowing – that is, being acquainted with – the subatomic particles. Finally, as John Hospers (1997, pp. 39–40) notes, it is sometimes argued that knowledge by acquaintance is not really knowledge at all. He says that from this point of view simply staring at or observing some entity is not knowledge. Knowledge requires that 'you have before your mind some statement that is either true or false'. For instance, the perception of the lake in Hyde Park only becomes knowledge when the proposition that 'there is a lake in Hyde Park' is formulated. In other words, all knowledge is knowledge by description. As Hospers says, from this perspective knowledge is always propositional (knowing that). Acquaintance is the raw material for knowledge, because one's knowledge of facts must be grounded in one's own or another person's observations, but is not itself knowledge. Whether or not acquaintance is really knowledge at all is thus a moot point.

Knowledge by acquaintance in Indian thought

Ancient Indian epistemology identifies perception (*pratyakṣa*) as a distinct means of correct cognition or knowledge (*pramāṇa*). By contrast, means of knowledge such as inference (*anumāna*), testimony (*śabda*), and so forth give knowledge of an entity without a perceptual encounter with the entity known. For instance, I know about the terrible floods that occur in Bangladesh perhaps through the testimony of the newspapers or the reports of my Bangladeshi friend, but this knowledge is a different sort from that which I would acquire by perception if I were to go to Bangladesh and see the floods for myself. This seems to correspond to the distinction between knowledge by description and knowledge by acquaintance. Furthermore, many Indian systems of epistemology give perception a foundational status. As Richard King (1999a, p. 147) remarks: 'Perception is considered by most schools to be the *pramāṇa par excellence* ... For instance in the case of the Nyāya school, inferential knowledge (*anumāna*) follows on from perceptual knowledge and lacks its immediacy (*aporokṣatva*).' For example, if I infer that there is a fire on the hill because I can see smoke, my inference 'follows on' from perception because I must both observe the smoke in order to infer the existence of unperceived fire and also I must have previous perceptual experience that 'where there is smoke there is fire'. And objects of perception have a vividness and directness that objects as known by inference cannot have.

The privileging of perception as the superior means of knowledge is certainly a characteristic of much Buddhist thought. Liberating knowledge is often described as *seeing* things as they actually are. It is said to be a *darśana*, that is, a vision or direct observation. Though the testimony of the wise and one's reasoning are often valued, they are usually thought to be simply aids to the final goal, that is, the unmediated perception of reality. This is evident, for example, in the common Buddhist division of understanding or wisdom (*prajñā*) into three types: the understanding that comes from listening to Buddhist teachings, that which develops by means of reflecting on the teachings and that which comes from meditation (see, for example, *Dīgha*

Nikāya 3, 220, trans. Walshe, 1987, p. 486). These three types are organized hierarchically, with the understanding from listening being the lowest, that which is developed by reflecting in the middle and that which comes from meditation as the highest. Clearly there is a process of internalization of Buddhist truths here, where what is simply heard from others is eventually transformed into something that, via reflection and finally meditation, one perceives for oneself.

It can be objected, of course, that perceptual knowledge is not a pristine, unmediated apprehension of the object perceived but involves a degree of conceptualization and judgement or interpretation. Thus, the idea of an entirely accurate perception is problematic. Perceptions may seem to acquaint one directly with the perceived object, yet in fact much of the perceptual situation is a contribution of one's own mind and perceptual apparatus. That the lake in Hyde Park, for example, is perceived in the way that it is (with a certain colour, shape, and so forth) has at least as much to do with the nature of one's sense organs and mind as with the lake in Hyde Park as it is independently of one's perceptual process. The world as it is really exists is not available via perception, because a perception is already an interpretation.

This is certainly a serious challenge to any epistemology which claims that perception has a privileged access to 'things as they really are'. And to a large extent the Buddhists agree with the objection. They think that the perceptions of Unawakened people are inaccurate and interpretation-laden. Thus, Buddhists have often criticized the Nyāya-Vaiśeṣika common-sense realism, according to which everyday objects such as tables, chairs, mountains and so forth exist mind-independently and are usually apprehended just as they really are. According to the Indian Buddhist philosophers Dignāga (480–540 CE) and Dharmakīrti (600–60 CE), though there is a bare perception that apprehends its object 'just as it is', without any distortion or contribution from the mind, for Unawakened people these bare perceptions are generally obscured and distorted by further mental activity (see Klein, 1998, p. 91; King, 1999a, pp. 178–9). That being said, there is a strong tendency within some Buddhist thought to claim that the Awakened person is able to recover the pure perception, stripping away any distorting, conceptualizing tendencies that characterize the Unawakened mind. Dignāga and Dharmakīrti thus refer to a yogic perception (*yogipratyakṣa*) which sees the true nature of things in a pristine fashion. Other Buddhist philosophers concur. For instance, as we will see in more detail in Chapter 5, Tibetan dGe lugs pa Madhyamaka stresses the importance of achieving an undistorted perception of reality. *Seeing* 'things as they really are' clearly has for many Buddhists a sort of foundational veracity, requiring no further justification and with direct, uninterpreted access to reality.

Knowledge by acquaintance and the three characteristics

So, the Buddhists might claim that those who understand the three characteristics and yet still crave and get attached to things have knowledge by description, which is deficient in so far as it is not knowledge by acquaintance. Hence, these Unawakened people continue to crave and to get attached. It is only when their perceptions are purified of distortions, so that their seeing of entities is in accord with their knowledge by description, that craving and attachment for these entities will be stopped. The notion here is that a perception of 'things as they really are' will have more potency or more effect on one's craving and attachment than does knowledge by description, just like perceiving a famine in Ethiopia is far more emotionally powerful than having a merely factual understanding that there is a famine in Ethiopia.

However, it might be protested that it is surely not true that Unawakened people fail to perceive the impermanence of things and their lack of a fixed nature. Nor do they fail to experience directly the suffering that results from craving. On the contrary, the impermanence of entities is normally accessible to people's perceptions. One perceives all sorts of changes, and numerous instances of entities coming into existence and passing away. And in the course of one's life, one often perceives the impermanence and lack of fixed nature of entities that are extremely dear to oneself. This often produces a direct experience of suffering. This is not merely knowledge by description. It is knowledge one has from direct perception. And yet one still craves and gets attached to these impermanent entities. So, even perceptual knowledge of the three characteristics, it seems, does not stop craving and attachment. If Unawakened people have powerful perceptions of the three characteristics and yet continue to crave, it does not seem plausible that the inability to have knowledge by acquaintance of the three characteristics is the root obstacle to liberation. How might the Buddhists deal with this objection?

Some Buddhists would reply that the pristine liberating perception attained by Awakened people is not simply of the impermanence of the objects of craving but, furthermore, that these objects are one and all fabrications. The common-sense things that we think we perceive are not just impermanent; in addition they do not exist mind independently at all. These Buddhists would say that Unawakened people might see everyday things as transitory but they fail to see that these objects are mental constructs. The knowledge by acquaintance required for Awakening is thus a very special and uncommon vision of the illusory nature of the objects of craving. In Chapter 5 I will return to this Buddhist attitude, a type of 'anti-realism' exemplified in various forms by Sarvāstivāda, Sautrāntika, Madhyamaka and Yogācāra Buddhism.

Omniscience

Another reply to the problem would be that, though people often gain the perceptual knowledge of the three characteristics, their knowledge is deficient in so far as they do not perceive that *everything* is impermanent, has no fixed self, and will cause suffering when craved. Perhaps, then, there remains room for craving and attachment so long as the perception of the universal scope of the three characteristics has not been achieved. Unawakened people have an insufficiently extensive knowledge by acquaintance. In other words, the eradication of craving and attachment is dependent on gaining omniscience, that is, the ability to see everything. Awakened people can perceive the all-pervasiveness of the three characteristics, and it is this extraordinary ability that allows them to cut off craving and attachment once and for all.

Indeed, it is a contention of many Buddhists that a Buddha does have omniscience (*sarvākarājñatā*). He can see all things past, present and future. Paul Griffiths (1994) has studied the notion of a Buddha's omniscience as it occurs in a variety of important Mahāyāna texts. Griffiths (1994, pp. 170–72) notes that a Buddha's omniscience is often understood to mean that the Buddha is aware of each and every thing without any effort, that is, without having to turn his mind to the thing known. This means, apparently, that a Buddha constantly knows each and every thing that exists, has existed and will exist. He is said to apprehend everything is a single moment (*ekaṣaṇika*).

Furthermore, according to Bhikkhu Bodhi (see Ñāṇamoli and Bodhi 1995, p. 1273 and p. 1292), there is a common Theravāda view that the Buddha is omniscient. However, the Theravāda notion of the Buddha's omniscience appears to be somewhat weaker than that found in some Mahāyāna sources. The Buddha is thought to be omniscient, but only in the limited sense that, though he can see whatever he chooses, he does not perceive everything simultaneously, but must turn his mind to whatever it is he wants to perceive. He can perceive whatever he adverts his mind to. According to the Theravāda tradition, the Buddha denies that anyone can see everything with one act of consciousness (*ekacitta*).

So, many Buddhists claim that a Buddha has omniscience, even if there are some subtle differences in how this omniscience is understood. Perhaps, then, it is this omniscience, the extraordinary ability to see all impermanence and suffering, that liberates a Buddha. It is Unawakened people's lack of omniscience that stops them from cutting off their craving and attachment. A perception of the entire universe as permeated by the three characteristics would conceivably have an emotional impact which merely limited perceptions of impermanence, not-self and suffering would not have. It seems quite possible that a perception of this magnitude might cause a basic change in affective attitude. Seeing directly that always and everywhere suffering is the fruit of craving for impermanent things might compel one to give up one's selfish, appropriate tendencies once and for all.

Is omniscience really possible?

However, the idea that human beings can become omniscient is obviously a highly contentious position. Modern scientific knowledge of the limitations of the human mind, and its dependence on the physical processes of the brain, surely provides strong evidence that an all-seeing awareness is impossible. Thus, the claim that the eradication of craving and attachment depends on such omniscience might seem to make liberation an unachievable task. That being said, perhaps we should not assume that modern science has a monopoly on knowledge. While it seems to be in the realm of fantasy to suggest, as many Buddhist texts do, that a human being can have a constant awareness of all things past, present and future, it does not seem quite so outlandish to entertain the idea that Buddhist practitioners can achieve, especially in concentrated meditative states, an occasional mystical vision of the whole universe as an impermanent, selfless process and of all sentient beings as suffering as a result of their craving. This might only be a temporary, fleeting vision, but it, and the memory of it, might conceivably be powerful enough to root out the practitioner's craving.

Alternatively, it is presumably open to Buddhists, perhaps especially of a modernist variety, to argue that the objection of the scientist is missing the point because Buddhist claims that Awakened people gain omniscience are not to be taken literally. It is enough for Buddhist practitioners to visualize the manifest entities of the world as impermanent, without self and to imagine vividly all the suffering caused by the craving of sentient beings for such things. It is not that the practitioners actually see the entire world but rather that they engage their imaginations to create a picture in the mind of what the entire impermanent, selfless world full of craving-induced suffering must be like. Perhaps such use of the imagination, especially when systematically cultivated in the context of deeply concentrated meditation, would have a powerful transformative effect on one's emotional response to the world, prompting one to relinquish craving and attachment once and for all.

Are Awakened people always thought to be omniscient?

It would be incorrect, I think, to suggest that Buddhists have generally considered omniscience to be vital to liberation. For example, the Theravāda tradition makes a distinction between Arhats and Buddhas. Usually, the title 'Arhat' is given to a person who is thought to have achieved Awakening by following a Buddha's teaching. By contrast, the title 'Buddha' tends to be reserved for those very rare individuals who are thought to attain Awakening on their own, that is, without an Awakened teacher to guide them. Arhats are considered to be free from craving and attachment, yet they are not thought to have the all-seeing knowledge sometimes attributed to Buddhas.

In Mahāyāna Buddhism, practitioners are sometimes said to be free of craving and attachment by the sixth stage (*bhūmi*) of the Bodhisattva path, often equated with the state of the Arhat and the attainment of the perfection of wisdom (*prajñāpāramitā*), yet omniscience is said to occur only when one has achieved Buddhahood and the path of no more learning (*aśaikṣamārga*), having traversed all ten stages of the Bodhisattva path (see Williams, 1989, p. 211). Indeed, it would appear that the omniscience of a Mahāyāna Buddha has more to do with enabling him to enact his great compassion for other sentient beings than with eradicating his own craving and attachment. Seeing all beings and their plights, and seeing fully their requirements both mundane and religious, a Buddha is in a superb position to offer them appropriate aid, either pragmatic or spiritual. He has a God's-eye view and is thus able to help sentient beings effectively. So, perhaps it is possible to overemphasize the connection between omniscience and liberation from craving.

Furthermore, some Buddhist texts in the Pāli Canon seem to depict the Buddha himself as *not* having omniscience. For example, there is the famous passage at *Majjhima Nikāya* 1, 426–32 (trans. Ñāṇamoli and Bodhi, 1995, pp. 533–6) where the Buddha is asked by the disciple Māluṅkyāputta whether the world has a beginning or end, both or neither, whether the *tathāgatha* exists or does not exist after death, both or neither, and whether the life-principle is the same as or different from the body. The Buddha's response is that he never said that he would give the answers to such questions. Rather, he had always said that he teaches the truth of suffering, its cause, that there is an end of suffering by eliminating its cause and the path to the elimination of suffering. Answering such metaphysical queries is not connected with the Buddhist goal of overcoming the problem of suffering. The passage does not state whether the Buddha knows or does not know the answers to the questions. It simply says that he does not answer them because of their irrelevance to the liberating path he has explained. But the possibility remains that the Buddha did not know the answers to the questions and thus his knowledge was limited. That is, he was not omniscient.

Furthermore, at *Saṃyutta Nikāya* 320–22 (trans. Bodhi, 2000, pp. 1773–4) it is related that some monks misinterpreted the meaning of a sermon of the Buddha concerning the 'foulness of the body'. The Buddha taught that the body inside the skin is ugly and repulsive and thus should not be an object of craving and attachment. The monks took this to mean that they should put an end to their bodies and thus committed suicide. As a result the Buddha formulated the monastic precept prohibiting suicide and declared that violation of this precept would lead to expulsion from the monastic community (see Harvey, 2000, p. 288). This story seems to indicate that the

Buddha did not realize, he did not foresee, the effect that his teaching would have on the monks. In other words, his knowledge was limited, at least in the sense that he could not see into the future on this occasion.

Finally, *Majjhima Nikāya* 1, 22–3 (trans. Ñāṇamoli and Bodhi, 1995, pp. 105–6) claims that when he became Awakened Siddhattha Gotama gained the 'three knowledges': (1) the ability to see his past lives and (2) the ability to see the past lives of others as they occurred in dependence on good and bad actions (*kamma*), and (3) the knowledge of the Four Noble Truths together with the knowledge of the destruction of his taints (*āsava*). This latter point means that he knew that craving and ignorance, the taints, had been eradicated and that there would be no more rebirth for him. This indicates that Awakening is not simply the eradication of one's craving and ignorance, but also the knowledge that one's craving and ignorance has been eradicated. In short, Awakened people know that they are Awakened.

While the three knowledges do indicate that the Buddha's perceptual capacity is thought to be far more extensive than that of ordinary human beings, they do not amount to omniscience, given that there would still be things that a Buddha could not perceive. For example, there is no suggestion that the Buddha can see into the future or has a detailed knowledge of the entire physical universe or of the minutiae of all individual people's daily lives and minds. Nevertheless, given that the Buddha (and presumably the Arhats too) can reputedly see *so much more* impermanence and suffering than do Unawakened people, perhaps this enables him to cut off his craving and attachment once and for all. And, as with the claims to omniscience, Buddhist modernists, faced with the challenge of adapting Buddhist ideas to the scientific worldview, might seek to interpret the three knowledges non-literally as an imaginative visualization that practitioners can produce in meditation in order to facilitate liberation.

Unconscious belief

So far, I have given a critical analysis of the theory that Unawakened people's knowledge of the three characteristics is deficient because it is not knowledge by acquaintance. However, there is another possible explanation of the deficiency. Perhaps Unawakened people continue to crave despite apparently understanding the three characteristics because they have an unconscious and false belief that things are permanent, have an abiding essence, and will not cause suffering if coveted. It is this unconscious and false belief that causes such people to crave and get attached. The unconscious false belief must be removed if liberation is to be achieved.

Is there much evidence for the idea of such an unconscious belief, as the root cause for craving and attachment, in the Buddhist tradition? I think that we can answer this question in the affirmative. For example, Padmasiri De Silva (1991, p. 43) claims that Theravāda Buddhism advocates that there are unconscious wrong beliefs which fuel one's craving. De Silva points to the notion, found in the Pāli *sutta*s, of the hidden proclivity (*anusaya*) towards (wrong) views (*diṭṭhi*). 'Wrong beliefs exist', he says, 'at the level of dormant dispositions (*diṭṭhānusaya*) and account for the unconscious roots of prejudices and strong biases which colour our emotional life.' Most important among these prejudices is the 'personality view' (*sakkāyadiṭṭhi*), the belief that one has a permanent self. The *Majjhima Nikāya* 1, 432–3, for instance, claims that: 'The young tender infant lying prone does not even have the notion "personality", so how could personality view [that is, the idea that he has a permanent self] arise in him? Yet the underlying tendency [*anusaya*] to personality etc. lies within him' (trans. Ñāṇamoli and Bodhi, 1995, p. 537).

One can find support in other parts of the Buddhist tradition for the notion of unconscious beliefs. For example, central to Yogācāra Buddhism is the concept of the storehouse consciousness (*ālayavijñāna*) which contains unmanifested seeds (*bīja*) of ignorance, not present to one's conscious mind, but nevertheless a cause of the craving, attachment and suffering which one experiences. The common Yogācāra metaphor is that these seeds colour or perfume consciousness until consciousness undergoes the transformation in Awakening, called the 'revolution at the basis' (*āśrayaparāvṛtti*), where the seeds are neutralized or exterminated, and the unconscious source of ignorance is thus finally overcome (see *Triṃśikā* 1–7, trans. Anacker, 1998, p. 186). There is also the common Tibetan notion, found for example in the writings of Tsong kha pa (see Napper, 1987, pp. 84–7) and his disciples (see, for example, Cabezón, 1992, pp. 128–35), of the innate (*lhan skyes*) misconception of reality, which is said to be harboured in the minds of all sentient beings whether or not they are aware of it. Even babies, animals and so forth are thought to have this innate misconception. And it is the innate misconception that is said to be the root cause of craving, attachment and suffering.

Can there be unconscious beliefs?

It is tempting to think, however, that the notion of an unconscious belief is an oxymoron, for a belief of which one is unaware seems not to be one's belief at all. Is it not essential to the notion of 'having a belief' that one is aware of one's belief? I think there is plenty of evidence to answer this question in the negative, however. The resources of contemporary philosophical reflection on the nature of beliefs are of some assistance here. Many epistemologists claim that a belief is essentially an attitude of acceptance of a proposition, where this attitude is a disposition rather than a currently occurring mental event. In other words, I might believe proposition x even though I am not presently having a mental episode in which I accept proposition *x*, so long as I would be disposed to accept proposition *x* if it were to come to my attention. In which case, our beliefs are not always transparent to us. That is, I might believe proposition *x* without being presently conscious of that belief.

Thus, Nicholas Everitt and Alec Fisher (1995, pp. 54–5) argue that there are beliefs which one has which are unconscious dispositions in the sense that one has *never* consciously entertained them. One holds the beliefs, even though one has at no time thought about or been aware of them. To use Everitt and Fisher's example, it is highly probable that I have never consciously entertained the belief or understanding that 'the world contains more than ninety-nine ants'. This is a proposition that, it is likely, I have never thought about. It is not that I once thought that 'the world contains more than ninety-nine ants' and now I have stopped thinking about it. It is rather that I have never had this thought. It has never been brought to my attention. And yet it is arguable that I do have the unconscious belief that 'the world contains more than ninety-nine ants'. Were a friend to tell me that 'the world contains more than ninety-nine ants' this would not be regarded by me as new information or a revelation. I would be disposed to accept the proposition. I would perhaps exclaim that 'I believe that, of course!' The proposition seems to be one that I believed already, though I had never attended to it.

Now, this sense in which beliefs might be unconscious is somewhat controversial because it seems to have the peculiar, counter-intuitive consequence that people actually have an infinite number of beliefs. There appear to be an unending number of propositions that people would assent to but which they have never thought about. For instance, not only do I believe that 'there are more than ninety-nine ants in the world', but I also believe 'there are more than one hundred ants in the world', and that 'there are more than one hundred and one ants in the world' and so on. And also I believe that 'there are more than ninety-nine fleas in the world' and so on. I have never thought about these propositions, but I would accept them if they were brought to my attention. As Paul Moser et al. (1998, pp. 53–4) point out, there are an infinite number of propositions to which one has never consciously assented, but which are presuppositions or consequences of beliefs one has consciously entertained. The belief that 'there are more than ninety-nine ants in the world', for instance, might be a consequence of a belief I have perhaps at some point consciously held, namely, that 'there are a very large number of ants in the world'. And, as Moser et al. say, if I consciously accept that $2 \times 5 = 10$, for example, then underlying this belief are a host of propositions about the number system and the mathematical laws which govern it which I might be said to believe even though I may never have considered them. Moser et al. claim that some philosophers 'bite the bullet' and accept that there are an infinite number of beliefs, but others would argue that here we need to distinguish a mere disposition to believe that *p* from an actual belief that *p*. For the latter philosophers, a proposition of which we have never been conscious but which we would be inclined to accept if it were brought to our attention is not a belief. It only becomes a belief when we have thought of it at least once. By contrast, Everitt and Fisher's claim that any proposition we would be disposed to accept is a belief even if we have never been conscious of it would seem to imply that, according to them, there are an infinite number of beliefs.

Now, the Buddhists might contend with some plausibility that some Unawakened people do believe that (some) things – for example, the soul and God – are permanent and so forth, yet have never thought about this belief. They have never consciously entertained the thought, yet, when asked, they might say that 'yes, of course I believe that'. It is as though they have always believed this, but have never turned their attention to their belief. Perhaps it has been imbibed by them from their cultural and religious environment, without any attention or reflection on their part. Or such a belief in the soul or God might even be an innate inclination, which is deeply engrained in the human psyche but has not necessarily been articulated and brought to the person's awareness.

Self-deception

However, the situation that we are addressing in this chapter is somewhat different. The Unawakened people we are considering are those who crave and yet apparently believe that things are impermanent, selfless and cause suffering when craved. Such people would deny that they have the belief that things are permanent, have a fixed self and do not cause suffering when craved. It is not that they have never thought about this belief but would happily accept that they have it when it is brought to their attention. On the contrary, such people would say that they actually believe that things are not permanent, do not have a self and will cause suffering if craved.

Once again Everitt and Fisher (1995, pp. 54–5) make a relevant point. It is arguable, they say, that there are beliefs that one has never consciously held and also that one would fail to recognize as one's beliefs, even if it were suggested that one does hold the beliefs in question. People would hold such beliefs without being able to admit that this is the case. They would deny that they hold these beliefs, and yet hold them they do. Everitt and Fisher give the example of beliefs that have strong and unpleasant emotional significance, such as the belief that 'my father hates me'. Some people who hold this belief might not be able to 'face up' to this belief. It might remain hidden from their consciousness and they might refuse to accept that they have this belief. They would not believe that they have this belief! Obviously this is the type of unconscious belief that modern psychoanalysis would posit and investigate and which is thought to be the cause of a variety of mental disorders.

Perhaps, then, it is open to the Buddhists to claim that Unawakened people might have such an unconscious belief when they apparently accept that the things they crave are impermanent, without self and cause suffering when coveted. Is it not possible that such people who claim to have the belief that things are impermanent, selfless, and will cause suffering when craved, actually believe that things are permanent, have a self, and will not cause suffering if craved? It is not that such people are simply lying to others about what they actually believe. Rather, they are not themselves aware that they have such a belief. They are self-deceived. Such people think that they believe things to be impermanent, selfless, and causes of suffering when craved, but in reality they do not. So, what they really believe without being aware of it is contradicted by what they mistakenly think that they believe. They may actually, unbeknownst to themselves, harbour the belief that things, or some things, have a permanent essence and thus there is no harm in craving them. Perhaps, it is too emotionally painful to admit this belief, and maybe the force of their craving and attachment is such that their minds have become clouded, as it were, so that they cannot see what their true belief is. This would explain why some people continue to crave and to suffer, while apparently (but not really) accepting the three characteristics of existence.

The problem of proof

However, there is a serious problem of verification with regard to such an unconscious belief. If one is not aware of, and will not admit, one's (supposed) belief that entities are permanent, have an abiding essence and do not cause suffering when craved, then how can one prove that it exists? It might be replied that, although one is not conscious of one's belief, it nevertheless governs one's responses to the world. This unconscious belief has enormous influence on one's attitudes and behaviour, despite being hidden from oneself. That is, the unconscious belief makes one crave and get attached. The proof of the unconscious belief that entities are permanent and so forth is thus precisely the fact that one continues to crave and get attached. If one did not have the unconscious belief that entities are permanent, have an abiding essence and do not cause suffering when craved, then one would not crave and get attached. One does, however, crave and get attached. Therefore, the unconscious belief that entities are permanent and so forth must exist.

But surely here is a vicious circle. The proof that one has such an unconscious belief cannot be the very behaviour of which the unconscious belief is meant to be the cause. If x is explained to have cause y, then x cannot itself be used as the proof for the existence of cause y. If craving and attachment are explained to have as their cause an unconscious belief, then it simply will not do to appeal to the existence of the craving and attachment as itself the proof that this craving and attachment is caused by an unconscious belief. There must be some other, independent means of verifying that the unconscious belief, rather than something else, is what causes the craving and attachment.

However, even granted that there is such a vicious circle, it might still be argued that, though indeed one cannot prove that there is such an unconscious belief that causes craving and attachment, this does not establish that it does not exist. To fail to prove that *y* is the cause of *x* is not to prove that it is not the case that *y* is the cause of *x*. There might be an unconscious belief, which causes craving and attachment, even though one cannot prove its existence. A hidden cause is not a non-existent cause.

While this is true, it nevertheless is dubious to posit as a cause of an observed phenomenon *x* another phenomenon *y* for which there is no proof. Surely it would be more reasonable to look for other causes for which there is some proof, rather than appealing to such an unproven explanation for the existence of phenomenon *x*. The attempt to explain the existence of craving and attachment as caused by an unconscious belief should give way to other explanations for which, at least, there is some justification.

Otherwise, an unconscious belief, not requiring any proof, might be posited as the cause for any sort of behaviour. Suppose, for instance, that I like doughnuts. A friend might claim that the cause of my liking doughnuts is my (false) belief that doughnuts are good for my health. I might object that I like doughnuts yet I do not have the belief that they are good for my health. Actually, I like doughnuts while at the same time believing that they are bad for my health. The friend might reply that I must in that case have an unconscious belief that doughnuts are good for my health. In which case, I do not really think they are bad for my health. I am self-deceived. If this were not the case, the friend might say, I would not continue to like doughnuts. If I object that I do not have such an unconscious belief, the friend might respond that in fact I do have the unconscious belief, but, as it is unconscious, I am not aware of it! But such a notion of an unconscious belief that doughnuts are good for my health is entirely unproven, and thus seems unhelpful and highly speculative as an explanation of the cause for my liking doughnuts. The friend would surely do better to admit that one must actually look elsewhere for the cause of my liking doughnuts! For instance, perhaps I like doughnuts because I find them delicious, and I therefore prefer to eat them despite knowing that they are bad for my health.

The explanation that one's craving and attachment are caused by an unconscious belief can be compared to the (highly dubious) claim that one's craving and attachment is a result of undetectable demons who possess one and compel one to crave and get attached. One can never prove that there are such undetectable demons which cause this behaviour because, even if they did exist, there would be, by definition, no way of detecting them other than by appealing to their supposed effects, that is, the observable phenomena of craving and attachment. But as it is precisely these effects that the demons are intended to explain, the effects themselves cannot be used as evidence for the existence of the demons. It is true that in failing to prove that there are any such demons causing one's craving and attachment, one has not proven that there are no such demons. However, in the absence of the evidence for their existence, it seems unreasonable and fanciful to suggest that they are in fact the cause of one's craving and attachment. It would seem reasonable to look for another explanation for which there is some evidence. Like this claim that demons cause one's craving and attachment, the notion that one's craving and attachment are caused by an unconscious belief seems to introduce a mystery in the guise of an explanation.

Making the unconscious belief conscious

However, the Buddhists might conceivably reply that this objection is quite unfair. Although it is true to say that one is not and has not been conscious of one's belief that entities are permanent, have a self and will not cause suffering when craved, this is not to say that this belief must remain inaccessible to one's awareness. On the contrary, one can become aware of the unconscious belief and this would be a proof of its existence. One may come to realize that one has such a belief, even though one had not admitted it to oneself previously.

The Buddhists might say that one can become conscious of this belief through the use of meditative techniques. Perhaps this ordinarily unconscious belief can come to one's awareness in the context of the mental absorptions (*dhyāna*) reputedly achieved in *śamatha* meditation, which is said to make the mind especially pliable and concentrated. Maybe this meditative training would give one the ability to plumb the depths, so to speak, of one's unconscious mind, so that one would see clearly one's ordinarily unconscious belief that entities are permanent, have a fixed self, and do not cause suffering when craved. One would no longer be self-deceived. Furthermore, continued reflection on the three characteristics of entities in this meditative context, where the ordinarily unconscious belief has been brought to one's awareness, might enable one eventually to eradicate this false belief once and for all, thereby providing a complete release from craving and attachment.

But here the proponent of the unconscious false belief that causes one's craving and attachment is appealing to a special experience as providing the proof that such an unconscious misunderstanding exists. Such an appeal must remain unconvincing to the uninitiated outsider who is not party to the experience. There is also the issue of whether such experiences are reliable or trustworthy. It remains doubtful, then, whether an inference from craving and attachment to an unconscious belief in permanence and so forth as their cause is really an inference to the best explanation.

Furthermore, it can be argued that the problem with the notion of such an unconscious belief is not just that there is no publicly accessible proof provided, but also that it seems unfalsifiable. Is there any evidence that would conclusively refute the theory that there is such an unconscious belief which is hidden to everyone including the believer? How could one ever establish that this unobservable unconscious belief does not exist? What evidence to refute the idea would be admissible in this case? And, following Karl Popper, we might argue that a theory which cannot conceivably be shown to be false by some test or potential counter-evidence is not in any meaningful sense true.

Alternatively, we might argue that this unconscious belief is falsifiable because many Unawakened people apparently assent to the three characteristics of existence on the basis of a considerable amount of personal experience of impermanence, not-self and suffering. Thus, it is not just that there is no proof that these people are self-deceived and have an unconscious belief in permanence and so forth. In addition, there is pretty strong evidence that they do really believe that things are impermanent, have no self, and cause suffering when craved. Very often such people seem deeply convinced that the three characteristics are the truth about phenomena. So, they might continue to crave and suffer, but it is implausible to suggest that this is caused by an unconscious belief that things are permanent and so forth.

Thus, either the Buddhists should conclude that there is probably not an unconscious belief in permanence and so forth motivating such people's behaviour or else they must claim that, despite the evidence to the contrary, such people are self-deceived and there are mysterious unconscious beliefs that lurk like undetectable demons in such people's minds. But in the latter case, they would seem to be saying that there is no evidence that would convince them that this is not the case. No matter how much experience of impermanence and so forth the Unawakened people's (apparent) belief in the three characteristics might be founded upon, and no matter how convinced of the truth of the three characteristics they would seem to be, the Buddhists would make the unfalsifiable claim that these people are self-deceived and actually believe things to have a permanent essence and to be causes of satisfaction rather than suffering.

Further thoughts on unconscious beliefs

However, the idea of unconscious beliefs is actually multi-faceted and there is more to be said about it. Everitt and Fisher (1995, pp. 54–5) notice that there are many beliefs one holds which one has been conscious of at some point in the past but of which one is not presently conscious. Take, for instance, my beliefs that 'Paris is the capital city of France' and that '2 + 2 = 4'. These are beliefs I hold and of which I have been conscious. For example, I was conscious of these beliefs when I learned them in school. However, I rarely think about these beliefs. I certainly am not continuously rehearsing them in my mind. For the most part they are unconscious beliefs, that is, beliefs that I am not thinking about. I can and do, when required, bring these beliefs to consciousness, and this is the proof that I do indeed have them. At any particular time most of one's previously consciously held beliefs will be below the threshold of consciousness, so to speak, in this way. One is explicitly thinking about only a minute amount of what one has at some point in the past consciously believed. Indeed, there are occasions, such as in deep sleep, when everything one has consciously believed is unconscious. Note, however, that it is not that such unconscious beliefs have been forgotten. They are still there, available to consciousness when required. It is just that they are not presently objects of consciousness.

There are clearly people who believe in permanence, an abiding self and that this self will be a cause of great happiness (for example, in an afterlife) and yet rarely think about this belief. In so far as these people accept that (some) things are permanent and so forth, they are usually unconscious of their belief. But such people have at times been conscious of their belief. It is just that they are not presently thinking about it. Christians, for instance, might usually believe that the soul and God are eternal, yet many of them, especially if they are not particularly devout, might only rarely bring this belief to mind.

Insufficient attentiveness and reflection

The Buddhists can also point out that there are also many Unawakened people who have the belief that things are impermanent, without self and cause suffering when craved but are unconscious of this belief in the sense that they rarely think about it. In other words, their belief that things have the three characteristics is something they have thought about from time to time perhaps, but they do not bring it to mind often enough. Perhaps this is the deficiency in their knowledge that prevents them from achieving liberation.

Indeed, people often hardly notice many of their beliefs. I glance out of the window and perceive a tree with green leaves, swaying in the wind and with a blackbird perched on one of its branches. I form the belief that there is a tree with green leaves, swaying with the wind and with a blackbird perched on one of its branches. Though I perceive these things, I am unlikely to give them very much attention. Very soon my mind moves on to other matters. It would be unusual for me to stop and think about the belief I have formed, that is, to hold it in my mind and give it some consideration. Similarly, many Unawakened people have, on the basis of their experiences, the belief that things are impermanent, without an abiding essence, and cause suffering when craved, but, according to Buddhism, they do not take enough notice of this belief. They are insufficiently attentive to what they believe. This belief is too often unconscious.

So, it is not enough to believe that all things have the three characteristics. One must also engage in systematic and sustained reflection on what one believes. Otherwise the facts of impermanence, not-self and suffering will have very little impact on one's mind. Contemplation on these three characteristics is, the Buddhists can point out, a relatively rare event. Perhaps such reflection is most common and poignant when we have the often traumatic experience of losing someone or something to whom or which we are very attached. At this point impermanence, selflessness and suffering come very sharply into focus and we are likely to reflect on them. But this attentiveness to the three characteristics usually fades rapidly. We do not sustain it.

Attentiveness and reflection in meditation

A particularly powerful opportunity for such reflection would take place in Buddhist meditation. According to a very common Buddhist meditation theory, 'insight' (*vipaśyanā*) reflections focused on the true nature of reality can be introduced in the context of the absorption and concentration produced by calming (*śamatha*) meditation. For the Buddhists, such reflections can be especially important in eradicating craving, because one is here thinking about the three characteristics while the mind is poised and pliable. In this special state of consciousness the psyche is thought to be receptive to transformation and the thoughts one has are more influential than normal.

Clearly such meditative contemplations might focus on the impermanent and selfless nature of phenomena, and practitioners might constantly turn over in their minds these realities. Furthermore, they might engage in sustained reflection on suffering, contemplating that continued craving for such impermanent, selfless entities will inevitability lead to disappointment and anguish. The repetitive attention to these truths in a concentrated state of mind might lead to a weakening and even the eradication of one's craving and attachment. In other words, such reflection would produce eventually the transformation of one's emotional orientation, allowing one to 'let go', finding composure in impermanence and selflessness, rather than continuing with one's covetousness.

Meditative reflection on interconnectedness

Furthermore, it might be argued that meditative reflection which focuses on and probes further into the not-self teaching in particular would be a very potent tool for stopping craving and attachment. It will be recalled that the Buddhist idea of not-self is not simply that no thing has a permanent, abiding essence. It also means that everything that exists does so in dependence upon causal conditions. Not-self has as its corollary the central Buddhist teaching of dependent origination or interdependence (*pratītyasamutpāda*). Nothing exists autonomously. There is no independent, self-standing entity. The world is in fact a vast web of interconnected phenomena. Everything that exists does so in dependence on conditions. In which case, what we call 'the self' is actually not separate from the world that it inhabits. No individual is an island unto him or herself. One's personality is formed, for example, by education, the values and attitudes of one's culture, the influence of family, friends and teachers. Furthermore, one's existence depends upon natural phenomena, such as the sun, air, water and foodstuffs.

Now, it might be argued that sustained, concentrated reflection on the interconnectedness of one's self with other things and people would naturally lead to a weakening, and perhaps finally an ending, of craving and attachment. The appropriative emotion of craving might be replaced by empathy and altruism, motivated by one's understanding that self and other are not autonomous, unconnected things. One's sense of separation from others would be reduced, the boundaries softened, and one's concern for other people and the natural world would increase. It is even conceivable that such sustained reflection, particularly when done in the context of formal meditation when the mind is deeply absorbed, might lead to a sort of extraordinary perception, in which the hard distinction between self and other is actually seen to fall away, replaced by a vision of one's interconnectedness with all that is normally thought to be outside and beyond the self. What this would be like is admittedly difficult to imagine, but it is not implausible that it might lead one to have a less appropriative, selfish attitude.

Indeed the claim that serious reflection on interconnectedness should lead directly to the weakening and eradication of craving and attachment seems to be a popular idea among some modern Buddhists, though I am unsure that such reflections occur very much in the earlier Buddhist tradition. They seem to be largely a new development, as a creative adaptation of some key Buddhist ideas in the face of distinctively modern preoccupations such as the conservation of nature, globalization and the growing sense of a shared cross-cultural human community. For instance, the Thai monk Buddhadāsa Bhikkhu promotes a form of environmental Buddhism, according to which reflection on not-self and interconnectedness leads to an abandonment of craving and attachment, and the stimulation of a concern for nature and other people. As Donald Swearer (1997, p. 27) comments:

> Caring in Buddhadāsa's dhammic sense ... is the active expression of our empathetic identification with all life-forms: sentient and nonsentient, human beings and nature ... To conserve (*anurak*) nature (*thamachāt*), therefore, translates as having at the core of one's very being the quality of empathetic caring for all things in the world in their natural conditions; that is to say, to care

for them as they really are rather than as I might benefit from them or as I might like them to be. Indeed, *anurak thamachāt* implies that the 'I' is not over against nature but interactively co-dependent with it. In other words, the moral/spiritual quality of non-attachment of self-forgetfulness necessarily implies the ontological realization of interdependent co-arising.

Meditative reflection on radical impermanence

Another perhaps more traditional meditative reflection would involve contemplation of the deeper meaning of the notion of impermanence. According to the Tibetan dGe lugs pa tradition (see Klein 1998, pp. 134–40), practitioners should be encouraged in their meditations to reflect not just on the impermanence of entities but also on the idea that all things change moment by moment. In other words, it is not just that things are impermanent, but that they are radically impermanent. No thing stays the same, even for an instant. This teaching is called the doctrine of 'subtle' impermanence, as opposed to the teaching of 'coarse' impermanence that recognizes that things change, but without acknowledging their momentariness. The understanding of coarse impermanence would be noticing that a tree, for example, changes over time and eventually ceases to exist whereas the recognition of subtle impermanence would involve discerning that the various material phenomena that constitute the tree are in constant flux. The tree has an apparent stability but, on closer examination, it is made up of many natural processes, many of which are on the microscopic level, which are never static.

Now, it is striking that, although people do perceive things as impermanent, they do not usually ascertain that the perceived things change moment by moment. According to the dGe lugs pas, sustained meditative reflection on the transitoriness of phenomena can eventually produce a supernormal, yogic perception (*rnal 'byor mngon sum*) that ascertains the constantly changing nature of things. Thus, sustained meditative reflections might lead to a 'more perceptive perception' that things are not just impermanent but also are ever-changing.

It might be argued that this perception that all things are changing moment by moment can result in liberation from craving and suffering. Seeing coarse impermanence – that is, that the things they covet are impermanent but nevertheless remain for a while, for a long time in some cases – people may still be inclined to crave them. Seeing subtle impermanence – that is, the constantly changing nature of these things – and thus sensing the extreme instability of every thing, people might have extra motivation to give up their craving for such radically changeable entities.

Whether such a supernormal perception is of course possible is debatable. Are human beings really capable of perceiving the minute momentary changes that all things (supposedly) undergo? It is perhaps rather hard to imagine what this would be like. Furthermore, it can be objected that human sensory faculties and the brain are not equipped to produce such a perception. This may or may not be true. However, the Buddhist modernists can again rebuff the objector here by claiming that they do not literally see things changing moment by moment. Rather, what they aim to do in their meditations is to produce, using the imagination, a vivid mental picture of things as a constantly changing stream of events. It is this lucid meditative vision which can perhaps help put an end to craving.

Mindfulness in daily life

Important as they are considered to be, Buddhism usually stresses that intensive formal meditations are not enough. In addition, there needs to be constant reflection in daily life on the three characteristics. The merely temporary and occasional reflections on impermanence, suffering and selflessness ideally need to be transformed into a permanent attentiveness. Only then will one's knowledge of the three characteristics be fully conscious and the deficiency which causes continued craving overcome.

The Theravāda tradition calls this attentiveness 'mindfulness' (*sati*) and thorough or wise attention (*yoniso manasikāra*). Commenting on the idea of *yoniso manasikāra* as it occurs at *Majjhima Nikāya* 1, 7, Bhikkhu Bodhi (Ñāṇamoli and Bodhi, 1995, p. 1169) writes that 'wise attention (*yoniso manasikāra*) is glossed as attention that is the right means (*upāya*), on the right track (*patha*). It is explained as mental advertence, consideration, or preoccupation that accords with the truth, namely, attention to the impermanent as impermanent, etc.' A good example of this common Buddhist emphasis on mindfulness is found in the forest monastery of the twentieth-century Thai monk Ajahn Chah, where the monks are encouraged to dwell on the truth of impermanence throughout the day, in all their activities (see Thompson, 1997). The Vietnamese Zen master Thich Nhat Hanh (1987) also stresses the importance of such constant mindfulness. Such mindfulness practices have a venerable pedigree. For instance, *Dīgha Nikāya* 2, 292 says:

> A bhikkhu applies full attention either in going forward or back; in looking straight on or looking away; in bending or in stretching; in wearing robes or carrying the bowl; in eating, drinking, chewing or savouring; in attending to the calls of nature; in walking, in standing, in sitting; in falling asleep, in waking; in speaking or in keeping silence. In all these he applies full attention. (trans. Rahula, 1959, p. 111)

This passage is from the influential Theravāda *Satipaṭṭānasutta*, 'The *Sutta* on the Foundations of Mindfulness', according to which monks (and nuns, presumably) are to develop a continual mindfulness of their feelings, their bodies, the physical things around them and their mental states. They are to be constantly aware that they and everything else are simply transitory conglomerations of physical and, in the case of sentient beings, psychological processes. They are to be mindful that clinging on to such impermanent phenomena will lead to suffering. It is this constant reflection on the three characteristics that puts an end to craving once and for all.

This Buddhist idea of mindfulness invites comparison with the thoughts of the German philosopher Martin Heidegger. In *Being and Time*, Heidegger (1962, pp. 279–311) contends that, for the most part, people live in an inauthentic relationship with the inevitable prospect of their own death. They know that they must die yet in everyday life they tend to be forgetful of their impending demise. Thus, life is lived on the whole in a state of inauthenticity and 'tranquillization', where reality is avoided rather than faced. Only at exceptional moments, for example, when a loved one dies or one is faced by a terminal disease, does the truth that one is going to die erupt into one's consciousness, so to speak, and only at such rare times does one achieve an authentic relation with the truth about one's finitude. The Buddhist attitude, it would seem, is to stay in an authentic relationship to death, and impermanence in general, at all times. Meditation techniques where practitioners reflect on the three characteristics are particularly intense periods of reflection on impermanence, but the aim is often to enable practitioners to bring this awareness of transitoriness into all their activities. Whatever practitioners do – eating, talking, walking, defecating – they are to remain mindful of 'how things really are'.

Mindfulness as a form of knowledge

It is common in Western philosophy to regard knowledge as a possession that one has whether or not one is presently cognizing what one knows. For instance, I have the knowledge that dinosaurs are extinct even when I am not thinking that dinosaurs are extinct. One does not generally say that I no longer know that dinosaurs are extinct simply because I am not presently thinking about this proposition. Let me call this sense of the term 'knowledge' – that is, knowledge as a possession that one has whether or not one is presently cognizing what one knows – knowledge (type 1).

In Indian philosophy, Buddhist and non-Buddhist, there is, by contrast, a tendency to think of knowledge as an actual correct cognition. As Bimalal Matilal (1986, pp. 97–101) has pointed out, this is particularly clear in the Nyāya epistemology, where knowledge (*pramā*) is identified as a particular type of cognition, distinct from erroneous cognitions, memories, doubts, and so forth. Hence '*pramā* 'is usually translated as 'knowledge-episode', 'valid cognition' or 'correct cognition'. In this sense, one knows that dinosaurs are extinct when one is presently thinking about this proposition. Knowledge is a mental event that occurs at a particular time and then passes away, to be replaced by further and often different mental events. I am presently having the knowledge-episode, the correct cognition, that dinosaurs are extinct. But soon this knowledge-episode will be replaced by other cognitions. Let me call this sense of knowledge, as a correct cognitive event, knowledge (type 2).

The Buddhist might argue that, although many Unawakened people indeed understand impermanence, suffering and selflessness, they most of the time do not have the cognition of these three characteristics. In other words, one has knowledge (type 1), but only rarely knowledge (type 2), of 'how things really are'. In which case, the Buddhist might claim that the knowledge of the impermanence of entities that eradicates craving and attachment is knowledge (type 2). In order to cut off craving and attachment, one must have frequent, possibly constant, cognitions of the three characteristics. It is this frequent or constant cognition of the impermanence, suffering and selflessness that is lacking in most people for most of the time. One is inattentive to the three characteristics, and hence one craves and gets attached to entities.

This does not entail, it is important to note, that, when one is inattentive to impermanence, suffering and selflessness, one at that time has the false cognition that entities are permanent, have an abiding essence, and are the cause of joy rather than suffering. To say, for example, that one is not currently attentive to the impermanence of entities is not to say that one has the (false) belief that entities are permanent. One's ignorance is a lack of awareness rather than an actual misapprehension. It is simply that one is not at the moment thinking about the impermanence of things, rather than that one is thinking that entities are permanent, just like, if I am currently not thinking that dinosaurs are extinct, I do not therefore (erroneously) cognize that dinosaurs are not extinct.

The knowledge that brings liberation from craving and suffering is thus the constant attentiveness to the three characteristics of existence. Of course, one might wonder whether this mindfulness throughout daily life is psychologically possible. Is the human mind strong enough to allow such unbreakable mindfulness? It might be that the Buddhists here have a rather unrealistic conception of the human ability to remain focused on 'things as they really are'. It is a moot point, then, whether the Buddhist goal of liberation from craving and suffering is in fact attainable. Sceptics might contend that the perfect mindfulness that is, according to this analysis, required for the ending of suffering is an ideal that, in reality, can at best be approximated. Craving probably can be reduced, and suffering can thereby be diminished, but the Buddhist *summum bonum* – that is, the total eradication of craving and attachment – is arguably beyond human reach. The question is, then, how much reality can humans bear?

CHAPTER FOUR

Moral Knowledge and the Buddhist Path

The possibility that perfect mindfulness of the three characteristics is not humanly achievable is not the only problem with the Buddhist account of liberating knowledge. The present chapter will examine two further difficulties. First, Buddhism seems to assume that one can derive an 'ought' from an 'is', in other words, that moral knowledge is entailed by the understanding of an ontological state of affairs. Second, it might appear that the Buddhists make the problematic claim that when moral knowledge of what one should do is achieved, then one will automatically do it. My argument in this chapter will be that the first of these difficulties is a serious one and the Buddhists' claim to objective moral knowledge that craving ought to be eliminated is questionable, given the challenge of moral relativism. The second problem, I will argue, can be resolved by viewing the Buddhist idea of liberating knowledge in the context of the Buddhist path as a whole, in which training in ethical conduct complements knowledge of 'how things really are'.

Getting an 'ought' from an 'is'

Many moral philosophers contend that there are moral principles that are universally applicable and objective. There are moral facts. Moral philosophies which make this claim are sometimes called universalist ethical theories and include rights ethics, utilitarianism, deontology and virtue ethics, among others (see Boss, 2002, pp. 19–40). Thus, a rights theorist might assert the universality of the right to free speech and/or the right to life and so forth, whereas a utilitarian might claim that actions that produce the 'greatest happiness for the greatest number of people' are objectively moral. A deontologist will focus on certain moral duties (for example, the duty to 'do unto others as you would have them do unto you') which they consider to be objective. A virtue ethicist will emphasize that there are various admirable character traits, that is, virtues, that benefit ourselves and others (for example, courage, friendliness, truthfulness and so forth) and are thus objectively morally desirable. These ethical universalists are united in their commitment to the objectivity of key moral values, even if there are serious disagreements about the precise number and nature of those moral values, how exactly we can know them (for example, by reason or intuition) and which ones have priority and greater weight (for example, whether justice is more important than happiness or vice versa).

By contrast, moral philosophers of a relativist persuasion make a sharp distinction between factual assertions and moral judgements. They claim that ethical evaluations ('ought' judgements) are not entailed by matters of fact (what 'is' the case). Given a particular fact or set of facts, people may and often do arrive at different legitimate moral judgements about them. There is nothing about the facts themselves that privileges one moral judgement as better than others. For matters of fact there is evidence that can count as proof or disproof. For example, a controversy about whether the earth is flat or spherical is about a factual matter. There are widely agreed standards of justification that can establish that the earth is spherical and is not flat. But, the moral relativists will point out, for values there are generally no widely agreed standards of proof. The same facts may elicit different moral judgements. And it is impossible to adjudicate between contradictory moral judgements because they often both seem to have been made on equally reasonable grounds. As the ethicist Philippa Foot writes, for moral relativism 'if a man is given good evidence for a factual conclusion he cannot just refuse to accept the conclusion on the ground that in his scheme of things this evidence is not evidence at all. With evaluations, however, it is different. An evaluation is not connected logically with the factual statements on which it is based.' For the moral relativists, a person can always claim that 'any statement of value always seems to go beyond any statement of fact, so that he might have a reason for accepting the factual premises but refusing to accept the evaluative conclusion' (Foot, 1978, pp. 110–11 and 121). Whatever moral evaluation is made about a set of facts can always be rejected by someone who chooses to make a different moral judgement.

For example, you may think that an abortion is justified, and I may think that it is not, based on the same information. The basic facts here would be that (1) a woman is pregnant and (2) this woman wants an abortion. One person might decide that the woman ought to have the abortion, because a woman has the right to choose what happens to her body. Another person might judge that the woman ought not to have the abortion, because the foetus has the right to life. Obviously, arguments for and against abortion can be and usually are far more complex than this. However, keeping the example simple here helps to illustrate clearly that different moral judgements have been reached, based on the same facts (1) and (2). These different moral judgements are made not on the basis of disagreement about the facts, but because of a difference in values. The first person places more weight on the right of a woman to choose what happens to her body. The second person puts more emphasis on the foetus's right to life. And, it can be argued, there is nothing 'in the facts themselves' which privileges one evaluation as superior to the other. The moral relativists would say that, to a dispassionate observer, neither moral judgement appears to be unreasonable. A responsible, rational human being might make either of these ethical evaluations.

To give another example, suppose that an expensive medicine will cure a disease by which one is afflicted. The facts here are that (1) there is an expensive medicine that will cure a disease and (2) one has that disease. The moral relativists will claim that the conclusion that one ought to take the medicine is not entailed by these facts. There is nothing about the facts themselves that necessitates that one has the obligation to take the medicine. One might decide that one ought to take the medicine, but this will presumably be on the basis of the moral judgement that this would be the best use of one's money. In other words, one might make the choice to buy the medicine on the grounds that eradicating one's own pain and discomfort is more valuable than other ways of spending the money. This would appear to be a reasonable evaluation but, like other moral judgements, it is added on to, rather than being contained in, the facts themselves. One might make a different judgement and, furthermore, this would not be unreasonable. For instance, maybe one would decide to bear the disease without taking the medicine on the grounds that the money might be better spent by using it to help other people. So, one might make the moral judgement that (1) one ought to bear the disease rather than spend the money on the medicine, or that (2) one ought to spend the money on the medicine rather than bearing the disease. The same facts can lead to opposing apparently rational moral evaluations. One's moral judgement here will depend on the relative value one attributes to overcoming one's own sickness versus helping other people. A sane, intelligent individual, the moral relativists will argue, might have defensible grounds to choose either moral evaluation (1) or (2). There is no sense in which one of these value judgements is objectively better than the other.

Getting an 'ought' from an 'is' in Buddhism

Now, I do not here wish to arbitrate between moral relativism and universalist theories of ethics as a whole. The relevant point is that Buddhism makes a negative moral judgement about craving and this evaluation is based on what Buddhists consider to be the facts of impermanence, not-self and suffering. Furthermore, it appears that the Buddhists think that the moral judgement that one ought not to crave and get attached to impermanent, selfless things is entailed by these matters of fact. Buddhists here seem content to derive an 'ought' from an 'is' in a fashion which suggests that for them the 'ought' is actually an 'is', that is, a moral fact. They think that it is objectively true that one ought not to crave impermanent, selfless things. People who fail to make this moral judgement have failed to see this objective truth. In other words, the Buddhists are here, it appears, advocating a universalist moral theory.

Moral relativists will protest that there is no such objective moral truth. Buddhists see that impermanent, selfless things cause suffering when coveted and judge that they ought not to be craved. Surely their moral claim that craving for impermanent, selfless things should be avoided does not mirror or correspond to an objective 'way things really are'? Surely this moral evaluation is something added on by the Buddhists who sees the three characteristics? Could not a (non-Buddhist) person who sees the three characteristics legitimately choose to make a different moral evaluation of craving?

The Buddhists might answer that their moral evaluation is the only reasonable one. For, is it not true that all human beings seek the avoidance of suffering? In other words, for Buddhism the value of eradicating suffering is fundamental and non-negotiable for all people. The ending of suffering, the Buddhists will contend, is simply and quite uncontroversially what every human being wants. It is the basic goal towards which human behaviour is orientated. Is it not the case, then, that the Buddhist moral judgement is objective, in the sense that human beings ought to avoid craving for impermanent things, given that they one and all desire to stop suffering? Surely, the Buddhists might say, this impulse is so basic and strong that the value of eradicating craving is beyond doubt. In other words, it is a moral fact.

Perhaps the Buddhists are right. There is a case, I think, for claiming that human beings do usually wish to achieve the ending of suffering and, put more positively, some sort of genuine happiness, even if they try to achieve this goal in very strange and often counter-productive ways (perhaps because of their ignorance of the three characteristics). However, the moral relativists will find this Buddhist position unconvincing and will doubt that the value of avoiding suffering is as absolute for human beings as the Buddhists contend. Do human beings really all seek to avoid suffering and is this the most important objective for them? I think the moral relativists can marshal evidence which might suggest otherwise.

Masochists, for instance, would presumably make a different moral judgement. They will choose to covet things precisely because of the suffering that this will bring them. Of course, it might be protested that the masochists here are simply the unreasonable exception that proves the rule. But the moral relativists need not appeal to the troubled masochists alone. They might argue that many rational, non-masochistic people would not judge that the avoidance of suffering is of the highest importance. Such people, even when they understand the three characteristics, would make a moral evaluation that differs from the Buddhists'. They might thus make the moral judgement, on reasonable grounds, that it is sometimes acceptable to continue to covet and be attached to things.

For instance, such people might judge that the suffering entailed by craving and attachment can sometimes open up avenues for fortitude and possibly aesthetic experience (see here the notion of the suffering artist) that would be closed down by cutting off this suffering. Thus, craving and attachment, as the source of suffering, ought not to be eliminated. Or people might decide that human relationships that necessarily involve some degree, sometimes very high degrees, of craving and attachment are intrinsically worthwhile, even though they admittedly also entail suffering of one degree or another. People might decide, for instance, that it is better to be attached to one's children, spouse, parents and friends and experience the (sometimes very considerable) suffering this entails, rather than to be cut off from this sort of relationship, yet free from suffering. From this point of view, craving can admittedly be extremely destructive, but it can also have a positive, life-affirming quality when properly controlled and regulated. So, the propensity to appropriative desire ought not to be eliminated, but channelled into constructive endeavours. The Jewish tradition, for instance, claims that humans' evil inclination to gratify their own wants and appetites, when employed appropriately, can lead to creative, good results such as procreation, marriage, success in business and so forth (see Ludwig, 2001, p. 113). Furthermore, some people might make the moral judgement that the suffering entailed by craving for and attachment to impermanent entities is simply part of the human condition and is thus to be accepted rather than transcended. It might be believed that surviving such suffering is a test of one's humanity and that one ought to experience this suffering rather than seek to avoid it. Maybe suffering is the human lot and the attempt to transcend it is an arrogant attempt to 'be like God', that is, to become more than human. Finally, it might be argued that the impermanence of entities ought actually to lead one to crave things more intensely, to make the most of the limited time during which one will have possession of these entities. And similarly, one's awareness of one's own impermanence ought to lead one to intensify one's desire for and attachment to the entities from which one will be inevitably separated by one's impending death. 'Making hay while the sun shines' would be the moral principle here. From this moral perspective, craving and attachment might be judged to be at the very core of life and to attempt to cut them off is precisely what one ought not to do if one truly values being alive. This does not seem to be an unreasonable position to hold.

Of course, what counts as reasonable or unreasonable, and how this is to be determined, is not clear. Masochists too might have their reasons and their grounds for the value judgement that they make, yet we are inclined to say that they are not good or reasonable reasons. Fully fledged moral relativists might argue that this is simply prejudice on our part. A less extreme moral relativism might seek in some way to distinguish between a range of moral judgements that are reasonable and those, such as the masochists', that are beyond the pale. How exactly the distinction might be drawn is not my concern here. My point is that, for the moral relativists, there are a number of reasons on the basis of which a non-masochistic, sane, intelligent and ethically sensitive person might reach the decision that craving and suffering can sometimes be morally acceptable.

So, the common Buddhist claim that one ought not to crave is far from being a self-evident truth. How can we be sure that the Buddhists' attitude to craving and suffering is the only right one? Perhaps the Buddhists' supposed moral knowledge is nothing more than an opinion? In short, the Buddhist might be accused of illegitimately universalizing the value of avoiding suffering. It is not clear that the importance of the ending of suffering is as fundamental to human beings as Buddhists seem to claim. It seems possible to make other value judgements, where the avoidance of suffering has less moral worth. Perhaps, then, the Buddhist is too concerned with overcoming craving and attachment and some people will legitimately decide to have these human experiences rather than trying to transcend them. Maybe, then, these people can, with justification, decide to 'let go' of the Buddhist emphasis on 'letting go'. Indeed, there are some traditions of Buddhism itself, notably Tantra, that seem to take this view, encouraging the practitioner to use craving creatively rather than attempting to eliminate it. I suppose also that certain Mahāyāna ideas, such as the identity of *nirvāṇa* and *saṃsāra*, could be used to support the idea that saṃsāric impulses such as craving are not necessarily an impediment to the gaining of Awakening. However, the moral judgement that craving ought to be eradicated rather than creatively employed seems to be the dominant one within Buddhism.

I am not suggesting that more positive evaluations of craving and suffering are objectively better than the common Buddhist one. My only claim is that the very diversity of legitimate value judgements here indicates that the moral relativist has a strong case for arguing that a reasonable person need not make the Buddhist moral judgement.

Faced with this difficulty, Buddhists might conceivably try to reason in a different way. They might claim that one ought not to crave and get attached because craving and attachment are selfish and appropriative emotions, and selfishness is always inherently bad. In relying on this argument, Buddhists would no longer be claiming that one ought not to crave and get attached to impermanent entities on the grounds that craving and attachment cause suffering. Rather, they would be saying that one ought not to crave and get attached because craving and attachment are essentially selfish. However, this approach clearly will not solve the problem. For the moral relativists can question the Buddhists' contention that it is always wrong to be selfish. A capitalist, for instance, might argue that self-interest can sometimes be right, and can have beneficial effects both for self and society, for instance, by making oneself rich and stimulating the economy. An evolutionary theorist might claim that selfishness is sometimes good, because it can enhance one's prospects for personal and genetic survival. Once again the Buddhists are trying to derive a value (that craving and attachment are wrong) from a fact (that craving and attachment are selfish), and moral relativists, while not necessarily doubting the fact, can raise their doubts about the objectivity of the value.

The *Anattalakkhaṇa sutta*

The Buddhist moral perspective is found very clearly in the *Anattalakkhaṇa sutta*, 'The Discourse on the Definition of Not-Self', found in *Mahāvagga* 1 of the *Vinaya*. This text is described by Paul Williams (2000, p. 57) as 'probably the single most important source for understanding the mainstream position of Buddhist thought in relationship to its soteriological project'. The main message of the *sutta* is that practitioners should come to know that there is no permanent abiding essence, that is, no self, which underlies the empirical individual. And this knowledge will liberate them from craving and suffering. Thus, the Buddha declares that such liberation is the practical consequence of the monk's understanding of not-self:

> Seeing thus, bhikkhus, a wise noble disciple becomes dispassionate towards material form, becomes dispassionate towards feeling ... [the text then goes on to say that there will be dispassion towards each of the other *khandhas*]. Becoming dispassionate, his lust fades away; with the fading of lust his heart is liberated; when liberated, there comes the knowledge: 'It is liberated.' He understands: 'Birth is exhausted, the holy life has been lived out, what was to be done is done, there is no more of this to come.' (trans. Ñāṇamoli, 1992, p. 47)

Williams (2000, p. 60), commenting on this passage, says that the *sutta* reveals that for the Buddhist, 'there is built into seeing how things are ("is") a transformation of moral response ("ought"). The Buddha seems to suggest that this transformation is an automatic response to seeing how things really are.' That is, seeing the truth that all things are devoid of self, practitioners, automatically it appears, know that they ought to be dispassionate towards and to cut off their lust, that is, craving, for these things. The *sutta* implies that the facts here entail a particular moral judgement. It is as though the correct attitude one ought to have towards impermanent things is an objective moral truth. All the practitioner has to do is to see the things correctly, and this seeing reveals not only that things do not have a permanent, unchanging self and cause suffering if craved, but also that they ought not to be craved. There is no indication that the moral judgement might be otherwise, or that someone who sees 'things as they really are' might legitimately come to a different moral judgement about them.

It is perhaps significant that the seeing of 'things as they really are' that occurs in this text would normally be the culmination of a systematic monastic training, one might say indoctrination, of the monk or nun. This is a process of intellectual and ethical discipline in which the moral judgement that craving and suffering are wrong and ought to be eradicated will have been inculcated into the monks or nuns and perhaps will have been become an unquestioned foundation of their world view. In other words, practitioners consider that craving and suffering are wrong and ought to be eliminated because their minds have been conditioned, by absorbing prevalent Buddhist moral attitudes, to view the world in this way. A critic might therefore wonder whether the supposed objective moral truth which the 'wise' monk or nun is thought to ascertain is in actuality a disputable moral judgement, acquired in the course of monastic training, which might seem to be 'how things actually are' to practitioners only because they have not critically examined it or at least are no longer doing so.

However, the Buddhists might respond that their training is not a blind indoctrination. For Buddhism, the moral teaching that one ought not to crave is an idea that needs to be tested by experience, and is not to be accepted uncritically. When practitioners come to see 'things as they really are', and this seeing includes the knowledge that one ought not to crave impermanent, selfless things, this is because the practitioners have observed themselves and other people and have come to the conclusion that, despite what the moral relativists say, human beings (even if they do not know it themselves) really do one and all consider the ending of suffering to be the highest value. And craving ought to be eradicated, given that it will frustrate them in this aim. Buddhist teachings about the undesirability of suffering and thus the need to avoid craving are not attempts to indoctrinate the practitioner but are simply meant to make them receptive to these objective truths about the human condition.

Maybe the Buddhists are right. However, it is also possible that there is an element of self-deception here. It might be that the practitioners tend to get the experience that they have been trained for. Experience is arguably not the final arbiter of the truth, given that the mind is often, perhaps always, busy in interpreting and constructing the experiences that we have. The Buddhists might experience themselves and others as valuing the ending of suffering as of paramount importance because they have been taught to experience themselves and other people in this way. The experience that human beings desire the cessation of suffering as the highest good, and thus craving should be eradicated, might seem to involve a discovery of an objective moral order, but in reality it may be the final step of instruction in disputable Buddhist moral opinions. If these Buddhists had been trained differently, and had imbibed different teachings, they might not have come to experience the avoidance of suffering as being of ultimate value to themselves and others, and hence the eradication of craving would not be the highest priority.

Perhaps some Buddhists could choose to accommodate moral relativism.

They might concede that there is no objective moral truth that one ought to stop craving and suffering. They might admit that it is a value judgement rather than 'how things really are'. Such Buddhists might face up to the moral uncertainty about how one should respond to the facts (if facts they are) of impermanence, not-self and suffering. They might accept the moral relativists' point that value judgements other than the Buddhists' can reasonably be made. The avoidance of suffering is not the only highest value for human beings. It is of course possible that this admission, which throws into doubt the key Buddhist claim that one ought to stop craving and suffering, would undermine the Buddhists' commitment to the Buddhist moral perspective. But it is also possible that such Buddhists might quite rationally continue to make the judgement that the avoidance of suffering is the highest value for them, and thus they should endeavour to eradicate their craving, while also being aware that this is their choice, and other people might reasonably choose differently. After all, one does have to make a choice of some sort! So, in this case Buddhism might take account of the moral relativists' insight (if it is an insight), and this might have the attractive consequence that such Buddhists would have a non-dogmatic commitment to their moral perspective together with a respect for and understanding of the different moral choices made by others.

Getting a 'will' from a 'should'

The *Anattalakkhaṇa sutta* is revealing about the connection between Buddhist views concerning knowledge and liberation in another way. It is not just that the text suggests that an 'ought' can be derived from an 'is'. It also seems to say that monks and nuns who see 'things as they really are' will actually act or behave automatically in accord with the moral knowledge that they have attained. The Buddha says that, having seen things to be without self, the 'wise noble disciple becomes dispassionate, without lust, and liberated'. The Buddha is claiming that knowledge of 'how things really are' will cause one to stop craving once and for all.

There appears to be a problem here, however. The Buddha does not seem to acknowledge that one might not do what one knows that one ought to do, and one might do what one knows that one ought not to do. He does not appear to admit any gap between knowledge and action, that is, that there can be a discrepancy between what one does and what one knows. He appears to claim that one's knowledge that one ought not to crave impermanent, selfless things is sufficient to stop one craving them. It seems that Buddhism is saying that having understood what one *should* do one *will* necessarily do it. Yet it can be protested that one need not do what one knows one ought to do. On some occasions, knowing what one should do, one will not do it, and knowing what one should not do, one will do it anyway. Even if it is true that one ought not to crave and get attached to impermanent entities, it seems untenable to claim that the sole cause of one's continued craving is the failure to understand that one ought not to crave. For, it might be suggested, a people can know thoroughly both (1) the three characteristics of entities, and (2) that one ought not to crave and get attached to such entities, and yet they do not necessarily stop craving and getting attached. One's thorough knowledge that one ought not to crave and get attached to impermanent, selfless entities is no guarantee that one will not crave and get attached to these entities, just like smokers' thorough knowledge that they ought not to smoke cigarettes is no guarantee that they will stop.

The problem here is essentially the same as that which occurs with the Socratic position that to know the good is to do the good. According to Socrates, no one does wrong knowingly. This position seems obviously faulty, in so far as people seem able to know what they ought to do, and yet refrain from doing it, and know what they ought not to do and yet cannot resist the temptation to do it anyway. As Portia famously declares in *The Merchant of Venice* (I, ii. 12–19):

> If to do were as easy as to know what were good to do, chapels had been churches, and poor men's cottages princes' palaces. It is a good divine that follows his own instructions; I can easier teach twenty what were good to be done, than to be one of the twenty to follow mine own teaching. The brain may devise laws for the blood, but a hot temper leaps o'er a cold decree. (Shakespeare, 1974, p. 256)

People are not simply rational beings, and emotions can pull them in an opposite direction to that recommended by their understanding. One's emotions are fickle; they do not automatically follow the intellect. One is often compelled by passion to do the wrong thing or to refrain from doing the right thing, despite knowing better. In which case, contrary to the Buddhist analysis as I have presented it in this book, it would appear that craving does have some autonomy from one's understanding and thus the craving for impermanent entities does not after all result only from a deficiency in one's knowledge. And, therefore, liberation from craving and attachment does not follow from the attainment of knowledge alone. Even knowing that entities are impermanent, selfless and cause suffering when craved, and that one ought not to crave and get attached to them, one might nevertheless often find oneself enslaved by craving. In other words, the Buddhist claim that knowledge of the three characteristics can bring about the eradication of craving seems unconvincing, even if this knowledge is thorough in the ways suggested in the previous chapter. I might stubbornly refuse to behave in the way that my understanding suggests that I should.

This is not to deny that there is a relation, often very strong, between one's cravings and one's understanding. It is reasonable to claim that cravings are not fully independent of one's intellect. They can be and often are influenced, even heavily influenced, by one's understanding. My craving for the attractive car in the parking lot, for instance, might be mitigated when I discover that it requires thousands of dollars of repairs, and my craving for the cake in the fridge might well diminish if I come to understand that it is well past its expiry date. But neither do cravings follow the understanding with total obedience. They can rebel. For example, I can crave chocolate and want to eat large amounts of it, even though I understand that this will be very bad for me and thus I ought not to indulge. Reflection on and attentiveness to the three characteristics might well be an important element in the attempt to overcome craving, but it does not seem likely that such thorough knowledge alone would suffice.

Knowledge and the Buddhist path

However, I think that Buddhism can accommodate this objection, powerful though it might seem. For the Buddhists can claim that their notion of liberating knowledge needs to be understood in the context of Buddhist spiritual life as a whole. The objection stems from examining Buddhist knowledge-claims in isolation from the other aspects of Buddhist practice. In fact, Buddhism does not think that knowledge alone brings about liberation. Rather, the Buddhists think that what one should do becomes what one will do when understanding is combined with effort and ethical endeavour. Liberating knowledge needs to be viewed as the outcome of a process of training and the thorough knowledge which finally ends craving is simply the last step of a path of discipline and reflection. Let me explain.

The Eightfold Path

The Buddhist spiritual discipline, as expressed in formulae such as the Eightfold Path, includes cognitive and non-cognitive dimensions. And the non-cognitive dimensions might be further divided into affective, volitional and behavioural sub-categories. Buddhism generally advocates a systematic training which is meant to transform the practitioner's intellect, emotions and will, as well as verbal and bodily actions.

Thus, the Eightfold Path includes as its first part 'right view' (*samyagdṛṣṭi*) as the cognitive aspect of the training. Buddhists are to transform their understanding, so that Buddhist truths such as the three characteristics are properly grasped.

The non-cognitive dimension of Buddhist spirituality is expressed in parts two through six of the Eightfold Path. The second aspect of the Eightfold Path is 'right intention' (*samyaksaṃkalpa*), traditionally glossed as a mind pervaded by non-craving as well as friendliness and compassion, emotions that indicate the establishment of a non-appropriative, altruistic attitude. Here we see clearly the affective part of the training. The next three dimensions of the Eightfold Path, 'right speech' (*samyagvācā*), 'right action' (*samyak-karmanta*), and 'right livelihood' (*samyagājīva*), involve a transformation of verbal and bodily conduct, so that one's outward behaviour becomes an expression of non-craving and non-attachment. The various formulations of Buddhist ethical precepts are a further expression of this aspect of the Buddhist discipline.

The sixth part of the Eightfold Path, 'right effort' (*samyagvyāyāma*), indicates that practitioners must exert themselves, especially in meditation, in order to stop unskilful mental states such as greed, hatred, jealousy, and so forth – all of which are rooted in craving – from arising and to eliminate those that have arisen. Further, they are to cultivate and maintain skilful mental states, all of which are devoid of craving. Here, then, the volitional dimension of Buddhist spirituality comes to the fore. The practitioner is exhorted to make an effort, that is, to engage the will in order to overcome craving. Indeed, many Buddhist writings stress the need for the practitioner to be diligent and to strive. As the *Dhammapada* 25 (trans. K.R. Norman, 1997a, p. 4) declares: 'By exertion, by carefulness, by restraint and self-control, a wise man would make an island, which a flood [that is, craving] does not overwhelm.'

The seventh and eighth aspects of the Eightfold Path, 'right mindfulness' (*samyaksmṛti*) and 'right concentration' (*samyaksamādhi*), are also expressions of the meditative dimension of Buddhism, where a variety of mental techniques are used to support the transformation of all four aspects of the person – intellectual, emotional, volitional and behavioural. For instance, insight (Sanskrit: *vipaśyanā*; Pāli: *vipassanā*) meditation is primarily focused on the intellectual dimension, where reflections are introduced on subjects such as not-self, impermanence and suffering. Calming (Sanskrit: *śamatha*; Pāli: *samatha*) meditations, by contrast, often work directly on the emotional and volitional. For example, the cultivation of loving kindness (*mettābhāvanā*) is a popular Theravāda *samatha* meditation aimed at producing emotions of love and empathy. These emotions in turn would stimulate a desire or volition to help others to express concern for others. This altruistic desire would naturally find expression in generous and considerate bodily and verbal actions. All of this would counteract selfish craving. As Damien Keown (1992, pp. 77–8) says:

> I wish to suggest that 'calming meditation' (*samatha-bhāvanā*) cultivates moral virtue and 'insight meditation' (*vipassanā-bhāvanā*) develops knowledge or insight ... The suppression of intellectual activity in *samatha* practice is a specialised technique for gaining access to the non-rational, emotional dimension of the psyche. It is a means of penetrating the deeper layers of consciousness and restructuring them in accordance with virtue rather than vice.

So, Buddhist liberating knowledge should not be viewed out of the context of this complex, multi-dimensional Buddhist training. Buddhism usually does not claim that knowledge alone can bring about the elimination of craving and suffering. To say otherwise is to intellectualize Buddhist spirituality in a way that distorts its true nature. In addition to understanding, the eradication of one's craving and attachment also requires detailed and systematic attention to and transformation of one's conduct, emotions and volitions. Buddhism is a path of effort and action as well as knowledge.

Relations between the elements of the path

Of course, there are here subtle interconnections between the non-cognitive aspects of the Buddhist path. The will, emotions and actions are closely related. For example, making the effort to stop craving is essentially an attempt to change one's emotional state, and would also naturally be expressed in endeavours to transform one's bodily and verbal conduct. And acting with body and speech in ways that are expressive of kindness and sensitivity to others, rather than selfish craving, would itself be a way of altering one's emotional state, making it less appropriative, and might also strengthen one's resolve to stop craving. Acting kindly and considerately can be a way to change one's mental state, just as changing one's mental state can result in more kind and considerate acts.

But there are also important interconnections between the cognitive and the non-cognitive parts of the Eightfold Path. They are not entirely separate and do exert considerable influence on one another. Suppose, for instance, that one acquires – perhaps by listening to Buddhist teachings – the right view that entities are impermanent, without self and cause suffering when craved. And maybe one has also acquired the conviction that one ought not to crave such entities. This understanding is arguably indispensable in order to make progress on the Buddhist path. Having acquired this right view, one would have a reason to undertake the other aspects of the Buddhist training. One needs to understand that entities are impermanent, selfless and cause suffering when craved, and one needs to understand that one ought not to crave and get attached to these entities. This right view is important as providing a justification for one's endeavours to eradicate craving and attachment. Without this understanding one would not try to put an end to one's craving and attachment. It gives one the rationale for making the attempt.

However, this initial right view is only a starting point. It is a long way from actually stopping one's craving. In order to make what one understands that one ought not to do into what one does not do, consistent endeavour and the cultivation of habitual virtuous emotions and behaviour are required. Craving and attachment will only be eradicated by making the effort to stop them as they manifest in one's every thought, word and bodily action. So, Buddhists might say that they do not think that the eradication of craving and attachment follows simply from the understanding – that is, the initial right view – of the three characteristics and that one ought not to crave and get attached. Craving and attachment can indeed continue, even when one has this understanding. Practitioners need to realign their will, emotions and actions so that they are in accord with their understanding. The whole character or personality of the practitioners is thereby transformed. Then they do not simply have an understanding that they ought not to crave. In addition, they actually weaken and eventually stop their selfish desire.

For Buddhism construed in this way, perhaps one might say that liberation is the result not of knowledge alone but rather of wisdom, the wise people being the individuals who apprehend the three characteristics, who understand or judge that they ought not to crave and be attached, and who, by means of constant attentiveness to and transformation of their mental, verbal and bodily conduct, do not crave and get attached. The Buddhists might here agree with the moral philosopher Philippa Foot (1978, p. 7) when she comments that wisdom is 'partly to be described in terms of apprehension, and even judgement, but since it has to do with a man's attachments it also characterizes his will'.

Knowledge is not merely preliminary

However, we must not be left with the impression that for Buddhism understanding, or right view, is simply a precursor, and is followed by the 'real work' of emotional, volitional and behavioural transformation. The cognitive aspect of Buddhism is not to be relegated to a merely preparatory role. It is not that right view just gets the path started, as it were, with the non-cognitive aspects of the path alone having the weightier role of actually eliminating craving. I would suggest that the Buddhist attitude to liberating knowledge is more complex than this. For the knowledge of the three characteristics I have been referring to so far is simply the initial right view which can give practitioners their first justification for undertaking the Buddhist training. However, the Buddhist practitioners' intellectual development does not stop there.

As we have seen in the previous chapter, an important part of Buddhist training is reflecting further on and being attentive to the three characteristics of existence. Indeed, I would suggest, that this is vital from a Buddhist perspective, in order to keep practitioners motivated in their efforts to eradicate craving. If Buddhists bear in mind the three characteristics, then they will remain aware of their reason for diligently practising the other aspects of the path. Without such reflection and mindfulness, the Buddhists' endeavours to stop craving would soon wane. If they become forgetful of the three characteristics, they are likely to become lax in their efforts to eradicate craving and easily diverted from the Buddhist path. For they will have forgotten the rationale for their endeavours. So, maintaining and improving reflective attentiveness concerning the three characteristics is extremely important.

Furthermore, it seems that the more the Buddhists manage to weaken craving and attachment, the more they will be able to reflect on and remain mindful of the truths of impermanence, not self and suffering. Why is this? Craving is a restless emotion, and a mind that is afflicted by craving is said in Buddhism to be unable to settle and thus is incapable of sustained concentration. Objects of craving easily distract it. So, as the hold of craving on the mind weakens, the ability of the mind to remain focused on the three characteristics will increase. And, as the mind becomes increasingly able to focus on the three characteristics, the practitioners' dedication to the task of eliminating craving can become stronger.

In other words, the cognitive and the non-cognitive parts of the path here go hand in hand. They are mutually assisting processes. As Padmasiri De Silva (1991, p. 29) aptly says, for Buddhism, 'man's desires influence his cognitive powers and his cognitions have an impact on his desires'. When one's understanding of the three characteristics becomes steadier and more constant, the effort to eradicate craving can grow stronger. As one becomes increasingly successful in eradicating craving, the steadiness and constancy of the intellect becomes easier to maintain. Understanding the three characteristics supports virtue, that is, the actual eradication of craving through effort in ethical and meditative practice, and the strengthening of virtue makes stronger the understanding, that is, one's consistent mindfulness of the three characteristics. In this regard, Keown (1992, pp. 38–9) has pointed to *Digha Nikāya* 1, 124 where the disciple Soṇadaṇḍa explains that:

> Where there is virtue there is understanding, and where there is understanding there is virtue. Those who have virtue possess understanding, and those who have understanding possess virtue, and virtue and understanding are declared to be the best things in the world. Just as, Gotama, one hand might wash the other or one foot wash the other, even so Gotama, is understanding washed around with virtue and virtue washed around with understanding. (trans. Keown, 1992, p. 39)

The Buddha expresses his approval of Soṇadaṇḍa's statement. For the Buddhists, then, the culmination of the mutually assisting processes of increasing virtue and understanding would be the wise man or woman, who is able to remain constantly mindful of 'the way things really are', because not distracted by craving, and whose absence of craving is itself supported by this constant mindfulness of 'the way things really are'.

Thus, perhaps the final liberating knowledge is, for many Buddhists, a state of unwavering reflection on and mindfulness of the three characteristics –

made possible because craving has already been greatly weakened through previous efforts on the Buddhist path – that enables one to make the final effort to eliminate any residual craving. This final liberating knowledge is attained by Buddhists who have already developed, by means of ethical and meditative discipline, extraordinary mental control and have thus significantly reduced their selfish desires. The final liberating knowledge acts as the metaphorical 'straw that breaks the camel's back'. It needs to be seen as the end of a process of training, with interconnected cognitive and non-cognitive dimensions, and it is able to bring about the cessation of craving once and for all because of the weakening of the propensity to crave which the prior stages of the process have already brought about. The Buddhist path culminates, then, in a state of being where the cognitive and non-cognitive dimensions of the person are both perfected, and have reached this perfection in dependence upon one another. There is completely mindful understanding of the three characteristics and, furthermore, the affections, and thus one's bodily and verbal conduct as expressions of these affections, are free from craving and attachment. The suffering which craving and attachment bring is thus terminated.

Liberating knowledge and introspection

There is, I think, a further role that knowledge plays in the Buddhist path to liberation. In order to diminish and finally eradicate craving, practitioners need to be aware of what their mental states actually are. One needs to know when greed, hatred, jealousy and so forth are actually present in one's mind, in order to do something about them. This awareness is an essential prerequisite if one is to stop craving in its tracks, so to speak. If one does not have this self-knowledge, one will be unable to apply appropriate ethical and meditative remedies for this craving. Furthermore, self-knowledge is required in order to identify skilful mental events, all of which are untainted by craving, so that Buddhist ethical and meditative techniques can be employed in order to maintain and encourage them. So, knowledge in the sense of introspective understanding is very important on the Buddhist path. An honest, authentic and constant appraisal of the contents of the mind is required.

Thus, for instance, at *Majjhima Nikāya* 1, 24–32 (trans. Ñāṇamoli and Bodhi (1995), pp. 108–14) practitioners are reminded of the need to *understand* their moral blemishes if they are to arouse the zeal, effort and energy required to abandon them. Again, at *Majjhima Nikāya* 1, 414–20 (pp. 523–6), the Buddha advises Rāhula to reflect on his bodily, verbal and mental actions (that is, his thoughts) and to constantly ask himself whether they will cause suffering to himself or to other people. If the answer is 'yes', then they should be confessed and avoided. Furthermore, Abhidharma analyses of mental states into numerous categories evolved, it would seem, as aids for practitioners, helping them to identify the contents of their minds and to determine whether these contents are skilful or unskilful.

Without this self-knowledge as a basis, the Buddhist practitioner will be unable to apply the Buddhist teaching in a transformative way. Without an understanding of and attentiveness to one's mental and emotional world, there presumably could be no progress towards the weakening and eradication of craving. Here there is once again a subtle interconnectedness between the cognitive and non-cognitive dimensions of Buddhist spirituality. For this self-knowledge can only occur if one is vigilant in maintaining one's mindfulness. That is, such self-understanding itself requires exertion, in order to maintain awareness of the contents of one's mind. But it is itself a necessary prerequisite for successful efforts to weaken and eliminate craving. One must have knowledge of the contents of one's mind before effort can be made to transform them, yet maintaining this awareness itself requires effort. Presumably, as the hold of craving weakens, practitioners become more able to remain mindful of their mental states. As the practitioners' awareness of the workings of their minds increases, they will become more successful at identifying whatever craving remains. And, once the craving has been noticed, efforts can be made to reduce and eliminate it. We see here another example of how knowledge and diligence operate in tandem.

Knowledge of the Four Noble Truths

While, as we have seen, Buddhist texts often describe liberating knowledge to be of impermanence, not-self and suffering, it is worth noting that there are also many texts that say that it is knowledge of the Four Noble Truths that is required. That is, Awakening is described as occurring when the practitioner thoroughly understands the truth: (1) of suffering, (2) of craving as the cause of suffering, (3) that suffering will cease with the end of craving, and (4) of the Noble Eightfold Path as the way to eradicate craving and thus suffering. Indeed, as we have seen already in Chapter 3, the stock account in the Theravāda scriptures of the Buddha's Awakening describes the knowledge of these Four Noble Truths as the culmination of his Awakening experience. This is a somewhat different, though not incompatible, Buddhist account of liberating knowledge. This version is worth examining in the present context, as it sheds further light on the relation between the cognitive and non-cognitive dimensions of Buddhist spirituality, as well as an important way in which liberating knowledge might be described as knowledge by acquaintance, as opposed to merely propositional knowledge. Let me explain.

I would suggest that the understanding of the Four Noble Truths begins for novice Buddhist practitioners as largely propositional knowledge, rather than knowledge by acquaintance. Knowledge of the Four Noble Truths is presumably mainly theoretical at the very beginning of the Buddhist path. It has probably been heard from a Buddhist teacher and/or text, but the practitioners' direct personal experience of the Four Noble Truths will be limited. Perhaps they will have had experience, even considerable experience, of the first Noble Truth, suffering, but probably not the other three truths. After all, they are still subject to much craving, so how could they know by acquaintance that completely stopping craving would indeed entirely stop their suffering? And it is only by stopping craving that they would know by acquaintance the second truth, that craving is the cause of suffering. That is, the best proof that craving is the cause of suffering is when suffering disappears with the elimination of craving. And complete novices have yet to embark on the Buddhist training which is the Eightfold Path, so how could they know by acquaintance the fourth truth, that the Eightfold Path is the way to eradicate craving and hence suffering?

Perhaps at best total novices have had some limited experience of the second and third truths. For instance, suppose I have yet to begin on the Buddhist path and I have noticed that I crave the big car that my neighbour owns. I notice that this craving causes my mind to be unsettled, and I notice that I suffer distress because I cannot have what I covet. However, at some point I somehow manage to let go of this craving. I manage to stop coveting my neighbour's nice new car. Suppose that I then have an experience of tranquillity and my suffering dissipates. This is an experience (albeit limited) of how the relinquishing of craving can alleviate suffering. Such glimpses are perhaps rare but might give one the motivation, that is, the initial confidence or faith (*śraddha*), to undertake a more concerted and systematic attempt to eradicate craving by means of the Eightfold Path.

When one begins to practise the Eightfold Path, one would gradually acquire what modern epistemologists refer to as 'competence knowledge', 'capacity knowledge', or 'knowing how'. That is, with experience and effort one would learn how to cut off craving and attachment by applying the Buddhist teachings about right action, right speech, right effort, and so forth. One would not simply know the theory; one would actually be doing it. And as one continued to apply the Buddhist teachings, one would presumably gradually gain more proficiency at cutting off one's craving and attachment. In this respect, the Buddhist training can be likened to the acquisition of a skill like riding a bicycle or learning to swim.

Assuming one's efforts are successful, craving would be weakened and one would see that suffering also diminishes. Thus, one's conviction that craving causes suffering and that cutting off craving is the way to eliminate suffering would become stronger. Furthermore, one would become convinced that the Buddhist path is the way to achieve this result. In other words, through one's experience, one would gain evidence for the knowledge claim that craving causes suffering, the eradication of craving will eradicate suffering and that the way to eradicate craving (and hence suffering) is by means of the Buddhist path. Furthermore, as these Buddhist teachings become increasingly experientially verified, this strengthening of one's knowledge by acquaintance will itself provide further justification for more effort on the Buddhist path. As their experiential evidence for the Buddhist analysis of the problem of and solution to suffering increases, practitioners will have more reason to carry on with their endeavours to eradicate craving by means of Buddhist ethical and meditative practices. Here we see again that understanding and endeavour, the cognitive and non-cognitive dimensions of Buddhism, are mutually supportive.

If Buddhism is right, the final result of this 'backwards and forwards' process of understanding leading to endeavour, and endeavour leading to further verification of understanding would be that one's endeavour would completely eradicate one's craving, and one's understanding would be completely experientially verified. One would have a fully justified true belief that craving is the cause of suffering, that all suffering ends with the end of craving, and that the Buddhist path is the way to achieve this eradication of craving and suffering. Endeavour gradually leads to a completely validated understanding, that is, a thorough knowledge by acquaintance. The practitioners come to know the second, third and fourth Noble Truths face-to-face, as it were. In addition, it is noteworthy that the common account of the Buddha's Awakening experience, as I explained in Chapter 2 and 3, gives the Buddha the extraordinary perception of the sufferings of sentient beings as they transmigrate in dependence upon their actions. If this is true (which is obviously a moot point), then an Awakened person also gains a far more extensive knowledge by acquaintance of the first Noble Truth, that is, suffering.

Eric Frauwallner's theory about craving and ignorance

Eric Frauwallner (1973, pp. 150 ff.) contends that the common Buddhist claim that ignorance is the cause of craving and knowledge is the means to liberation is absent from the very earliest form of Buddhism. He suggests that the Buddha's initial teaching was about craving as a habitual response to the contact between the senses and their various objects. Thus, the elimination of craving was to be achieved by cultivating continuous attentiveness to the contents of one's mind in order to identify and eradicate whatever craving arises through contact with sense objects. In the beginning, the Buddha simply taught that practitioners can, through constant mindfulness, stop the habitual reaction of craving. It was only later that the Buddha or the Buddhist tradition started to teach that ignorance – of the Four Noble Truths, the three characteristics and so forth – is the root cause of craving and hence suffering.

As Williams (2000, p. 46) notes, Frauwallner's suggestion that there are these two distinct phases of the Buddha's or early Buddhism's account of liberation is controversial. A serious assessment of it would require a detailed examination of the earliest texts, and, given our uncertainty about their provenance, might well be inconclusive. I do not want to engage in such an appraisal here. Whether or not Frauwallner's claim that craving rather than ignorance as the root cause of suffering was the teaching of the earliest form of Buddhism, I would argue that the developed Buddhist position sees craving and ignorance as interwoven and mutually supportive. They cause one another, and the weakening of one results in the weakening of the other.

Furthermore, it seems to me that even in Frauwallner's proposed earliest stage of Buddhism there are important senses in which knowledge must play a role. For mindfulness, as I have already explained, is a form of knowledge, and unmindfulness is ignorance. So, in order to stop craving by noticing and eradicating it when it arises, practitioners must at least have introspective knowledge, that is, awareness of their mental states. Thus it seems correct to say that ignorance, in the sense of failing to watch the contents of the mind in order to stop craving when it does arise, must be implied as a cause of craving and hence suffering. Also, in so far as early Buddhist practitioners, according to Frauwallner's theory, undertook to stop craving by developing mindfulness, they must have had some *understanding* that (1) craving is a cause of suffering, and (2) craving and suffering can be eliminated by applying Buddhist teachings about mindfulness. And presumably ignorance of (1) and (2) would be one reason why some people failed to undertake to stop craving by developing mindfulness.

In addition, as Frauwallner's earliest practitioners became more adept at mindfulness and cutting off craving, it seems that their understanding of (1) and (2) must have become firmer, in the sense that it would be increasingly attested by their experience Would not this firmer understanding provide further justification for their attempts to be mindful? Seeing in their personal experience that mindfulness is effective in reducing craving (and hence suffering), practitioners would have more reason to practise this mindfulness. The culmination of this process would be a thorough knowledge by acquaintance of (1) and (2). Craving would be known by personal experience to be the cause of suffering, because the practitioners' craving has been removed completely and suffering has thereby ended. Buddhist teachings about mindfulness as the way to end craving and suffering would be known by experience to be true, because the practitioners have applied them, and they have resulted in the cessation of craving and hence suffering. In other words, even in Frauwallner's account of the earliest stage of Buddhism, it appears that knowledge and ignorance must have an important role, even if it is the case that the Buddha did not initially point this out. The cognitive and the non-cognitive are inextricably linked in the Buddhist path, though it might conceivably be the case that in the earliest Buddhism these links had not yet been made explicit.

The Mahāyāna understanding of the Buddhist path

This chapter has focused on sources from the Theravāda and wider non-Mahāyāna tradition which illustrate the important dynamic between knowledge and the other aspects of the Buddhist path. However, it must not be overlooked that Mahāyāna Buddhism explains the Buddhist training primarily in terms of the Bodhisattva path and the cultivation of six (or ten) perfections (*pāramitā*), rather than the Eightfold Path. Nevertheless, the underlying principle is the same, namely, that the Buddhist discipline involves some aspects that facilitate cognitive development and others that enable non-cognitive transformation. For instance, in the list of six perfections, the practitioner develops the perfections of giving (*dāna*), ethical conduct (*śīla*), patience (*kṣānti*), energy or effort (*vīrya*), meditation (*dhyāna*) and understanding (*prajñā*). Both non-cognitive (the first four perfections) and cognitive (the sixth perfection) aspects of the practitioner are to be developed, as well as meditation (the fifth perfection) as an aid to both.

As we will see in greater detail in Chapters 5–7, Mahāyāna Buddhists understand liberating knowledge differently from Theravāda and other non-Mahāyāna Buddhists, emphasizing that insight into the emptiness (*śūnyatā*) of phenomena is required. Nevertheless, they usually share the Theravāda conviction that liberating knowledge is the outcome of a long training and needs to be seen in the context of the Buddhist path as a whole. This training involves many ethical and meditative practices that aim to reshape the personality, making it increasingly unsusceptible to craving and attachment. For example, Tibetan Mahāyāna Buddhism emphasizes a meditation, called 'exchanging self and others', based on verses from Śāntideva's *Bodhicāryāvatāra*. One is instructed to reflect that, like oneself, all sentient beings want to avoid suffering and achieve happiness. Furthermore, there is nothing special about oneself and one is vastly outnumbered by other sentient beings. So, objectively, it makes sense to help other sentient beings rather than oneself. The meditator also reflects that one's own happiness comes from helping others, and being selfish and inconsiderate is actually the cause of one's misery. Here the function of the meditation is clearly to bring about a reduction in selfishness and craving, and to cultivate an other-regarding, altruistic attitude. Indeed, this meditation is usually considered to be a means of developing the Mahāyāna *bodhicitta*, the aspiration for Awakening for the sake of all beings (see Williams, 1989, pp. 201–2).

Furthermore, it seems that the Mahāyāna Buddhists would claim that the level of concentration and mindfulness required for the sustained *śamatha* meditation that, together with *vipaśyanā* meditation, is usually said to produce the liberating knowledge of emptiness, would require that craving has already been severely mitigated. Without sustained ethical and meditative practice aimed at the reduction of craving, distraction and unmindfulness would prevent the meditator from achieving the requisite absorption and attentiveness. Thus, by the time that the liberating insight into emptiness is achieved, the hold of craving and attachment on practitioners would already be so weakened, and the moral attitude that empty things ought not to be craved would have become so ingrained, that, like in the Theravāda tradition, the Mahāyāna liberating knowledge is best viewed as the end of a process and causes a final rupture with the propensity to crave, rather than doing all the work on its own.

Buddhist ethics and Awakening

In this chapter I have presented Buddhist ethics – understood broadly as the endeavour to eradicate unskilful mental states, which are all rooted in craving, and to act verbally and bodily in ways that are not expressive of such mental states – as an essential part of Buddhist Awakening. However, James Whitehall (2000, p. 21) claims that some Buddhists, especially of the Zen persuasion, fall into what he calls 'the transcendence trap'. This is the (according to Whitehall) misguided idea that Awakening is a 'non-rational' realization, where the categories of morality no longer apply and in which the Awakened practitioner has gone beyond good and evil. Ethics is a stage to be passed through and then left behind. It is a step on the path, but not part of the goal itself.

Such an approach, Whitehall suggests, diminishes the ethical dimension of the Buddhist Awakening and focuses only on its character as a cognitive apprehension of 'things as they really are'. In fact, Whitehall maintains, the Buddhist Awakening is better seen as a perfection of human character as a whole, a state in which both intellectual and moral virtues are fully developed. The Buddhist trains in ethical conduct as a means to Awakening. But Awakening itself is not a transcendence of ethical conduct. Rather, Awakened practitioners transcend *training* in ethical conduct, because their morality is now perfected.

This is not necessarily to deny the Buddhist idea of skilful means (*upāyakauśalya*) – found especially in the Mahāyāna tradition – that Awakened and other very spiritually developed people might in some exceptional cases break traditional Buddhist ethical precepts against lying, stealing, sexual misconduct and even killing. For such occasional violations of the rules are thought to occur not out of disregard for ethical action but as an expression of it. That is to say, Buddhas and advanced Bodhisattvas are thought to have sufficient wisdom to recognize that on occasion it is more compassionate to act contrary to conventional Buddhist moral prohibitions rather than to follow them dogmatically. Lying, stealing, sexual misconduct, killing and so forth are arguably sometimes, very rarely, more compassionate than the alternative. For example, the assassination of a psychotic despot might be deemed justified out of compassion for the tyrant's victims and perhaps also to prevent him or her from accruing enormous bad *karma*. In such circumstances, Buddhas and advanced Bodhisattvas break the precepts not motivated by selfish craving but rather by selfless compassion.

I do not wish here to debate the validity of this idea and in which precise circumstances such actions might be deemed appropriate (see Williams, 1989, pp. 144–5). The relevant point is that there is not thought to be a transcendence of genuinely ethical conduct here. Rather Buddhas and advanced Bodhisattvas simply recognize that concern for the welfare of others is the highest ethical principle and it occasionally overrides the moral rules against stealing, lying, sexual misconduct, killing and so forth that are normally expressions of it.

It must also be acknowledged that for many Buddhists ethical conduct is undertaken for the sake of a better rebirth by the production of merit (*punya*), rather than the achievement of liberation from craving and suffering. Melford Spiro (1982), in his study of the Theravāda tradition, has called this 'kammatic' Buddhism which is opposed to 'nibbanic' Buddhism. It is undoubtedly true that for many Buddhists, laity and monastics, the immediate aim of their good actions (*kamma/karma*) is a good rebirth rather than Awakening or *nibbāna* itself. Awakening is seen to be a distant goal and not presently attainable.

However, Spiro (1982, p. 69) makes the further, more controversial claim that for Theravāda Buddhism ethical conduct (*sīla*) is only part of kammatic Buddhism, whereas meditation (*bhāvanā*) is the activity engaged in by practitioners interested in nibbanic Buddhism. As Keown (1992, p. 85) says, Spiro argues for a radical discontinuity between the two spheres of activity, where the practitioner in pursuit of Awakening by means of meditation is no longer interested in ethical conduct. In other words, Spiro seems here to fall into Whitehall's transcendence trap. Contrary to what Spiro claims, the fact that Buddhists often undertake ethical conduct for the relatively mundane purpose of achieving a better rebirth does not negate the fact that ethical conduct is also both a means to achieve the Buddhist liberation from suffering and, in so far as the Awakened people have perfected their behaviour by eradicating all craving, is part of Awakening itself. Those practitioners in pursuit of Awakening try to behave ethically for the purpose of finally eradicating all craving and attachment rather than simply for the sake of gaining a good rebirth. As Keown (1992, p. 22) has pointed out, ethics and knowledge can thus be seen as both constitutive of Awakening. He comments that 'ethical perfection is a central ingredient in the Buddhist *summum bonum*. The two basic values or categories of human good which are recognized by Buddhism are moral and intellectual excellence.'

Ethical conduct is not simply preparatory to liberating knowledge. Both ethical conduct and understanding of 'how things really are' are present and perfected in Awakening, and both are causes of this Awakening. And they both support one another. When Awakened, practitioners do what they ought to do – that is, they stop craving completely – because they have complete knowledge which is combined with perfect ethical conduct.

CHAPTER FIVE

Buddhist Anti-realism

In this chapter I will examine the third characteristic of existence, that is, not-self, in more depth. I will argue that, according to many Buddhist philosophers, there is a further dimension to this teaching. For these thinkers, things are without a self or essence in the sense that they are unreal or fabrications. These Buddhists are thus 'anti-realists'. It is not simply that entities are devoid of self in the sense that they are dependently originating and have no permanent, abiding nature. In addition, they are mental constructions. They do not exist independently of the mind. And knowledge of this unreality of things is, as the deepest meaning of the third characteristic of existence, thought to be necessary for liberation from craving and suffering. My initial focus will be on Madhyamaka school of Mahāyāna Buddhism and its teaching of emptiness (*śūnyatā*). I will then discuss Sarvāstivāda Abhidharma, Sautrāntika and Yogācāra Buddhism as varieties of anti-realism.

Interpreting Madhyamaka

Madhyamaka texts are difficult to unravel and they have stimulated numerous interpretations, both by Buddhist thinkers and in modern times by academics. The plethora of readings of Madhyamaka Buddhism by modern Western scholars – as nihilism, pragmatism, deconstructionism, scepticism, mysticism and so forth – has been well charted by Andrew Tuck (1990), as has the tendency for these interpretations to depend on the fashionable philosophical currents of the time. This interpretive openness can sometimes be explained by wishful thinking and inattentiveness to what the textual evidence actually suggests. However, I think that it is also the case that Madhyamaka works present more than one philosophical outlook. There are inconsistencies between and even within texts. Here one must remember, of course, that Madhyamaka is a tradition, or set of traditions, with a long history, and which has been transplanted into diverse cultures and expressed in various languages. It would be far from surprising (one might argue it is inevitable) that understandings of Madhyamaka shifted with the change in historical and cultural circumstances. Furthermore, there are genuine ambiguities in many Madhyamaka texts and it is not clear that the possible implications of what is stated were always transparent to the authors themselves. Madhyamaka texts are thus often philosophically underdetermined.

With this important proviso, I want to explore here a particular reading of the Madhyamaka notion of emptiness which seems to have considerable plausibility. That is, there are many texts which support it. According to this interpretation, Madhyamaka is what might be called a very strong form of anti-realism, which advocates that the knowledge required for liberation is the perception of the entirely fabricated nature of all things.

Emptiness and dependent origination

A common Madhyamaka explanation of emptiness is that it means that things lack inherent existence (*svabhāva*). That is, they are empty of inherent existence. Nāgārjuna (second century CE), who is considered to be the founder of Madhyamaka thought, says that for a thing to have inherent existence it would have to exist independently of causes and to be uncreated, that is, to have existed forever. Entities with inherent existence would not dependently originate. They would have autonomous existence:

> [Things with] inherent existence do not occur by way of conditions and causes. [Things with] inherent existence that are produced by causes and conditions would be created. But how could [something with] inherent existence be created? For [things with] inherent existence are uncreated, and independent of other [things]. (*Madhyamakakārikā* 15, 1–2)

But, according to Nāgārjuna, there are no such inherently existing things. All entities are empty of inherent existence. That is, they are all dependently originating. Thus, Nāgārjuna's commentary to *Vigrahavyāvartanī* 70 declares that emptiness and dependent origination are synonyms. All things are empty in the sense that they are not self-sufficient. As Nāgārjuna says at *Madhayamakārikā* 24, 19: 'Since no entity is not dependently arisen, there is certainly no non-empty entity.'

Emptiness and conceptual construction

This teaching seems innocuous enough and, it might be thought, is merely a restatement of a central Buddhist tenet. However, it appears that this is not the full story about emptiness because many Madhyamaka statements make the more radical and contentious claim that all entities also lack inherent existence in the sense that they are completely conceptual constructs.

Buddhists have often recognized the role of conceptual construction in Unawakened experience. Thus, as Bhikkhu Ñānananda (1971) has discussed in detail, early Theravāda Buddhism identifies *papañca* (the Pāli form of the Sanskrit word *prapañca*) – sometimes translated as 'conceptual diffusion' – as the tendency of the mind to proliferate concepts which lead the mind further and further from its actual perceptions, and further and further into the realm of fantasy and delusion. Most importantly, the Unawakened mind is thought to distort 'things as they really are' by imposing concepts such as permanence and satisfactoriness, where in fact there is only impermanence and unsatisfactoriness. But the Madhyamaka claim, according to the anti-realist reading, is much stronger. It is not just that Unawakened people tend to misconceive these entities as permanent, satisfactory and so forth. In addition, they do not understand that the entities are entirely fabrications and are thus conceptual constructs through and through.

Thus, according to some Madhyamaka texts, all entities are simply conventions (*saṃvṛti*, *sāṃvṛta*). For example, Nāgārjuna's *Acintyastava* 6 gives the following praise of the Buddha: 'Oh protector, you declare everything born out of conditions to be conventional.' And *Acintyastava* 35 says that the true Buddhist position is that entities have a merely nominal existence: 'You [the Buddha] sonorously declare that the whole world is name-only (*nāmamātra*).' Other passages from texts attributed to Nāgārjuna say that entities are the result of conceptualization (*vikalpa*) and imagination (*kalpanā*, *parikalpa*). For instance, *Acintyastava* 36 states: '[The Buddha] has declared all entities to be merely imagination (*kalpanā*).' And *Lokātītastava* 19 says: 'You [the Buddha] have fully understood that this world is produced from imagination (*parikalpa*). It is unreal, unarisen and is not destroyed.' In addition, *Yuktiṣaṣṭikā* 37 asks: 'Why not accept that this world is conceptualization (*vikalpa*), as the Buddhas speak of it as having the causal condition that is ignorance?' Furthermore, Mādhyamikas often compare all entities to illusions, dreams, mirages and so forth. That is, entities are, like these fantasy objects, simply fabrications. They are merely appearances to the mind that have no existence beyond this:

> Just as, because it is simply a delusion of the mind, an illusory elephant does not come from anywhere, goes nowhere, and does not endure really, so too the world, which is like an illusion, does not come [from anywhere], goes nowhere, and does not endure really, because it is simply a delusion of the mind. (*Ratnāvalī* 2, 12–13)

This is presumably why in Madhyamaka texts one finds statements that dependently originating entities do not really originate. As *Yuktiṣaṣṭikā* 48 declares: 'The best of knowers of reality [that is, the Buddha] said the dependently arisen is not arisen.' In other words, the whole world of dependently originating entities is simply a phantasm or a mental creation. In Tibetan Madhyamaka (see Hopkins, 1996, pp. 35–41), things are said to have no 'existence from their own side' (*rang ngos nas grub pa*) and no 'existence from the side of the basis of designation' (*gdags gzhi'i ngos nas grub pa*). Entities are declared to 'mere imputations of thought' (*rtog pas btags tsam*) and to have a conceptual existence (*btags yod pa*).

Dependent origination and conceptual construction

But how do the Mādhyamikas reach this conclusion? What is their justification for the emptiness teaching? Madhyamaka texts, from the *Madhyamakakārikā* onwards, present numerous refutations of the inherent existence of various entities, such as causes, motion, the senses, the *skandha*s, the self, time and so forth. These refutations, it seems, are intended to show, first of all, that these entities cannot have independent existence and, second, that being dependently originating phenomena, they must be unreal. In other words, the basic Madhyamaka contention appears to be that the dependent origination of entities actually entails that they are conceptual constructs. This is because things, by virtue of their origination in dependence on various factors, can always be analysed into these causal conditions. Thus, according to the Mādhyamikas, entities are simply names attributed to a conglomeration of causes. So, Candrakīrti (seventh century CE) – in his commentary on *Madhyamakakārikā* 24, 18 – says that dependent origination and dependent designation (*upādāyaprajñapti*) are synonyms (*Prasannapadā* 504). That is, dependent origination means that the dependently originated entity (and that is every entity) is not a real thing, but is simply a convenient label for complex bundles of interrelated phenomena.

The Mādhyamikas would challenge us to examine any entity whatsoever. A tree, for example, is made up of various components – the trunk, roots, branches, bark, leaves and so forth. And the tree is also dependent on various external factors, such as soil, sunshine, water and so forth. The Mādhyamikas contend that, if one examines the entity that one calls 'tree', one finds that, in reality, there is nothing there other than these various parts and external causal conditions operating in conjunction. There is not in fact a separate 'tree-entity'. As Atiśa's *Satyadvayāvatāra* 21 puts this point, when an entity is analysed it is actually unfindable. When one searches for the tree-entity, for instance, it dissolves, so to speak, into its components and external causal conditions. The Mādhyamikas would say, then, that the entity which we call 'tree' is simply a concept which the mind attributes to these various factors. There is no mind-independent tree-entity.

Buddhism is well known for carrying out this sort of analysis with regard to the common notion of the self (*ātman*) as a separate reality underlying the body and our mental and emotional states. The Buddhists commonly claim that, if we examine ourselves, we discover that we are composed entirely of the five ever-changing psychophysical aggregates or 'bundles' of phenomena (*skandha*s). What one calls 'the self' is simply their interplay and continual flow. If one looks closely at one's experience, there is no additional factor, it is argued, which might be called the self. The self is, then, just a concept that is attributed by the mind to these ever-changing psychophysical processes. Thus, the *Milindapañha* (trans. Horner, 1990, pp. 34–8) famously compares the self to a chariot, which, it is claimed, is simply a name imputed to the collection of its parts – the axles, wheels, frame, reins, yoke and so forth. There is no extra chariot-entity in addition to the various components. The Mādhyamikas apply this reasoning to each and every thing. Just as the self or a chariot cannot withstand analysis, so it is with every entity. If one examines any thing, it can be reduced to its internal and external causal conditions. The entity itself will be found to be nothing more than a name that is used to label the conjunction of these causal conditions. And these causal conditions will themselves be found to be mere names or concepts used to label their own causal conditions, and so on. In no case are entities anything real in themselves. They do not exist inherently, that is, mind independently. In other words, in all cases things will be found to be empty.

Liberation and emptiness

The distinction between propositional knowledge and knowledge by acquaintance, discussed in Chapter 3, is crucial, I think, in understanding the purported liberative effect of the emptiness teaching. It is clearly one thing to have the propositional knowledge that things are empty and quite another to have the perception or knowledge by acquaintance of this emptiness. It appears that many Mādhyamikas consider knowledge by acquaintance to be required for liberation to occur. One needs to *see* that things are fabrications. Such seeing will, it is thought, have more transformative power than a mere reasoned understanding that things are empty. Mādhyamikas often contend that this perception is to be induced by meditation. The dGe lugs pa tradition of Tibetan Buddhism, for instance, provides extensive explanations of meditative techniques that are designed to bring about such a perception. Here is not the place to offer any detailed description or evaluation of these procedures (see Hopkins 1996). However, the basic principle is that *vipaśyanā* (Tibetan: *lhag mthong*) meditation – consisting of reflections on emptiness, including the rehearsal of various arguments to establish emptiness from Madhyamaka sources such as the *Madhyamakakārikā* – is thought eventually to produce a perception of emptiness if conjoined with the extremely concentrated, quiescent state supposedly attained through *śamatha* (Tibetan: *zhi gnas*) methods.

So, for the Mādhyamikas, liberating knowledge is the perception of not-self understood as the absence of inherent existence of things. Craving and attachment can be eradicated only by the knowledge by acquaintance of the deeper meaning of not-self – that is, that the entities one craves are without an essence in the sense that they have an entirely fabricated nature. Tsong kha pa (*Lam rim chen mo* 414) quotes a passage from Candrakīrti's commentary on *Catuḥśataka* 12, 12 that expresses succinctly this special Madhyamaka perspective on not-self and liberation:

> The complete destruction of attachment is the cause of the attainment of *nirvāṇa* and no teaching can be the cause of the complete destruction of attachment in this manner except the view that [entities] lack inherent existence. For just that [reason] this selflessness which has the characteristic of absence of inherent existence occurs as the door of quiescence without a second. This is the single, matchless door for the entry into the city of *nirvāṇa*.

Perceiving things to be fabricated is clearly quite different from perceiving things to be impermanent. One might see, for instance, that a flower is impermanent without perceiving that the flower is a conceptual construct – that is, something that, like a hallucination or dream, does not exist independently of the mind. And unlike the impermanence of entities, which is ordinarily perceived by many Unawakened people, the fabricated nature of entities is certainly not normally seen. One does not usually perceive flowers, for example, to have an entirely mind-dependent existence. The Mādhyamikas can claim, then, that it is this failure to see the emptiness of phenomena which causes people to continue craving.

But why would the perception of the fabricated nature of entities be any more effective at cutting off craving than the perception of entities' impermanence? One theoretical possibility is that the people who have the perceptual knowledge of entities as fabrications thereby stop experiencing these entities at all. If this were so, it is presumably true that craving and attachment for entities would be stopped because these fabricated entities would have been dispelled. They would no longer exist at all, even as appearances for the mind. One would thus have no objects of consciousness which to crave. But then the Mādhyamikas would have achieved the cessation of craving and attachment at a very high price indeed, namely, the complete obliteration of the entire everyday world of entities. They would have cut off craving by eradicating the world that they might crave. Such 'liberation by annihilation' no doubt would be an effective but also a very drastic and arguably an unappealing solution to the problem of suffering. Is this not a case of 'cracking a walnut with a sledgehammer'?

Few Buddhists, I suggest, would countenance this form of liberation. The Awakened person, after all, is usually depicted as still active in and cognizant of the conventional world. And we must remember that Madhyamaka is a form of Mahāyāna spirituality, according to which Awakened people who perceive entities as empty continue, out of compassion, to function in the world and to be accessible to Unawakened people for an indefinitely long period of time. It seems, then, that Awakened Mādhyamikas who have the perceptual knowledge of entities as fabrications might continue to experience these entities whilst perceiving them to be fabrications. Thus, the everyday world of entities would continue to appear to the Awakened Mādhyamikas, but, unlike ordinary, Unawakened people, they would not take it to be real. They would see the existence of entities to be far more tenuous than when they perceived merely the impermanent nature of things. Fabricated things clearly have a weaker type of existence than unfabricated entities. Seeing an entity to be transient, one might still crave and get attached to it, but perceiving the entity to have a merely nominal existence would surely, the anti-realist Mādhyamikas might say, stop one's craving and attachment once and for all (though, it should be noted, one might still object that it is quite possible to crave and be attached to an object that one knows to be a fantasy!).

Anti-realist Mādhyamikas who have achieved the perception of things as empty would thus continue to function in the world, but, insofar as they see entities as fabrications, would be without craving and attachment. The everyday reality would be like a magic show in which they participate. However, unlike the other participants, they would see the magic show for what it is; they would not be taken in or tricked by it. They would see the conventional (and that includes everything) to be merely conventional. As Candrakīrti remarks at *Madhyamakāvatārabhāṣya* 107–9, entities, which delude Unawakened people, are for Awakened people 'mere conventions' (*kun rdzob tsams*) because they see that these entities dependently arise like illusions and so forth.

The perception of emptiness in the everyday world – a problem

It is, however, a moot point whether it would be psychologically feasible for a person to continue to function in the everyday world whilst perceiving that the entities which constitute that world are fabrications. Might it not be that one's engagement with the conventional reality must be based on the assumption that it is not simply a fabrication? Could one really continue to function in a world of entities which one has seen to be entirely conceptually constructed? Is it psychologically possible, for instance, that I might have a conversation with you, whilst perceiving you (and, indeed, myself!) to be entirely fabricated? And could I really continue to sit on chairs, eat food, walk down roads and so on that I see to be completely illusory? Would not my interactions with the world become impossible? It is arguable that the effect of such a perception would in fact be a sort of paralysis in which ordinary activities would become meaningless. In which case, perceivers of things as fabricated might well be free from craving and attachment but they would most likely be found in a mental hospital! Whether or not Mādhyamikas who perceive the fabricated nature of entities would be able to preserve their sanity and continue to function is thus disputable. There seems here to be a fine line between Awakening and madness and is it not possible that the Mādhyamikas have crossed it?

However, in reply to this objection, it is noteworthy that the ability in daily life to see entities and at the very same time see their emptiness is, according to dGe lugs pa account of Madhyamaka at any rate, an extremely exalted and rare state. It is not achieved until the attainment of Buddhahood which usually requires very many lifetimes of meditative practice on the Bodhisattva path. At a much lower but still exalted stage (the first *bhūmi*), the Bodhisattvas are said to gain the ability to perceive emptiness in their meditation. However, when they rise from their meditation, they still perceive entities as having inherent existence, though they of course continue to have the merely propositional knowledge that these entities are empty. They cannot yet simultaneously perceive everyday entities and their emptiness. They must alternate between perceptions of emptiness in meditation and perceptions of entities in non-meditative experience (see Newland, 1992, p. 17; Williams 1989, pp. 73–4).What this account suggests is that Awakened people – that is, Buddhas – who have achieved the ability to see entities as fabrications in everyday life and not just in periods of meditative absorption are considered to be very rare and extraordinary beings who are in many ways quite unlike ordinary, Unawakened people. Indeed, they are depicted as having remarkable powers, including great ability as wonder-workers or magicians. Their perception of things as fabrications is thought to give them the ability to manipulate at will, with compassionate intentions of course, the magic show that is the conventional world. I make no comment on whether such a magic-wielding Awakened person could actually exist, a possibility that it is perhaps rather difficult for a modern Westerner to concede. What is clear, however, is that the Mādhyamikas, or the dGe lugs pa variety at any rate, consider people who are able to see the fabricated nature of all things in everyday life to be very different from and so much more mentally capable than ordinary Unawakened people that questions about whether they could preserve their sanity while seeing all things as empty are perhaps misplaced. But then one might wonder whether these Mādhyamikas have made liberation so lofty that it is in reality unattainable.

Innate and philosophical misconceptions

Perhaps one of the clearest examples of the Madhyamaka emphasis on knowledge of emptiness as the key to liberation occurs at *sTong thun chen mo* 132–40 (see trans. Cabezón, 1992, pp. 128–35) by mKhas grub rje (1385–1448), one of the most important disciples of Tsong kha pa. Here he claims that the misunderstanding that entities are permanent is a merely philosophical or contrived (*kun brtags*) misconception. It is one dreamt up by misguided intellectuals and not shared by people unfamiliar with philosophical tenets. Most people, mKhas grub rje contends, unless they have been introduced to ideas of the *ātman* (the permanent self or soul) and so forth as propounded by deluded philosophies (such as the orthodox Hindu *darśanas*), do not have such a mistaken view. Thus this misconception cannot be the root cause of craving and suffering, for many people do not have such a view and yet still crave and suffer.

mKhas grub rje claims that it is an innate (*lhan skyes*) misconception, shared by deluded philosophers and all non-philosophical people, which is the root cause of craving and suffering. The innate misconception is, mKhas grub rje claims, the mistaken understanding that things have 'true existence' (*bden par yod pa*) and 'existence from their own side' (*rang ngos nas grub pa*), which are synonyms for inherent existence. That is, Unawakened people have the erroneous conception that entities are real when in fact they are merely nominal. Tsong kha pa, who also writes extensively about innate and philosophical misconceptions, comments that the person with the innate misconception 'apprehends external and internal things as existing by way of own-essence and as not merely established by the power of convention' (*Drangs nges legs bshad snying po* 68).

The innate misconception is, mKhas grub rje claims, a pre-reflective error that is common to all Unawakened beings – the philosopher, the child, the animal, and so forth. He says that 'the innate [misconception] belongs without distinction from beginningless time to all sentient beings'. Most people and other sentient beings perceive entities to be unfabricated. It is not that they usually articulate this misconception or have a consciously held belief that this is so. Indeed, animals and young children are incapable of articulation or consciously held beliefs. Nevertheless, they do see things as real. That is, they discriminate objects which they treat as mind independent, even if it has never occurred to them that this is what they do. People and other sentient beings are, we might say, by nature ontological realists and it is this realism, rather than the relatively uncommon belief in permanent entities that mKhas grub rje thinks is the fundamental cause of craving and suffering. Thus one's meditations should be aimed primarily at cutting off this innate misconception by producing the perception that things lack inherent existence.

However, it is not the case that mKhas grub rje thinks it is unnecessary to refute the philosophical misconception of permanence. On the contrary, he thinks that it is a pernicious deluded view, a cause of eventual suffering for those who hold it, that needs to be eradicated whenever it occurs. His point is that such a refutation can only be an ancillary (*yan lag*) to the expurgation of the innate misconception which lies at the heart of Unawakened people's suffering.

mKhas grub rje, commenting on Candrakīrti's *Madhyamakāvatāra* 6, 140–41, says that refuting the contrived, philosophical misconception that there is a permanent self in order to eradicate the innate misconception that things lack inherent existence would be, as Candrakīrti says, 'like someone seeing a snake living in a hole in the wall of his own house [attempting to] remove his fear and eliminate his terror of the snake by the thought "here the elephant does not exist"'. One will never remove the subtler, less obvious (snake-like) misperception that things have inherent existence simply by meditating on their impermanence and thereby removing the gross and obvious (elephant-like) misconception that things are permanent. Given that it is the innate misconception that is the fundamental cause of one's craving and suffering, it must be the principal aim of one's meditation to produce the perceptual knowledge of things' absence of inherent existence.

Sarvāstivāda and Sautrāntika anti-realism

Madhyamaka is not the only form of Buddhist anti-realism. Both the Sarvāstivāda Abhidharma and Sautrāntika forms of non-Mahāyāna Indian Buddhism claim that all entities with parts are simply conceptual constructs on the basis of their parts. However, unlike Madhyamaka, they contend that there are partless material and mental entities, called *dharma*s, out of which all other entities are constructed. These *dharma*s include mental events such as feeling, mental engagement, jealousy, belligerence, doubt, shame, conscientiousness, mental pliancy and so forth (see Hopkins, 1996, pp. 238–68) as well as physical phenomena such as hardness, viscidity, fluidity, heat, motion and so forth (for a detailed study see Karunadasa, 1967). The important point here is that the *dharma*s are not fabricated. They are ultimate truths (*paramārthasatya*) and not conventional truths (*saṃvṛtisatya*). They have real existence (*dravyasat*) and not conceptual existence (*prajñaptisat*). All other things have merely conceptual existence and not real existence (see Burton, 1999, pp. 90–92). *Abhidharmakośa* 6, 4 says, 'a conventional truth is [any phenomenon] an awareness of which no [longer] operates when [that phenomenon] is broken or mentally subdivided' (trans. Klein, 1998, p. 34). In other words, whatever can be broken apart or analysed into constituents is merely nominally existent. The Sarvāstivādins and Sautrāntikas think that there is no infinite regress here because there are some fundamental entities, the *dharma*s, which cannot be physically dissected or mentally subdivided. They are the real building blocks out of which the fabricated world of everyday things is constructed.

For these Buddhists, then, the atomic *dharma*s are really there and conglomerations of the material ones are perceived as bits of sensory information – colours, sounds, smells and so forth. The Sarvāstivādins contend that these collections of *dharma*s are perceived directly, that is, the mind apprehends, via the sense organs, the *dharma*s themselves. By contrast, the Sautrāntikas uphold a representational theory of perception, according to which the assemblages of *dharma*s are not perceived directly but the contact of the sense organs with them stimulates mental images (*ākāra*) which are the actual object of perception (see King, 1999a, p. 159). Though they disagree here on the actual mechanics of the perceptual process, the two schools are united in their position that everyday objects such as tables, chairs, mountains and rivers are not real. The mind creates these entities on the basis of the perceived *dharma*s or, in the case of Sautrāntika, the perceived images of the *dharma*s.

This *dharma* theory bears comparison with Bertrand Russell's theory that what we actually perceive are sense data – sounds, smells, colours and so forth – on the basis of which the mind infers the existence of commonsense objects such as tables, chairs, mountains and rivers (see Cooper, 1999, pp. 232–4). In other words, according to Russell, we never have knowledge by acquaintance of any external objects other than the sense data. Thus, Russell thinks that I cannot know by acquaintance, for example, the lake in Hyde Park. I would have perceptual knowledge of various bits of sensory information and would infer on that basis that there is a lake in Hyde Park that causes these sense data. However, a big difference between Russell's view and that of these Buddhists is that Russell has strong realist inclinations and claims that there is very strong reason to believe that there are real everyday objects causing the perceived sense data (see Cooper, 1999, p. 233), whereas the Sarvāstivādins and Sautrāntikas say that only the *dharma*s really exist, and the everyday objects are actually mental creations.

I am here calling these two Buddhist philosophical schools forms of anti-realism. However, it should be noted that, from another vantage point, it would be legitimate to label them as realists of a sort, in so far as they do say that there is a mind-independent world, albeit one of atomic *dharma*s rather than tables, mountains, trees and so forth. Whether one calls the middle ground they occupy 'critical realism' or 'moderate anti-realism' is thus a moot point. They are certainly not naive realists, who would affirm the mind-independent existence of everyday objects, nor are they extreme anti-realists, who would completely deny the existence of a mind-independent world, claiming that it is all merely conventional. These Buddhists reject the Madhyamaka idea that everything is empty. I am labelling them anti-realists to stress that for them the commonsense world is a fabrication.

It is arguable that the Sautrāntikas' anti-realism is somewhat stronger than that of the Sarvāstivādins because the Sautrāntikas claim that the *dharma*s themselves, though real, are impermanent in a very radical sense. They are not simply impermanent. They are also momentary. Indeed, they are said to have no duration at all because any persistence in time would compromise their instantaneous nature, the idea here apparently being that any duration can always be divided into smaller moments! By contrast, the Sarvāstivādins advocate that, though the *dharma*s' present existence is momentary, a moment is characterized by origination, duration, decay and cessation (see *Abhidharmakośa* 2, 45). In other words, a moment does endure.

Furthermore, the Sarvāstivādins say that the momentary *dharma*s have an inherently existing essence (*svabhāva*) that persists through all three times, past, present and future. *Dharma*s thus have a permanence of a sort (see *Abhidharmakośa* 5, 25 ff.). This might seem a peculiar reversal of the ordinary Buddhist emphasis on transitoriness, but it seems that the Sarvāstivādins say that past and future *dharma*s cannot be absolutely non-existent in so far as they can continue to be objects of consciousness, through memory or expectation (see Williams, 2000, p. 114). When a *dharma* is remembered or anticipated, according to the Sarvāstivādins, it is the ever-existing *svabhāva* of the *dharma* which is brought to mind. In addition, the Sārvastivādins thought that it was necessary to assert that past *dharma*s continue to exist in order to explain causal and karmic continuity. That is, how can a momentary *dharma* from a past life, for instance, exert an influence on the present consciousness if it does not somehow still exist? The Sarvāstivādins say that it is the *svabhāva* of the otherwise momentary *dharma* which continues and has this karmic influence. Sautrāntikas, by contrast, reject the continuing existence of past *dharma*s, arguing that the momentary wholesome or unwholesome past mental events have karmic result by modifying or 'perfuming' the subsequent causally connected series of momentary mental events. The image used is of a seed planted in the mental continuum which later comes to fruition as a karmic effect. The unwholesome or wholesome *dharma* does not last for more than a moment, but it deposits a trace which is reproduced in all subsequent momentary mental *dharma*s of the continuum until it comes to maturation as a karmic effect.

The relative strength of the Sautrāntikas' anti-realism is also evident in their rejection of various types of *dharma*s accepted by the Sarvāstivāda Abhidharma tradition. For instance, the Sautrāntikas refute the Sarvāstivādin claim that shape (*saṃsthāna*) is a *dharma* and they also refute the Sarvāstivāda claim that there is a *dharma* called 'possession' (*prāpti*) which acts as an impersonal, metaphysical glue, binding specific qualities (for example, one's karmic inheritance and basic disposition) to a particular stream of consciousness (see King, 1999a, p. 88). In other words, there is a tendency in Sautrāntika Buddhism to reduce the number of *dharma*s and to claim that some phenomena granted substantial existence by the Sarvāstivādins in fact have only conceptual existence.

As with other Buddhists, the Sarvāstivādins and Sautrāntikas are interested in 'seeing things as they really are', and this perception is thought to have a liberative effect. The *dharma* theory is, then, intended as an aid in meditation and reflection, in order to bring about understanding of things in their true nature. Liberation requires that we distinguish what is real from what is unreal and realize that the everyday things that we crave are merely conceptual constructions on the basis of their atomic constituents.

Yogācāra anti-realism

Yogācāra Buddhism – which is, like Madhyamaka, a form of Mahāyāna philosophy – can also be construed as a form of anti-realism. In this case, the anti-realism amounts to ontological idealism, that is, the view that only the mind really exists. As with the Madhyamaka sources, Yogācāra texts are open to a variety of interpretations, and might not present an entirely consistent philosophical message. There are numerous Yogācāra thinkers and they did not all necessarily advocate precisely the same philosophical position at all times. We will see in Chapter 7 a reading of Yogācāra which challenges the idealist interpretation. That being said, it is plausible and has been popular to understand many Yogācāra texts as advocating that only the mind exists (see, for example, Williams, 1989, pp. 82–90; Williams, 2000, pp. 156–60). So, the idealist interpretation is worthy of consideration.

Read in this manner, the Yogācāra position is that the entire external world is a fabrication. By contrast the momentary mental events that make up the stream of consciousness (*citta/vijñāna*) are real. In other words, experiences themselves are unfabricated, but the notion that these experiences refer to actually existing external objects is incorrect. For instance, if I perceive a tree, according to the Yogācārins, this experience is real – that is, I am having a tree experience – but there is no externally existing tree which corresponds to the experience. Hence, Yogācāra is also known as the Cittamātra (consciousness or mind-only), Vijñaptimātra (cognition-only) and Vijñānavāda (doctrine of consciousness) school.

The early Yogācārin Vasubandhu (fourth century CE) compares the experience of external objects to a hallucination produced by an eye disease. As *Viṃśatikā* 1 says, 'all this [that is, the entire external world] is cognition-only, because of the appearance of non-existent objects, just as there may be the seeing of non-existent nets of hair by someone afflicted by an optical disorder'. And he goes on, at *Viṃśatikā* 3–4, to employ the dream analogy in order to explain our experience of external objects. That is, just as in a dream we think that we experience and interact with external objects when in fact we do not, so it is in waking life. Thus, *Triṃśikā* 25 identifies suchness (*tathatā*), a synonym for reality or 'things as they actually are', with cognition only (*vijñaptimātra*).

Vasubandhu also argues, at *Viṃśatikā* 11 ff., that whatever supposed external object is experienced can always be analysed into its parts, and thus does not really exist. And he says that the parts themselves are unreal as they can be reduced to their own constituents. It might be claimed, with the Sautrāntika and Sarvāstivāda Buddhists, that eventually we are left with irreducible and unanalysable atoms, the smallest and imperceptible pieces of external reality. However, Vasubandhu disputes the existence of such atoms. He argues that if they join together in part, then they are capable of further division into these parts and are not really atoms. Yet, if the atoms combine totally, rather than in part, then they would never take up the space of more than one atom, and they would remain imperceptible! This reasoning is not without its weaknesses. For example, it is not clear to me why atoms that combine totally would take up only the space of one atom. I do not wish here to give a detailed assessment of Vasubandhu's logic, however. What is significant in the present context is that he appears intent on demonstrating that external perceptible objects, and the imperceptible *dharma*s which supposedly constitute them, do not really exist.

Further support for the idealist interpretation of Yogācāra is found at *Madhyāntavibhāga* 1, 22 which refers to the luminousness of consciousness (*citta*) which is identified with emptiness. It is said to be by nature unafflicted and pure. For the Yogācārins, then, reality is emptiness which here is to be construed as a 'luminous' flow of consciousness. It is presumably empty in the sense that it is inherently devoid of impurities and defilements. Similarly, at *Mahāyānasūtrālaṃkāra* 13, 19 Asaṅga declares that consciousness (*citta*) is always luminous by nature. This luminous consciousness is declared to be the *dharmatācitta*, which might be translated as the 'consciousness which is reality'. The commentary, which might be by either Asaṅga or Vasubandhu, identifies this luminous consciousness, which it too calls the *dharmatācitta*, with the sphere of reality (*dharmadhātu*), and with suchness (*tathatā*). *Dharmatā*, *dharmadhātu* and *tathatā* are common epithets for 'things as they really are'.

Another doctrine which seems to express the idealism of the Yogācārins is the three aspects (*trisvabhāva*) teaching, found, for instance, in the *Saṃdhinirmocana sūtra* and Vasubandhu's *Trisvabhāvanirdeśa*. The three aspects are identified as the dependent aspect (*paratantrasvabhāva*), the imagined aspect (*parikalpitasvabhāva*), and the perfected aspect (*pariniṣpannasvabhāva*).

Trisvabhāvanirdeśa 2 says that 'that which appears is the dependent aspect, because it depends on conditions'. In verses 4 ff., Vasubandhu appears to identify this dependent aspect with consciousness (*citta*). It is 'dependent' in the sense that each moment of consciousness originates in dependence upon previous ones. When Vasubandhu says that this dependent aspect is 'that which appears' he seems to mean that it is a flow of consciousness-events or experiences.

The imagined aspect, *Trisvabhāvanirdeśa* 2 continues, is 'how it [the dependent aspect] appears'. And, it says that, unlike the dependent aspect, this imagined aspect is 'imagination-only' (*kalpanāmātra*). In other words, the dependent aspect is not a fabrication. Experience itself is real. However, the manner in which it appears in the Unawakened state is a fabrication. *Trisvabhāvanirdeśa* 3 explains that how the dependent aspect appears is 'in the form of dualities'. So, the imagined aspect is the really existing flow of consciousness as it is misconstrued by Unawakened people who wrongly take their experiences to refer to external objects. They do not realize that in fact what they take to be external objects are only mind-produced images. And it is because they think that these images are real that they crave for and get attached to them. This is why the Yogācārins identifiy the dualism 'grasper-grasped' (*grāhaka-grāhya*) as central to the imagined aspect. Unawakened minds become graspers of objects that are thought worthy to be grasped. They are thought worthy to be grasped because they are thought to be real whereas, unbeknownst to Unawakened people, they are actually fabrications. Unawakened experience is thus afflicted by the duality of subject (the mind or consciousness) set over against, and seeking to appropriate, objects.

What, then, is the perfected aspect? At *Mahāyānasaṃgraha* 2, 4, Asaṅga (fourth century CE) says that the perfected aspect is the total absence of objects in the dependent aspect. And *Trisvabhāvanirdeśa* 3 says that the perfected aspect is the constant absence of 'how it appears' (the imagined aspect) in 'that which appears' (the dependent aspect). In other words, the perfected aspect is the fact that there is no real subject-object duality in the flow of consciousness. That is, the perfected aspect is the truth that external objects are merely fabrications and the dependent aspect is only the flow of consciousness. Emptiness here can be construed as the absence of the subject-object duality, because external objects are in fact simply fabrications. The flow of consciousness is in reality empty of the subject-object duality. It is this fact that Awakened people come to know. Thus, they purify their flow of consciousness, no longer misconstruing its images to be really existing external objects. So, the Awakened mind is no longer afflicted by the grasper-grasped dualism. That is, seeing that the objects of craving are fabrications, it stops seeking to appropriate them. The soteriological import of the Yogācāra mind-only doctrine is thus clear.

Madhyamaka and Yogācāra

I have described both Madhyamaka and Yogācāra as forms of anti-realism which deny the mind-independent existence of the external world. The natural question, then, is how exactly is Madhyamaka philosophically different from Yogācāra? This is a controversial issue. In Chapter 7 we will see that there are some interpreters who claim that there is no substantial philosophical disagreement. However, there is also a plausible interpretation, which I will now present, that there is a real point of difference and that the Madhyamaka anti-realism is more extreme than that of Yogācāra.

Indian Madhyamaka texts from about the sixth century onwards – such as the *Bodhicittavivaraṇa* 26 ff. (see Lindtner, 1982, pp. 192 ff.), Bhāvaviveka's

Madhyamakahṛdayakārikā, *Tarkajvālā*, *Prajñāpradīpa*, *Karatalaratna* and *Madhyamakaratnapradīpa* (see Lindtner 1986a; 1986b) as well as Candrakīrti's *Madhyamakāvatārabhāṣya* 6, 45–97 – offer strident and sustained refutations of Yogācāra philosophy. In addition, Śāntideva in the *Bodhicaryāvatāra* 9, 11 ff. confronts a Yogācārin opponent and Śāntarakṣita also criticizes the Yogācāra in his *Madhyamakālaṃkāra* 44 ff. In these critiques, the Mādhyamikas say that both consciousness and its objects lack inherent existence. For example, the *Madhyamakāvatāra* 6, 71 declares that 'just as the object of cognition does not exist, likewise the mind also does not exist', and the auto-commentary explains that what is meant is that neither the object of cognition nor the mind have inherent existence. These Madhyamaka texts seem to insist that absolutely everything is empty, including even the constructing mind and its constituent mental events.

The Mādhyamikas contrast their position with that of the Yogācārins, whom they depict as advocating the inherent existence of consciousness. Although the Yogācārins admit that objects of consciousness lack inherent existence, they say, according to the Mādhyamikas, that the flow of consciousness is not a fabrication; it exists in a real, substantial way. Consciousness is for the Yogācārins, according to these Mādhyamikas, the inherently existing reality that still exists when all false imaginings have been abolished. As we have seen, for the Yogacārins the dependent nature, that is, the stream of consciousness, is real. But the Mādhyamikas protest that there is no such inherently existing mind. As the *Bodhicittavivaraṇa* 55 declares: 'From the very beginning consciousness has never had inherent existence.'

Madhyamaka and the ontological paradox

Hence, it seems that the Madhyamaka anti-realism goes a step beyond that of Yogācāra Buddhism. But there is a serious philosophical difficulty entailed by the Mādhyamikas' position that everything is fabricated including consciousness itself. For surely the fabrication would never get started, so to speak, because such fabrication requires a fabricator which or who is logically prior to the fabricated entities. It seems necessary to claim that fabrication requires an agent of the fabrication, someone or something that is doing the fabricating, which is not him/her/itself a fabrication.

Furthermore, it can be objected that it simply does not make sense to say that everything is fabricated, because there must be some foundation, some basic stuff, which is not fabricated and on the basis of which fabrication takes place. In Sarvāstivāda Abhidharma and Sautrāntika Buddhism, this foundational stuff is the *dharma*s, whereas for the Yogācāra school it is the flow of consciousness. But fabrication by the human mind out of nothing real at all, a sort of creation *ex nihilo*, seems to be a highly questionable proposal.

It is certainly one that the Mādhyamikas' Buddhist opponents would not have countenanced. Indeed, some Yogācāra texts state quite explicitly that the position that absolutely everything is conceptually constructed is a misconception. For example, Asaṅga's *Bodhisattvabhūmi* (1966, p. 31) says:

> Having heard the abstruse teachings with a non-definitive meaning of the *sūtra*s associated with the Mahāyāna and associated with profound emptiness, not understanding the meaning of the exposition as it actually is, conceiving [of it] incorrectly, with mere conjecture which arises because of error, some people think that 'all this is only conceptual construction. This is reality. He who sees in this way sees correctly.' If this were so, on account of the non-existence of even the mere substratum that is the basis of conceptual construction even the conceptual construction itself would not exist at all. How could the reality that is mere conceptual construction be considered to exist? Therefore, in this manner these [people] negate both reality and conceptual construction.

The *Bodhisattvabhūmi* goes on to accuse these opponents of being the principal or most important nihilists. Given the text's statement that these people come to their nihilistic view as a result of their misunderstanding of the *Mahāyāna* teaching of emptiness, it is quite likely that these principal or most important nihilists are the Mādhyamikas though they are not named as such. mKhas grub rje, at any rate, is sure about the identity of the opponents when he comments on this passage. He says, at *sTong thun chen mo* 28, that this section from the *Bodhisattvabhūmi* teaches that the Mādhyamikas commit the fault of nihilism by asserting that all entities are only conceptual constructions.

The Yogācāra position, it appears, is that it does not make sense to claim, as Madhyamaka extreme anti-realism appears to say, that the flow of consciousness, that is, our experiences, lack inherent existence. Yes, the Yogācārins admit, it is true that the external world is a fabrication, but it cannot be the case that the experiences which falsely take the external world to be real are themselves unreal. Experience is an ontological bedrock which cannot be negated. It is what remains in emptiness. Indeed, the Yogācāra position might be bolstered by the Cartesian point that the very doubting of the existence of experience is itself an affirmation of the reality of experience, because doubting is a type of experience. One cannot successfully doubt that experience is real. The Madhyamaka contention that even experience is a fabrication seems illogical and nihilistic.

The Madhyamaka response to the problem of nihilism

In fact, one needs to look no further than Nāgārjuna's own works, such as the *Madhyamakākarikā* 24, 1–6, the *Vigrahavyāvartanī* 1–20, and the

Śūnyatāsaptati 15, to find the accusation of nihilism made by his opponents. If everything is empty, the opponents contend, then nothing exists at all. Madhyamaka philosophy thus destroys the entire world. Nāgārjuna is quick to refute this claim that the emptiness of things means that these things do not exist at all. However, I am not sure that his refutation is very convincing.

He warns against such a nihilistic misunderstanding of emptiness, saying that by this misperception of emptiness 'a person of little intelligence is destroyed, like by a snake wrongly seized or a spell wrongly cast'. His intention is not to negate the existence of the world. Emptiness means, Nāgārjuna says, not that entities are non-existent but rather that they are empty of, that is, lack, independent being. Emptiness denotes that the existence of entities is always dependent on many causal conditions.

Thus, Nāgārjuna is able to claim, in the *Madhyamakārikā* 24, 36, that it is only because things are empty that they can come into existence in dependence upon various conditions. It is the rejection, rather than the acceptance, of emptiness that in fact destroys all entities. If things were not empty of autonomous existence then there could be no explanation of the manifold dependently originating entities that undeniably do occur. The world would be static which is evidently not the case. So, the Madhyamaka claim is that everything is made possible by emptiness. The contention that entities are not empty contradicts the empirically verifiable reality that things change when the factors upon which these things rely alter. As *Vigrahavyāvartanī* 70 says: 'For whom emptiness exists, all things are possible. For whom emptiness does not exist, nothing is possible.' The teaching of emptiness is actually an affirmation of the dynamic interconnectedness of all things. Candrakīrti's *Prasannapadā* 368 expresses this Madhyamaka rejection of the accusation of nihilism succinctly:

> Some people insist that the Mādhyamikas are not different from nihilists, since the Mādhyamikas say that good and bad acts, the agent, the consequences of acts and the entire world are empty of an inherently existing nature. As the nihilists also say that these things do not exist, the Mādhyamikas are the same as nihilists. We reply that this is not the case. Why? Because Mādhyamikas are proponents of dependent origination. Having apprehended causes and conditions, they explain that the entire present and future world is without inherent existence, because dependently originated.

However, it seems to me that this Madhyamaka response to the accusation of nihilism does not address the real problem. For, as we have seen, Mādhyamikas claim not only that everything is dependently originating but also that these dependently originating things are fabrications. Yes, things are said to dependently originate, but it is also said that the entire manifold world of dependently originating entities is a show, a 'merely appearing' dependent origination. How does simply asserting that they accept dependent origination solve the Mādhyamikas' problem that, if all these dependently originating things are fabrications, then there is no unfabricated basis out of which the fabrication can take place, and no unfabricated agent of fabrication? If everything has conceptual existence, then it seems that nothing can exist at all. This is nihilism.

One way out of this conundrum is to give a 'soft' reading of Madhyamaka, according to which the point of the emptiness teaching is not to claim that things are fabrications, but rather that the attribution of autonomous, independent existence (*svabhāva*) to entities is a fabrication. Thus, Madhyamaka is not nihilistic because emptiness is the affirmation of the dependently originating existence of things. A selective reading of Madhyamaka passages might support this soft interpretation and would render Madhyamaka philosophically harmless and unremarkable, for all they would be asserting would be that all things are interconnected. This is not nihilism. But this strategy does not, as far as I can see, really deal with the radical nature of many Madhyamaka statements, which seem to make the claim that the interconnected entities themselves – and not just the independent, autonomous natures sometimes attributed to them – are fabrications.

Another possible solution would be to appeal to the doctrine of the two truths. Indeed, Nāgārjuna does precisely this in *Madhyamakārikā* 24. Here he seems to claim that from the ultimate perspective (*paramārthataḥ*) things are all empty, that is, they are fabrications. However, there is also the truth of worldly convention (*lokasaṃvṛtisatya*) which is also accepted by Mādhyamikas. This is the truth of custom, ordinary life and common practice (*vyavahāra*) which the ultimate truth of emptiness is not intended to negate. From this conventional point of view, entities exist as dependently originating phenomena, and the Mādhyamikas, like everyone else, continue to interact with them though, unlike other people, knowing that these phenomena are ultimately unreal. So, nihilism is supposedly averted because through the teaching of the two truths everyday, ordinary activity and the whole world of phenomena is preserved.

Perhaps the Mādhyamikas are right here. However, my suspicion is that the two truths doctrine does not really solve the problem of nihilism. For, if everything is fabricated, as the perspective of the ultimate truth shows us, then how is it possible that entities can exist for everyday, conventional purposes? It seems puzzling that anything at all exists, even in everyday, conventional terms. For, as I have said previously, there is for Madhyamaka no unfabricated stuff out of which fabrication can occur and no unfabricated agent of the fabrication. Even experience itself, it appears, is being negated as merely illusory. The two truths doctrine shows that Mādhyamikas clearly want to preserve the existence of empty things for conventional, everyday purposes, but it is not clear that they are entitled to do so. To assert a distinction between the two truths is not the same as to give an explanation of how entities, which are said to be from the point of view of ultimate truth entirely illusory, can also continue to exist from the perspective of conventional truth. Might the Mādhyamikas not be accused here of wanting to have their cake and eat it?

Maybe a solution of sorts to this conundrum is for the Mādhyamikas to accept the inexplicability of their own position, and to admit that it is a puzzling ontological paradox, a sort of holy mystery, that all entities are fabrications and yet they still arise, as fabrications fashioned out of nothing and without any unfabricated fabricator. Indeed, there is some evidence that this appeal to inexplicability was an option that some Mādhyamikas were sometimes willing to countenance. For instance, Candrakīrti says, in the *Catuhśatakaṭīkā* 94–7, that it is astonishing that consciousness originates in dependence on sense faculties and sense objects, that sprouts arise from seeds, that *karma* produces effects and so forth. Objects, such as vases, cannot possibly exist, and yet, as dependent designations they perform functions such as 'containing and scooping honey'. In fact, the whole world, Candrakīrti says, is 'amazing for the wise'.

The passage is admittedly obscure, but it seems plausible to suggest that here Candrakīrti is expressing his astonishment that everything is a fabrication, and thus reason tells us that nothing can exist, and yet the world continues to appear as a dependently originating complex of phenomena. It is inexplicable that this should be so. The fantasy show of fabricated entities, seemingly connected to one another through myriad patterns of interdependency, has no real basis and no unfabricated agent who does the fabricating, and seemingly should not exist at all, and yet it carries on. How can this be? This is not a question that Candrakīrti can answer. He admits that it is astonishing, strange. It is amazing and puzzling that the world of dependently arising things occurs and yet is entirely without inherent existence. Dependent origination is like a magic show with the peculiar and puzzling feature that the magician, the audience and the props are entirely illusory. There is nothing outside the magic show on which it is based. Of course, it might be objected, especially by someone with rationalist inclinations, that this appeal to an inexplicable mystery is intellectually irresponsible and a failure to admit that there is a real and irresolvable problem with the Madhyamaka philosophy of emptiness. A far better and more intelligible response might be to relinquish the teaching of universal emptiness that produces the ontological paradox.

A Madhyamaka criticism of other Buddhist anti-realists

Whether or not the Madhyamaka extreme anti-realism is tenable is thus a debatable point. What is clear, however, is that, from the Madhyamaka point of view, the Sarvāstivādins, Sautrāntikas and Yogācārins still posit a very subtle basis for craving and attachment. They have not gone far enough in their anti-realism. That is, for the Sarvāstivādins and Sautrāntikas, it would be the unfabricated *dharma*s and, for the Yogācārins, the flow of consciousness-events. Craving and attachment can only be completely eradicated, the Mādhyamikas might contend, when even these entities have been shown to be empty. Here the Mādhyamikas would agree with the *Prajñāpāramitā* scriptures, of which Madhyamaka is often considered to be the systematic exposition. As the *Ratnaguṇasaṃcayagāthā* 1, 5–6, says:

> In form, in feeling, will, perception, and consciousness
> Nowhere in them they [Bodhisattvas] find a place to rest on.
> Without a home they wander, dharmas never hold them,
> Nor do they grasp at them – the Jina's Bodhi
> they are bound to gain. (trans. Conze, 1973, pp. 9–10)

Are not the Sarvāstivādins and Sautrāntikas 'held' by the *dharma*s which they consider to be real and are not the Yogācārins still 'resting on' consciousness which they assert to be unfabricated? Perhaps the Mādhyamikas have a point. However, it might also be that this Madhyamaka objection is misguided. Their Buddhist opponents might argue that people do not usually get attached to *dharma*s or non-dual consciousness events; it is the world of everyday objects constructed on the basis of these unconstructed entities that people crave and to which they get attached. I do not crave and get attached to the atomic parts of my new car, for instance, but I certainly may crave and get attached to the new car that has these atoms as its parts. Is it not possible, then, that one needs only to perceive the conceptually constructed nature of the everyday entities that are the normal objects of one's craving and attachment? Indeed, even if one did somehow crave and become attached to *dharma*s or non-dual consciousness events, it might be possible to deal with that craving and attachment without taking the drastic step of asserting that they are merely fabricated. Perhaps, for instance, the craving could be eradicated by reflecting on the momentary nature of the real *dharma*s or non-dual consciousness events. So, it seems possible that the Mādhyamikas' criticism of their fellow anti-realist Buddhists can be rebutted. Liberation from craving arguably does not require a commitment to such extreme anti-realism.

The realists' objections

But it is not the Mādhyamikas alone who make some questionable claims. I would suggest that all the forms of Buddhist anti-realism that I have explored in this chapter share a highly contentious ontological commitment. It is far from evident that these Buddhists – Yogācārins, Sarvāstivādins, Sautrāntikas and Mādhyamikas – are right to say that the world of everyday things is a fabrication. These anti-realists, it might be objected, seem to give the mind inordinate power. It is arguable that these Buddhists have been far too parsimonious in their ontology and the mind-independent world of everyday things cannot be so readily reduced to a mental creation. Indeed, many of their opponents in ancient India, such as the Nyāya-Vaiśeṣika and Sāṃkhya schools, advocate realist philosophies that maintain the mind-independent existence of the commonsense world.

So, for instance, realists can object that the Mādhyamikas' conclusion that all entities are nothing more than names does not follow necessarily from their premise that all entities exist in dependence on their parts and external causal factors. The Madhyamaka equation of dependently originating existence with conceptually constructed existence is questionable. Surely it is at least plausible that entities, or some entities, could be mind-independent realities, but nevertheless depend for their existence on a variety of external causal conditions and essential components? For the whole might be greater than the sum of its parts, and an entity which is dependent on others might nevertheless be a new, real phenomenon that is not merely a mind-produced label. It can be argued that a tree, for instance, might exist independently of the mind even though it is dependent on numerous external causal conditions and components for its existence. It is not necessarily simply a concept, entirely reducible to the intrinsic and external factors on which its existence depends. It is worth noting, then, that it would not be unreasonable to resist the Madhyamaka claim – a form of extreme ontological reductionism – that all entities have a merely conceptual existence. Philosophers of a realist persuasion need not be persuaded by the Madhyamaka equation of dependent origination with dependent designation and could accuse the Mādhyamikas of over-emphasizing the power of the mind in constructing reality. Similarly, the Sarvāstivāda and Sautrāntika reduction of the everyday world to *dharma*s might be questioned on the same grounds. It does not follow, the realists can claim, that because commonsense objects depend for their existence on their consitutent *dharma*s, that they are nothing more than mind-created names applied to these *dharma*s.

Furthermore the realists can claim that the Yogācārins and the Mādhyamikas have difficulty in providing a convincing explanation for the shared experience of everyday entities. If the mind creates these things, then why do I experience trees, mountains, rivers, tables, and so forth in the same places and at the same times as do you and other people? Shouldn't it be the case that we all live in private worlds of our own creation?

This problem is perhaps less acute for the Sarvāstivādins and Sautrāntikas, in so far as they can say that there are shared constructions at least partly because certain conglomerations of material *dharma*s tend to get constructed into specific sorts of entities. Thus, a particular grouping of *dharma*s might prompt human minds to construct a tree, whereas a different arrangement of *dharmas* might lead to the construction of a mountain or a river and so forth. These philosophers thus provide some mind-independent basis for a common experience of the world.

The store consciousness

The Yogācārins, for whom there are no such mind-independent *dharma*s, do nevertheless attempt to address the realists' objection. Their explanation is based on their theory of the store consciousness (*ālayavijñāna*). We find in the *Triṃśikā* 1 ff. that the store consciousness is envisaged as a subconscious level of awareness, described as a torrent or current of water. It is thought of as a constantly changing substratum which underlies seven other forms of consciousness. These are identified as the five sense consciousnesses (which enable us to see, hear, smell, taste and touch), the mind consciousness (*manovijñāna*), which apprehends psychic events such as emotions and ideas as well as processing and organizing the information from the sense consciousnesses and, finally, the afflicted mind (*kliṣṭamanas*) which is responsible for all sorts of false constructions, most notably the view that there is a permanent, unchanging self underlying the empirical individual. Significantly, numerous seeds (*bīja*) are said to be planted within the store consciousness. Many of these seeds are said to be common to all store consciousnesses and it is their ripening which is said to explain the inter-subjective world. There is thus no need for an appeal to external objects in order to explain the shared world of experience. That is, we all experience rivers, mountains and trees in the same place at the same time because of the simultaneous ripening of similar seeds (river, mountain and tree seeds?) from our store consciousnesses.

But how is it that these same seeds have come to be present in each and everyone's store consciousness? It is clear that, according to Yogācāra, many seeds in the store consciousness are the result of previous *karma*. Thus, previous bad actions in countless lives have deposited seeds which will come to fruition as a bad or unpleasant experience of some sort. Good actions in past lives will produce good or pleasant experiences when the seeds yield their result. Often Yogācāra texts, such as Vasubandhu's *Viṃśatikā*, give the impression that all the seeds in the store consciousness are karmic and thus all experiences of objects can be explained as the fruition of past actions. Humans construct very similar worlds because of the similarity of karmic seeds stored in different individual conscious streams. Other types of sentient beings, such as gods and those who live in the hell realms, construct very different worlds based on their past *karma*.

However, is it not strange to suggest that all people construct a particular object – say, a tree – rather than something else because of their past actions? What peculiar kind of past action, which all people have done, would cause people to fabricate trees at the same time in the same place? It is hard to imagine. And then other specific sorts of past actions, done by all people, would be required to explain why all people construct rivers, and mountains and so on. And would trees, rivers and mountains be produced by good or bad *karma*? It is difficult to understand how specific phenomena such as these could be the fruit of particular past actions of any sort.

Faced with this difficulty, perhaps the Yogācārins might make the somewhat different claim that the ripening of common *karma* causes people to be born as human beings rather than gods or hell beings, and so forth (states of existence accepted by the traditional Buddhist cosmology). Furthermore, all human beings have minds which share a structure, or 'hard-wiring', which causes them to fabricate the world in very similar ways. In this case, it is not that particular seeds of past good or bad actions directly cause the construction of specific objects in the human world, but rather the seeds of past actions (good ones primarily, in that human rebirth is meant to be a relatively fortunate) do cause one to be reborn as a human, and all human minds are somehow 'pre-set' to construct similar objects at similar times and places. Experiencing a tree, for example, would then not directly be a consequence of a particular past good or bad action, but (mainly good) *karma* does result in human rebirth and human minds are programmed, as it were, to construct trees at similar times and places.

The seventh-century Chinese Yogācārin Hsüang-tsang (1973, pp. 117–21; see also Williams, 1989, p. 91) claims that not all of the seeds in the store consciousness are the result of *karma*. Some seeds are simply present in all store consciousnesses and always have been. They have been latent in the store consciousnesses since beginningless time. It seems plausible, then, that much of the inter-subjective world might be explained as the fruition of these shared non-karmic seeds. So, trees, mountains and rivers are products of the non-karmic (tree, mountain and river) seeds common to everyone's store consciousness and which form the basic 'program' which governs how the world is fabricated by us.

Still, it might be objected that it seems peculiar and rather convoluted to suggest that all human minds are programmed to fabricate the same trees, mountains, rivers and so forth in the same places at the same times. The Yogācārins are committing themselves to the highly contentious notion of a collective aspect of the mind which has the extraordinary power to make all people fabricate a similar world of objects. Might it not be simpler and more straightforward to take the position that people have inter-subjective experiences of trees, mountains, rivers, and so forth because there is some mind-independent basis for their experience of these things? Or so anyone with any realist inclinations would probably contend!

The ontological debate

Of course, the dispute between such ontological realism and anti-realism is long, nuanced and unresolved. Here is not the place to discuss it at length, but the very existence of such a perennial disagreement indicates that the Buddhists' anti-realism is not unproblematic. So, craving and attachment might be stopped by the anti-realist Buddhists' perception of the fabricated nature of most or all entities, but it has not in fact been established that most or all entities indeed have a fabricated nature. In which case, if one somehow convinced oneself and even perceived that, in the case of Madhyamaka, all things are fabrications, or that, in the case of Sarvāstivāda, Sautrāntika and Yogācāra, most entities are fabrications, one's conviction might be quite wrong, and one's perception might be erroneous. One might become liberated from craving and attachment but it might be liberation based on ignorance rather than knowledge!

The difficult business here is to provide the proof that reality is as these anti-realist Buddhists claim it to be, for without such proof their supposed perception of things as they actually are may simply be a mistake. Which is not to say, of course, that without the proof their perception is necessarily wrong. But given that, as the Buddhist anti-realists themselves admit, everyday entities appear to be, on the whole, unfabricated, the realist can claim that the onus is surely on these Buddhist anti-realists to prove their point. Otherwise, for these Buddhists liberation from craving and attachment depends on what is actually an unsubstantiated knowledge-claim.

However, we should not be too quick to dismiss the anti-realist perspective. After all, modern natural science maintains that the everyday objects we think we perceive are in reality composed of complex combinations of atoms or even smaller constituents such as quarks and antiparticles and so forth. Perhaps the Madhyamaka is excessive in claiming everything to be fabricated. Perhaps Yogācāra Buddhism goes too far in completely negating the external world. Maybe the Sarvāstivāda Abhidharma and Sautrāntika categorization of the types of material *dharma*s which ultimately exist (for example, solidity, fluidity, heat and motion *dharma*s and so forth) is rather primitive and inaccurate. However, it is clear that modern scientific theory can support a philosophical view that the actually existing external world is very different from that which we ordinarily perceive and often assume to be real. And, at least in broad outline, modern scientific theories about atoms, quarks and so forth bear a striking resemblance to the Buddhist *dharma* theory. Furthermore, the insights of modern biological theory support the idea that our common evolutionary past causes us to have a shared experience of entities we call trees, mountains, rivers and so forth. That is, our perceptual organs and brains have developed through natural selection and shared genetic constitution in such a way that we perceive things similarly. This arguably amounts to a form of anti-realism, which acknowledges that the commonsense world that we usually take to be mind-independently real is in many ways created by our biological constitution. However, it is worth noting that such evolutionary theory, even if it has anti-realist tendencies, contradicts the extreme anti-realism of Madhyamaka and the idealism of Yogācāra, because it presupposes an external world that was there before and during our evolution, and that our evolution happened within a pre-existing world that is outside us. We did not create it; on the contrary, it plays a large part in creating us.

Whether they are right or wrong, the Buddhist anti-realists' emphasis on the constructing activity of the mind is philosophically important because it raises difficult questions about just how much of what we perceive is really there, and how much of it is a contribution of the perceiving mind. The philosophical benefit here is that, having considered the Buddhist anti-realist ideas, even if one rejects them, any tendency one might have towards unreflective, naive realism would be corrected.

Are Buddhist anti-realists actually pragmatists?

Philosophically alert Buddhists might claim that the idea that things are fabricated is a pragmatic truth claim, and is not actually intended to be a statement about an ontological state of affairs. Here the truth of the assertion is measured by its usefulness rather than by its correlation to 'things as they actually are'. The criterion for usefulness in this context is, of course, the ability to cut off craving, attachment and suffering. That is, the idea that things are fabricated is true if by believing it one can be liberated. Whether things actually are fabricated is irrelevant, so long as the idea does its soteriological work.

Truth here is to be measured by efficacy rather than by correspondence with a state of affairs. The claim that the world is a fabrication might not mirror or accurately picture 'the way things really are', yet it is a useful means to overcome craving and suffering. The point is to change the mind and its habits, not to set out a correct ontology. The effect of the vision that the world is a fabrication might here be compared with poetic statements that convey ideas and images which are not literally true but can have a transformative effect by captivating the imagination. Perhaps the Buddhist anti-realists' claims that things are like illusions, magic shows, dreams and so forth are metaphors which are meant to move people to give up craving and attachment. Whether things are literally illusions and quite unreal is beside the point.

However, my suspicion is that the claim that things are fabricated is thought to be 'the way things really are' by the Buddhist philosophers I have considered. It is not that the truth of the claim is equated with its usefulness, but rather that the claim is thought to correspond to reality and thus it is useful. I do not see much evidence that these Buddhists are advocating a pragmatic theory of truth. I suspect that on the whole these Buddhists' stated intention to see 'things as they really are' is to be taken at face value.

Nevertheless, there is nothing to stop modern Buddhist practitioners from appropriating these anti-realist ideas in a pragmatic fashion, using them simply as therapeutic tools to cut off craving. One might wonder, however, about how useful these tools would be, if such Buddhists tried to use the idea that things are fabrications without the conviction that it corresponds to 'things as they really are'. If they doubt that things are really fabrications, how effective could the idea be in cutting off their craving? As José Cabezón (2000, p. 150) asks, in his evaluation of the strengths and weaknesses of such a pragmatic approach to Buddhist truths, 'to what extent can we will ourselves to believe, act upon and internalize doctrines whose metaphysical reality we doubt?'

For instance, it might be useful for me to believe in Awakening, but if I doubt seriously that Awakening is really possible, what transformative power would the notion of Awakening have? Or, to take another example, it might be useful for me to believe in *karma* and rebirth, for it might pacify my anxiety about being obliterated at death and might encourage me to act well in order to gain a good rebirth. Yet if I have serious doubts that there actually is *karma* and rebirth – that is, that these ideas correspond to 'things as they really are' – then it is hard to see what psychological conviction I could muster for them and thus the practical benefits would likely be lost. Similarly, without holding the belief that things truly are fabricated, it is difficult to understand how this idea could be efficacious in eradicating craving and hence suffering. It seems likely, then, that the Buddhists must consider the proposition that 'things are fabrications' to correspond to 'how things really are' in order for it to have any significant pragmatic value in the pursuit of liberation.

CHAPTER SIX

Buddhist Scepticism

We have seen already that when studying Madhyamaka Buddhism one is often faced by the problem of interpretive uncertainty. While the anti-realist reading of Madhyamaka that I have presented is supported by many textual passages, it need not be the only understanding that can be countenanced. Even though the anti-realist interpretation gives a credible account of many Madhyamaka texts, it is worth investigating other ways in which the Madhyamaka philosophy of emptiness might be construed. In the present chapter, I will consider an interpretation that takes Madhyamaka to be a form of scepticism, and will examine the rather different understanding of knowledge and liberation that this entails. In addition, I will argue that it is possible to find evidence for such a sceptical soteriology in the early Buddhism of the Pāli Canon as well.

Madhyamaka and the experience-reality gap

There is, it has often been claimed, a serious epistemological problem in establishing how the world exists independently of one's perceptions of it, for one's apprehension of the world is necessarily of the world as perceived, not as it is 'in itself'. One can never step outside one's perceptions, so to speak, in order to see the world as it really is, for this very seeing would itself be a perception. This epistemological problem has, of course, been much discussed in Western philosophy, and has led some thinkers, most notably Immanuel Kant, to deny that one has the ability to know the mind-independent world. In the *Critique of Pure Reason*, Kant (1965) argues that one does not have access to 'things in themselves', because in all experiences the 'things in themselves' are reshaped by the mind's own concepts such as space, time, cause and effect, substance and accident, quantity and so forth. For Kant, human beings one and all impose these concepts, which do not inhere in the 'things themselves'. This explains our shared experience of the world. That is, experience is always spatial and temporal, always of causes and effects and so forth, not because this is the way the mind-independent world is, but because these are the interpretive structures that minds always and in every case employ.

I have explained that for the Mādhyamikas all things are fabrications. That is, they are conceptual constructions and thus merely conventional. They do not have inherent existence. Now, it might be that the Mādhyamikas are here pointing out that entities *as experienced* are apprehended by minds that always structure their experiences in terms of various concepts. For instance, like Kant, the Mādhyamika might claim that the mind apprehends the world in terms of cause and effect, time, space, substance and attribute and so forth. These are concepts that are universally applied by the mind. Experience is always formed in these ways. In which case, entities lack inherent existence in that the mind always contributes to our experience of them. We do not have access to 'things in themselves', which lie hidden behind the veil which is the mind's interpretive framework. There is an unbridgeable gap between experience and reality.

Madhyamaka as scepticism

This position might be described as a form of scepticism. Scepticism here is understood broadly to mean the philosophical position that we do not and cannot have knowledge of reality. The Mādhyamikas are saying that we do not and cannot know how the world beyond our experience really is. All we have access to is the world as it appears to us, in which whatever mind-independent world exists has been filtered, so to speak, through our cognitive apparatus.

This sceptical version of Madhyamaka is quite different from the anti-realist reading. Understood as anti-realism, Madhyamaka is saying that entities are conceptual constructs in the sense that they are totally fabricated, with no grounding at all in a mind-independent reality, for there is no mind-independent reality for them to be grounded in. By contrast, the sceptical Mādhyamikas say that the experienced world is not entirely a mental fabrication, for it has a foundation in 'things in themselves'. Nevertheless, our conceptual imputations, such as space, time, cause and effect and so forth, are so basic to our experience that it is impossible to discern what is actually the case about the mind-independent world.

The sceptical interpretation has the effect of solving the ontological paradox that, as I explained in the last chapter, confronts the anti-realist reading of Madhyamaka. It thus avoids the charge of nihilism. For, the Mādhyamikas, construed as sceptics, are saying not that everything is fabricated, but that there is an unfabricated though unknowable reality that stands behind, as it were, the fabricated world of experience. They are claiming that there must exist an unfabricated reality ('things in themselves') that gets interpreted by the mind. It is the basis for fabrication or the raw material which the mind re-fashions, as it were. Without it nihilism would be entailed. However, we cannot know anything about this basis, other than that it must exist. The Madhyamaka philosophy of emptiness here treads the Middle Way between the nihilistic claim that everything is totally a fabrication and the naive epistemological realists' contention that one has undistorted access to the unfabricated world.

Textual evidence for the sceptical reading

Now, it might be objected that this sceptical reading of Madhyamaka is a crude attempt to turn Madhyamaka into a species of Kantianism. It is thus anachronistic. This accusation certainly has some weight. One needs to be very careful not to assimilate thoughtlessly and carelessly philosophies from different times and cultures to ways of thinking that are influential in one's own time and culture. Nevertheless, one should not go too far in this caution. It is surely possible that philosophies from very different times and cultures can have similar insights. Scepticism, it can be argued, is a cross-cultural, trans-historical phenomenon. It is one of the basic human philosophical responses to the world. Thus, one should not be surprised to find similar sceptical ideas in, for instance, Kant and Madhyamaka Buddhism.

Indeed, it is arguable that Madhyamaka philosophy belongs to a tradition of Indian scepticism, which also includes thinkers such as Jayarāśi Bhaṭṭa (c. 650 CE) in the *Tattvopaplavasiṃha* and the Advaita Vedāntin Śrīharṣa (twelfth century CE) who both rejected the various means of correct cognition (*pramāṇa*) accepted by other schools of Indian philosophy (see King, 1999a, p. 137). Furthermore, as I will discuss later, it is also possible that earlier, non-Madhyamaka Buddhism sometimes displays a similar sceptical tendency.

And considerable textual support can be mustered for a sceptical reading of Madhyamaka. For instance, *Madhyamakakārikā* 1 refutes all possible theories of causation, namely, that things originate from themselves, from other entities, from both themselves and others or from neither. *Madhyamakakārikā* 19 is focused on refuting the inherent existence of time. It seems plausible to read these critiques as intended to prove that causality, time and so forth are simply conceptual diffusion (*prapañca*). The point of these arguments might be to demonstrate that entities as experienced lack inherent existence because they are always experienced as causally linked, occurring in time and so forth, and the notions of causality and time originate in the mind rather than being features of the 'things in themselves'.

Furthermore, there is Nāgārjuna's critique at *Vigrahavyāvartanī* 30–51 of the means of correct cognition (*pramāṇa*) and objects of correct cognition (*prameya*). The *pramāṇa* theory had been developed by the Naiyāyikas who were staunch philosophical realists, believing that four means of correct cognition – perception (*pratyakṣa*), inferential reasoning (*anumāna*) and testimony (*śabda*) and analogy (*upamāna*) – can and do give the human mind undistorted access to 'things in themselves'. Thus, according to Nyāya philosophy, when I observe an object such as a fire, perception functions as the means by which I apprehend a mind-independent fire entity. When I see smoke over a distant hill and reason that there must be a fire on the hill, inference gives me the correct cognition that there is a mind-independent fire on the hill. When a reliable friend has seen the fire on the hill and tells me about it, this testimony also produces my correct cognition of the mind-independent fire on the hill. Analogy functions as a means of correct cognition when I come to understand an entity that I have never perceived by means of comparison with things that I have perceived. For instance, I can have a correct cognition of and recognize a tiger, supposing that I have never perceived one before, if I am told that it is like an extremely large cat with stripes, yellow fur and so forth. Nyāya thus has great confidence in the ability of the mind to know 'things in themselves' by these four means of correct cognition.

In the *Vigrahavyāvartanī*, Nāgārjuna seeks to demonstrate that there is no way of proving that the *pramāṇa*s do actually apprehend objects correctly. In other words, it is impossible to establish that the means of correct cognition are in fact means of *correct* cognition. Here a 'correct cognition' would be one that apprehends mind-independent entities as they really are. Any attempt at such a proof will, Nāgārjuna contends, result in fallacies such as an unestablished assumption, infinite regress and circular reasoning. How, for instance, is testimony to be proven to be reliable? Perhaps on the basis of perception? For example, if a friend tells me that there is a fire on the hill, this *pramāṇa* might be proved to be accurate if I were to go to the hill and observe the fire for myself. But how do I know that my perception is accurate? One possibility would be simply to assert its accuracy without proof, but this is, according to Nāgārjuna, to commit the fallacy of unestablished assumption. Perhaps then I can seek further *pramāṇa*s (for example, further perceptions, by myself or others, of the fire) to support and validate my perception? But then, Nāgārjuna claims, there is the issue of how those further *pramāṇa*s are to be proven reliable. There would appear to be an infinite regress of *pramāṇa*s being proved by *pramāṇa*s which themselves need to be proved by more *pramāṇa*s and so forth. Thus, the veracity and reliability of none of the *pramāṇa*s is proven, as they are not anchored in any firm, reliable foundation. A third option would be to say that my perception is correct because the object of the cognition (the *prameya*) accords with the perception. That is, I perceive the fire on the hill and the accuracy of the perception is established because there is a fire on the hill. However, this is, Nāgārjuna contends, circular reasoning because the *pramāṇa*, that is, the perception, is being used to prove the existence of the fire on the hill and the existence of the fire on the hill, the *prameya*, is then used to prove the correctness of the *pramāṇa*. This means, according to Nāgārjuna that neither the *pramāṇa* nor the *prameya* is established. It is a case of unverified means of correct cognition being used to verify the objects of cognition, and then these very unverified objects being used to verify the means of correct cognition! This is a vicious circle.

I make no comment on the cogency of Nāgārjuna's reasoning and whether he has successfully refuted the Nyāya *pramāṇa* theory. What is significant in the present context is that the point of this critique, it seems, is to prove that there is no way of establishing that our cognitions do apprehend entities as they might exist independently of the mind. Note that this critique does not establish, even if it is successful, that cognitions do not apprehend mind-independent entities, for it is possible that a cognition might be correct without being able to prove its correctness. I might have a correct cognition of a tree, for instance, without being able to demonstrate conclusively that the cognition is indeed correct. However, the inability to prove that cognitions do apprehend mind-independent entities at least raises the strong possibility that the mind does not have access to them. The means of correct cognition might lead only to cognitions of objects of experience, complete with the mind's contributions to that experience, rather than to cognitions of objects as they are mind independently. Nāgārjuna's critique is, it seems, designed to produce chronic, irresolvable uncertainty about the possibility of cognitions of 'things in themselves'.

In addition, *Vaidalyaprakaraṇa* 2, another early Madhyamaka work often attributed to Nāgārjuna, stresses the mutual dependence of the means of correct cognition and the objects of correct cognition. Candrakīrti, at *Prasannapadā* 75, makes a similar point:

> And those [*pramāṇa*s and *prameya*s] exist by means of mutual dependence. When there are *pramāṇa*s, then there are objects which are *prameya*s and when there are objects which are *prameya*s, then there are *pramāṇa*s. But certainly the *pramāṇa*s and *prameya*s do not have inherent existence.

The precise meaning of these passages is admittedly opaque. However, perhaps the point is that a cognition requires an object in order to be a cognition of something, and yet the object as known, as opposed to how it is 'in itself', is altered and contributed to by the very act of cognizing it. Thus, the means of cognition and the object as cognized depend on one another. Objects as cognized are conventions and lack inherent existence in so far as the entity as it is 'in itself' remains concealed behind the screen of the mind's own interpretive activity. And the *pramāṇa* too, if understood as a reliable means of apprehending 'things in themselves', is thus a fabrication and hence lacks inherent existence.

These passages on the *pramāṇa*s and *prameya*s thus offer resources for a sceptical reading of Madhyamaka, according to which the mind is so active in its conceptual imputations that it may be cut off from whatever mind-independent reality there might be. The mind, caught in its webs of fabrication, is unable to discern the world as it is 'in itself'.

Madhyamaka scepticism and liberation

But what are the implications of this scepticism for liberation from suffering? Presumably the sceptical Mādhyamikas would seek to achieve – via their arguments such as those found in the critique of the *pramāṇa*s and those refuting the inherent existence of causality, time and so forth – the knowledge that the spatio-temporal, cause-effect world of experience is a conceptual construction. These arguments might be reflected on in the context of meditation, in order to induce perceptual knowledge, so that the Mādhyamikas would come to see the world of experience, the only world to which we have access, to be a fabrication. On the basis of such perceptual knowledge, practitioners would give up their craving and attachment, realizing that fabricated things are not worth coveting.

In addition, the Awakened sceptical Mādhyamikas would presumably give up all claims to knowledge about the character of the 'things in themselves'. This too might be liberating. They might claim that, in realizing that they cannot know the character of 'things in themselves', they are emancipated from the attachment to views about reality, and from their hankering to know the true nature of things. They might 'let go' of this craving and attachment. Thus, the sceptical Mādhyamikas might claim that liberation is a result not of knowledge of 'things in themselves', but rather of the realization that we cannot have such knowledge.

This is why, on a sceptical reading, the Mādhyamika claims to hold no views. Views about 'things in themselves' are but misguided speculations. They are simply a web of fabrications, rather than being expressive of the world as it really is. Attachment to views and the disputes that such attachments entail between people who hold differing views are a futile pursuit, for one's views about the nature of 'things in themselves' are just conceptual proliferations that teach us nothing except about how the mind spins its web of fantasies. Emptiness in this context means that views about the nature of the world as it is independent of our experience are empty. That is, they are fabrications and devoid of meaning. The Awakened person's letting go of, and the danger of adhering to, views is well expressed in the *Yuktiṣaṣṭikā* 49–51. Nāgārjuna seems to indicate that views – that is, knowledge claims about 'things in themselves' – lead to craving and attachment, from which Awakened people are freed by having no thesis or standpoint:

> For those who suppressed by false knowledge take the untrue for true a series of seizing and contention etc. will arise. The magnanimous [that is, the Awakened] have neither thesis nor contention. How can there be an opposing thesis to those who have no thesis? By taking any standpoint whatsoever one is attacked by the twisting snakes of the passions. But those whose minds have no standpoint are not caught. (trans. Lindtner, 1982, pp. 115, 117)

Liberation as *ataraxia*

The Madhyamaka soteriology would thus be akin to that found in classical Western scepticism, as recorded for example by Sextus Empiricus in the *Outlines of Scepticism*, in which numerous arguments are employed to demonstrate that one does not have knowledge of phenomena as they exist in their real nature (*phusei*). Indeed, it is striking that there are many formal parallels between the arguments of the classical Western sceptics and those found in Madhyamaka texts. For instance, the classical Western sceptics use various arguments to refute the science of causes (aetiology) developed by the Stoics that advances various theories about the causal laws governing things in their real nature. Mādhyamikas also refute various theories of causation. Some of these arguments are almost identical. For example, there occurs in both traditions an argument meant to show that a cause cannot precede, follow, or exist simultaneously with its effect (see *Outlines of Scepticism* 3, 26–7; *Vaidalyaprakaraṇa* 12). Also, in classical Western scepticism it is argued that attempts to establish a knowledge claim, that is, to prove that it apprehends phenomena in their real nature, entail an unestablished assumption, an infinite regress or circular reasoning, which are identified, at *Outlines of Scepticism* 1, 164–77, as three of the five Modes of Agrippa. Remarkably, as we have seen already, *Vigrahavyāvartanī* 30–51 claims that attempts to establish the means of correct cognition will entail an unestablished assumption, an infinite regress or circularity. There are many other formal similarities between Madhyamaka and ancient sceptical arguments (see Garfield 2002, who explores some of them further), but these examples will suffice for our present purpose.

The classical Western sceptics' arguments are meant to show that one has access only to impressions or experiences (*phantasia*). The practical purpose of these arguments is to induce suspension of judgement (*epoche*) concerning, and non-assertion (*aphasia*) of views about, things in their real nature. The psychological effect of this non-assertion is said to be equanimity (*ataraxia*), which, Sextus Empiricus says, follows *epoche* like a shadow follows a body. The point here appears to be that one stops hankering after knowledge of reality and simply acquiesces in the impressions or experiences that one has, without the emotional investment in them that one might have if one did not realize that they are merely impressions or experiences (see *Outlines of Scepticism* 1, 19–24; 1, 29; 1, 192–3). Perhaps the arguments found in Madhyamaka are designed to have the same effect, that is, to propel one into a state of calm, free from craving for knowledge of and attachment to views about 'things in themselves'. One would realize just how futile such craving and attachment is. This realization, combined with the perception that the world as experienced is a fabrication, would produce a state of equanimity, free from craving and attachment.

However, it might be objected that the Mādhyamika sceptics are not justified in claiming that equanimity is the result of such non-assertion. Realizing that one cannot gain knowledge of things in their true nature would not necessarily lead to contentment. On the contrary, it might just as easily lead one to become distressed, when one realizes that one is cut off from reality. So, there seems to be an unexplained gap between the realization that one cannot know 'things in themselves' and the affective response – the equanimous giving up both of views and the desire for knowledge of reality – that this realization is meant to engender. There is not a necessary connection, it seems, between the two phenomena.

But maybe the Mādhyamikas' claim here needs to be understood in the context of the Buddhist path as a whole. The Buddhist practitioners train to have an attitude of contentment, calm and equanimity that is produced by ethical practice and *śamatha* meditation. Having done serious work to establish this attitude, it seems likely that the practitioners' response to the realization that there can be no knowledge of 'things in themselves' would be more likely to be tranquil acceptance rather than anxiety. *Ataraxia* in a Buddhist context needs to be understood against this background of practice which has already moulded the practitioner's emotional life.

Madhyamaka as mitigated scepticism

Though in this chapter I have depicted Madhyamaka as a form of scepticism, it should be noted that its scepticism, at least as I have explained it so far, is not total. The Mādhyamikas may deny many knowledge claims about 'things in themselves' but it would appear that Mādhyamikas do not necessarily abandon all knowledge claims whatsoever. Indeed, as I have explained their position, the Mādhyamikas might claim that they do know some things. Their scepticism is thus mitigated. Let me explain.

First of all, the Mādhyamika sceptics would presumably accept that there is a mind-independent world, that is, the 'things in themselves', as the otherwise unknowable basis for conceptual construction. Is this not a knowledge claim? That is, the Mādhyamika sceptics hold that a mind-independent reality *exists*. What they are refuting is any and all views that purport to tell us anything definite about *the character* of this mind-independent reality, that is, anything other than that it must exist. They allow the existential assertion but no predicative assertions. This position is analogous to the claim of rather agnostic theologians who might say that they know that God exists, but they do not know any of the characteristics of God – for example, whether God is wise, benevolent, omnipotent, a creator of the world, male, female and so forth.

A stronger form of scepticism would deny that one can know whether or not a mind-independent reality exists. Note that this stronger scepticism does not deny that a mind-independent reality exists. Rather, it makes no ontological commitment whatsoever, either to the existence or the non-existence of the mind-independent reality. It is completely agnostic. For the stronger sceptics, the rejection of all views would thus include even the views that there exists or does not exist a mind-independent reality. By contrast, I have suggested that the Mādhyamika sceptics might be inclined to accept that there must be an (otherwise unknowable) mind-independent reality in order to avoid the problem of nihilism.

Furthermore, the sceptical Mādhyamikas, it seems to me, might accept that we do have knowledge of our experiences. There is, they might concede, no doubt that we have these experiences. Their intention is only to refute knowledge of 'things in themselves'. Knowledge of our experiences is not within the purview of their critique. That I am having an experience of *x* is a type of knowledge the Mādhyamikas might admit. That I am having an experience of the 'thing in itself' *x* is the sort of knowledge claim that Madhyamaka scepticism seeks to refute. For example, the sceptical Mādhyamikas would not deny my tree experience. However, they would deny that this tree experience corresponds to a mind-independent reality. The mind-independent reality which provides the raw material for the tree experience is always unknowable, given that it is filtered by our own concepts of time, space, substance and so forth.

Indeed, it seems plausible that, in so far as all human beings are said to have similar interpretive frameworks that they apply to 'things in themselves', the Mādhyamikas might, like Kant, accept that there can be knowledge about the shared world of experience. That is, it can be ascertained whether *a* does cause *b*, because everyone accepts the categories of cause and effect, time, space and so forth. These categories are a mutual fabrication that all people superimpose, and must superimpose, on the 'things themselves'. What the Mādhyamikas are rejecting is any claim that this 'conventional knowledge' that *a* causes *b* corresponds to 'things in themselves', given that the very concepts of cause and effect, time and space and so forth are simply part of the interpretive framework shared by human beings. So, the Mādhyamikas would not necessarily have to reject knowledge of conventions as long as they are understood to be truths about experience, rather than truths about inherently existing things. Indeed, it is possible that this is Nāgārjuna's point in *Madhyamakakārikā* 24, when he emphasizes that his teaching about emptiness is not meant to negate conventional truth and that emptiness is misunderstood if the validity of everyday knowledge is not recognized. Perhaps therefore, it is not surprising to discover that Candrakīrti, at *Prasannapadā* 75, says that he accepts the four means of correct cognition (*pramāṇa*) as worldly (*laukika*) or conventional methods of gaining knowledge. Maybe he thinks that the means of correct cognition do produce knowledge about the shared world of appearances. The mistake of the Unawakened people is to believe that they thereby have knowledge of 'things in themselves'. The problem is, the Mādhyamikas would contend, that Unawakened people do not see that such knowledge is of entities as experienced – that is, as these things appear to human minds – and consider it to be knowledge of a mind-independent reality.

Finally, the Mādhyamikas might want to mitigate their scepticism by claiming that they do know that all things as experienced are fabrications. And they know that they do not (and presumably cannot) have knowledge about the character of 'things in themselves'. In other words, Mādhyamikas might claim that they have no views which assert the inherent existence of things as experienced but that they do hold the view that things as experienced lack inherent existence. This view is not a fabrication. It is the ultimate truth about entities. Indeed, some statements attributed to Nāgārjuna support this stance. For instance, *Śūnyatāsaptati* 68–9 declares that: 'The incomparable *tathāgata* taught the dependent origination of things [that is, the things of experience], since they are empty of inherent existence. The ultimate (*paramārtha*) is no more than that.' And *Acintyastava* 52 says: 'This is the ultimate truth (*paramaṃ tattvaṃ*): The teaching that objects [that is, objects of experience] are without inherent existence.' For the sceptical interpretation of Madhyamaka, this means that the proposition that 'all things as experienced are fabrications' is the ultimate truth. Presumably the Mādhyamikas would claim that they have knowledge of this ultimate truth? After all, their arguments refuting the inherent existence of universal features of human experience, such as time, space, cause and effect and so forth, are, it would appear, intended to prove that things as experienced are fabrications. Is this not a claim to knowledge that emptiness is the true nature of experienced objects?

A more radical scepticism?

However, it is not clear to me that Madhyamaka consistently advocates the knowledge claim that emptiness is the ultimate truth. For there are passages from Madhyamaka texts which appear to suggest a more radical version of scepticism. Most importantly and famously there is *Madhyamakakārikā* 13, 8. In this verse, Nāgārjuna says that: 'The Victorious Ones [that is, Awakened people] proclaimed emptiness to be the remedy for all views. But those for whom emptiness is a view were declared to be incurable.' What does this puzzling statement mean? First of all, it is quite plausible that in the first sentence Nāgārjuna is suggesting that the teaching of emptiness is a remedy for all views about the character of 'things in themselves', which are concealed by the fabricating activity of the mind. Emptiness means that all objects of experience are fabrications and that any view which asserts anything about the character of the 'things in themselves' is also a fabrication. This is in agreement with the mitigated scepticism I have explained above. However, it is worth noting that if emptiness is the remedy for *all* views, then it is also possible that Mādhyamikas *do not* claim to know even that the otherwise unknowable 'things in themselves' exist. In this case their scepticism is stronger than I have so far suggested. It might be that they at least sometimes reject even existential assertions about 'things in themselves', not just predicative assertions. Their scepticism entails that not only do they not know anything about the character of 'things in themselves' but also they do not know whether or not 'things in themselves' exist. However, it is worth noting that if the Mādhyamikas' scepticism is this strong, then they have not provided a sure bulwark against nihilism, because as long as the possibility that 'things in themselves' may not exist is left open, the ontological paradox that the world as experienced is a fabrication without any unfabricated foundation remains a threat.

But there is a further and even more radical possible reading of the Madhyamaka claim that emptiness is the remedy for all views and this, it appears, is drawn out in the second sentence, which says that emptiness itself is not to be taken as a view. It seems that here Nāgārjuna might be claiming that the teaching of emptiness is itself merely a convention or fabrication. That is, it is not the ultimate truth! Those who take emptiness to be a knowledge claim are said to be incurable. This would be scepticism so strong and consistent that it rejects even its own apparent knowledge claim that we experience only fabrications and never 'things in themselves'. Candrakīrti's commentary (*Prasannapadā* 248–9) on *Madhyamakārikā* 13, 8 is illuminating. In order to explain Nāgārjuna's statement, Candrakīrti uses an analogy taken from the *Ratnakūta Sūtra*: if a physician were to give a sick man a medicine and, having cured the man's sickness, the medicine were to remain in his stomach, then in fact the man's illness would become more intense. This is analogous to the situation of the man who takes emptiness, which is the remedy for all views, as itself a view. For the sceptical reading of Madhyamaka, what this passage indicates, perhaps, is that the teaching of emptiness – that is, that 'all entities as experienced are fabrications' and that 'there can be no knowledge of "things in themselves"' – is the medicine that dispels all views, that is, all knowledge claims, about 'things in themselves'. Once these views have been eradicated, the view that 'all entities as experienced are fabrications' and 'there can be no knowledge of "things in themselves"' must itself be dispelled, like the medicine must be removed from the man's stomach. As Candrakīrti says elsewhere (*Madhyamakāvatāra* 6, 185–6), emptiness itself is empty, which perhaps means that it too is a fabricated view which must be finally given up. So, perhaps the Mādhyamikas do not even claim to know that 'all entities as experienced are fabrications' and, furthermore, that 'there can be no knowledge of "things in themselves"'? This is scepticism so thorough that it turns upon itself.

Interestingly, Candrakīrti's commentary is remarkably similar to an analogy given by the Pyrrhonian sceptics. According to Sextus Empiricus, they say that the statement that there is no knowledge of things in their true nature is not itself a knowledge claim; like a medicine it is to be flushed out when its curative work is accomplished:

> In the case of all the sceptical phrases, you should understand that we do not affirm definitely that they are true – after all, we say that they can be destroyed by themselves, being cancelled along with what they are applied to, just as purgative drugs do not merely drain the humours from the body but drive themselves out too along with the humours. (*Outlines of Scepticism* 1, 206)

No *pratijñā*

It is perhaps significant in this respect that Nāgārjuna, at *Vigrahavyāvartanī* 29, claims that he does not have any thesis (*pratijñā*). He says this in the context of his critique of the Nyāya epistemology, according to which the *pratijñā* is the first of the five members of a valid inference, followed by the cause or reason (*hetu*) for the thesis, the statement of the example (*udāharaṇa*) supporting the thesis, the application (*upanaya*) of that example to the thesis and, finally, the conclusion (*nigamana*). Thus, in the stock example typically employed to illustrate this five-membered valid inference, the thesis is that 'there is a fire on the hill', the cause or reason is 'because it has smoke', the example is 'an oven' (as a previously observed case of something having smoke also having fire), the application of the example is the statement 'there is smoke on the hill, which is associated with fire' and the conclusion is that 'the hill has fire'.

Much could be said about the precise structure of this ancient Nyāya valid inference and its relation to Aristotelian syllogisms (see, for example, Ganeri, 1996). However, the relevant point for the present discussion is that debaters were required to set out their thesis and then go on to establish its veracity by means of the other four members of the inference. What Nāgārjuna is saying here is that he has no thesis to establish. It appears that this means that his interest is only in refuting whatever thesis his opponents advance. This is the point of the various arguments which he employs. If it is objected that such pure refutation implies that Nāgārjuna, even if he does not state it, has the thesis that all theses about 'things in themselves' are fabrications, he would say that, no, even this thesis must be refuted. To say otherwise would be inconsistent with his radical scepticism.

Svātantrika and Prāsaṅgika

There were some later Mādhyamikas, most notably Bhāvaviveka, who accepted the need to set out independent (*svatantra*) argumentation. That is, they thought that the Mādhyamikas need to establish the thesis of emptiness using the five-membered inference in the context of debate. The Tibetan tradition identifies this as the attitude of the Svātantrika sub-school of Madhyamaka which they contrast with the method of the Prāsaṅgika sub-school of thinkers such as Candrakīrti and Śāntideva, who apparently did not accept that Mādhyamikas should attempt to establish their own thesis in the debating context, but simply refuted the positions of others using only *reductio ad absurdum* (*prasaṅga*) arguments. Presumably the Prāsaṅgikas do not assert their own thesis because they think that they do not have one, recognizing that the view of emptiness itself needs to be rejected.

If Nāgārjuna is indeed a radical sceptic, who refutes even the ultimate truth of emptiness itself, then the Svātantrika position might be seen as a degeneration of early Madhyamaka into a milder form of scepticism which finally accepts, rather than refutes, the ultimate truth of emptiness. But, as I have indicated previously, Nāgārjuna himself seems sometimes to assert that emptiness is the ultimate truth, and is thus not to be refuted, so there seems to be some support for the Svātantrikas' milder scepticism even in his writings. That is, all views except the emptiness teaching are to be rejected as merely fabrications. Emptiness is the exception to the rule. The theory that the Svātantrika position is thus a departure from that of Nāgārjuna, and the Prāsaṅgikas represent the unadulterated, original teaching, is thus arguably an over-simplification which does not recognize that Nāgārjuna's writings admit of diverse readings.

That being said, it is not entirely clear to me that, unlike the Prāsaṅgikas, the Svātantrikas were claiming that the emptiness teaching is, unlike other knowledge claims, immune from refutation. For, it is possible to interpret the Svātantrikas as radical rather than mitigated sceptics who are simply making a pragmatic accommodation to the debating rules and standards of their time. Maybe Mādhyamikas, refusing to abide by the rules of discussion accepted by most other schools, had had trouble being taken seriously or having their voices heard. It seems likely that the claim that they have no thesis at all, and that they simply refute the theses of others, was incomprehensible to many other thinkers. As Richard King (1999a, p. 139) comments: 'The Svātantrika stance allowed the Madhyamaka tradition to maintain its involvement in the wider scholastic context and disciplinary framework of Indian philosophical debate (*vāda*) in a manner that would have been prohibitive, strictly speaking, on Prāsaṅgika grounds.' So, perhaps, the Svātantrika Mādhyamikas resolved initially to assert the ultimate truth of emptiness for the practical purpose of engaging in the debates of the day and to win over potential converts. The final aim, however, would be, as with the Prāsaṅgikas, to refute even the thesis of emptiness itself, leaving the practitioners with absolutely no ultimate truth claim on which to rely. They would not even hold the position that they have no ultimate truth claim, for this too would be a view! In this case, the disagreement between the two sub-schools is not about the strength of scepticism which they uphold, but rather about the appropriate and most efficacious methods of argumentation (*prasaṅga* versus *svatantra*) for compelling others to become radical sceptics.

An epistemological paradox?

It is difficult to know what to make of such radical scepticism. For it seems to result in an epistemological paradox. The Mādhyamikas here appear to claim that the view that 'all entities as experienced are fabrications' and 'all views about "things in themselves" are fabrications' is itself a fabrication. It does its work of refuting all views about 'things in themselves' and is then to be refuted itself. In which case, the view that 'all views about "things in themselves" are fabrications' is both true, because it is used to refute all views about 'things in themselves' and is false, because it is itself to be refuted. In other words, the Madhyamaka scepticism, if it is this radical, is self-contradictory. Furthermore, there is a troubling infinite regress here, because the consistent radical sceptic must presumably also say that the view that 'the view that all views about things in themselves are fabrications is a fabrication' is also a fabrication! And so forth.

It is, of course, possible that the sceptical Mādhyamikas are being intentionally paradoxical. They do not claim that their total scepticism can be made sense of. They are in fact delighting in the puzzle and inviting us to experience the sense of amazement and dislocation that it induces. They do not claim to have a coherent position of their own. They simply reject all views and establish no stance themselves. This is scepticism with a vengeance, so extreme that it is happy to accept that it is self-contradictory. The paradox, they might say, just goes to show how very feeble the human mind is. Maybe, then, Mādhyamikas think that the epistemological paradox should be embraced rather than solved. The fact that we cannot make sense of this paradox is not a good reason for shying away from it. In this case, the Mādhyamikas are acknowledging a mystery and not offering a solution.

Alternative interpretations

However, in accepting the paradox the Mādhyamikas might be accused of capitulating to irrationality. For those who find such apparent non-sense repellent, perhaps there are interpretive alternatives. Maybe, for instance, instead of being so radically sceptical, the Mādhyamikas are simply expressing some epistemic modesty. Knowledge, after all, is sometimes thought to involve indubitability and irrefutable justification. Or, even given a more relaxed definition of knowledge, a very high degree of warrant or evidence is often thought to be required. Perhaps the Mādhyamikas' point is simply that they do not have the requisite justification for their claim that 'all entities as experienced are fabrications' and 'all views about "things in themselves" are fabrications' to count as knowledge. Maybe they are admitting that, though they have justification for their belief – for example, through the various sceptical arguments that they employ – it is not sufficiently strong to make their justified belief a case of knowledge. So, *Madhyamakārikā* 13, 8 is saying that Mādhyamikas should not hold the teaching of emptiness as a view, where a view is to be understood as an irrefutable or very strongly justified knowledge claim.

This, indeed, seems to be a response by the Pyrrhonian sceptics to the sceptical paradox. They contend that their sceptical claims are statements of undogmatic belief rather than knowledge. As the passage quoted on page 117 says, 'in the case of all the sceptical phrases, you should understand that we do not affirm definitely that they are true.' Given the admittedly controvertible evidence they have accumulated, it appears to them that 'there can be no knowledge of things in their true nature' and they acquiesce in that appearance. But they acknowledge that they might well be wrong. They may have some warrant for their belief but not enough for it to count as knowledge.

There is a problem here, however, as I am not sure that the Mādhyamikas really do generally exhibit the suggested epistemic modesty. Madhyamaka sources sometimes seem to show little sign of uncertainty that they have knowledge of emptiness. Indeed, *Acintyastava* 40–41 declares that emptiness is the incontrovertible (*avisaṃvādin*) truth. And, if the understanding that the things of experience are fabricated is to be matured through meditation into a perception that liberates one from craving and attachment, the Mādhyamikas must think that they can achieve very strong justification for this belief. If *Madhyamakakārikā* 13, 8 is actually a call for epistemic modesty, it does not seem to be heeded always by the Mādhyamikas themselves. Perhaps the lesson here, once again, is that we should not seek to find an entirely consistent message in all Madhyamaka sources.

It also seems to me that the passage can be understood in three other ways, none of which entails that the sceptical Mādhyamikas give up their claim to knowledge of emptiness.

First, maybe 'taking emptiness to be a view' means (belligerently) *asserting* one's position that 'all entities as experienced are fabrications'. The point would be that, having refuted all views about the character of 'things in themselves', the Awakened Mādhyamikas are not interested in asserting their own position. Why not? 'Assertion' here is a shorthand for arrogant, proud and confrontational advocacy of one's knowledge claim. Asserting the view of emptiness might be equivalent to being conceited about one's knowledge, and expressing it in a manner which displays one's conceit. Such conceited people are 'incurable' in that they have not 'let go' of their craving and attachment. The issue then is not the ultimate truth of the Madhyamaka emptiness teaching (which is to be accepted), but rather the psychological attitude which should not accompany one's knowledge of this truth. Such knowledge should not be wielded as a weapon to crush others who do not share one's view and to inflate one's sense of self-importance. The lesson here is a very practical and ethical one, namely, that the manner in which one teaches the truth, and the emotional attitude one has to those one thinks do not have the truth, is at least as important as the truth itself.

This suggests another way of interpreting *Vigrahavyāvartanī* 29, where Nāgārjuna says that he has no thesis (*pratijñā*). As I have already noted, the *pratijñā* was the first step in the traditional Indian five-membered inference which was employed in debates between rival schools. Nāgārjuna's claim here might actually be a refusal to engage in such debates, which he perhaps regarded as breeding grounds for arrogance and conceit. It is not that he literally had no thesis or view, but rather that he did not choose to assert his position in the context of the traditional Indian debate, with all its attendant rivalries and aggression.

Second, it is noteworthy that Candrakīrti, at *Yuktiṣaṣṭikāvṛtti* 23, claims that the Mādhyamika should gain the vision (*darśana*) of emptiness which he contrasts with the view (*dṛṣṭi*) of emptiness. This suggests another possible interpretation of *Madhyamakakārikā* 13, 8. Perhaps the person who takes emptiness as a view is someone who settles for a merely theoretical, propositional knowledge of emptiness, and fails to make efforts to achieve the perception of the fabricated nature of things as experienced. They are 'incurable', that is, they will never be liberated from craving and attachment. Their propositional knowledge festers like a purgative medicine in the stomach because it has not been changed into knowledge by acquaintance. It is not that the theoretical, propositional knowledge is wrong, but rather that it is not sufficient for the attainment of liberation.

Finally, is it not possible that, when Nāgārjuna says that those who take emptiness to be a view are incurable, he might be warning against misunderstanding emptiness as referring to an inherently existing, autonomous and eternal Absolute Reality underlying or transcending the illusory world, akin to the *brahman* of the *Upaniṣads* and the (post-Nāgārjunian) Advaita

Vedānta school? Candrakīrti's claim that emptiness is itself empty can likewise, according to a common interpretation, be construed as a warning against such Absolutism. That is, emptiness is the ultimate truth but, as it is the ultimate truth about entities as experienced it is dependent on them for its existence and in this sense is itself empty. Emptiness is always the emptiness of the pot, of the chair, of the person and so forth. It is never an independent, autonomous reality. Like everything else, it is dependently originating. So, taking emptiness to be a view means misconstruing it as referring to an Absolute Reality. It is this misunderstanding of emptiness which turns the teaching into a metaphorical poison. Maybe, then, Nāgārjuna and Candrakīrti do not mean to make the radically sceptical point that the teaching of emptiness is itself merely a fabrication? If properly understood, emptiness is genuinely the ultimate truth about experienced things.

Such readings are admittedly an interpretive stretch and, it might be objected, it would be better to take Nāgārjuna's statement at *Madhyamakakārikā* 13, 8 at face value, meaning that, at least sometimes, he was a radical sceptic. Perhaps he did mean to refute even the teaching of emptiness as itself a false view, like all other knowledge claims, which stands in the way of genuine *ataraxia* and must therefore be finally relinquished regardless of the paradox that this entails. But Nāgārjuna's statement, and also Candrakīrti's commentary on it, are laconic. The meaning is not obvious, and it is not surprising that attempts to make sense of the passage might not all lead to the same conclusion. And it is interesting to speculate on philosophical directions in which Madhyamaka thoughts might be taken, even if it is not clear that historically the Mādhyamikas did intend them to be taken in that way!

Early Buddhist scepticism

The disparaging of views by Mādhyamikas might be part of a venerable tradition of Buddhist scepticism. For it is remarkable that *Yuktiṣaṣṭikā* 49–51 and *Madhyamakārikā* 13, 8 resemble quite closely statements made in the section of the *Sutta Nipāta* called the 'Chapter of Eights', which is probably one of the earliest parts of the Pāli Canon. Here, at *Sutta Nipāta* 824–34, it is declared that adherence to views leads to disputes which in turn produce various mental poisons, such as the distress of defeat and the hatred of one's opponents (trans. Norman, 1984, pp. 138–9) and, at *Sutta Nipāta* 785, that 'clingings to views are not easily overcome' (trans. Norman, 1984, pp. 131–2, slightly modified). The Awakened person, according to *Sutta Nipāta* 800, 'would not depend even upon knowledge. He indeed does not follow any faction among those who hold different views. He does not believe any view at all.' (trans. Norman, 1984, p. 135)

Now, it might be claimed that the views to be relinquished here are not literally *all* views but only all wrong views – such as the view of a permanent self and so forth. There are 'right views' – such as 'things are impermanent', 'things have no independent, unchanging self' and 'things cause suffering when craved' – that are thought by these early Buddhists to be expressive of 'things in themselves' or 'things as they really are' rather than being merely conceptual proliferation. Such right views interpret correctly the basic unfabricated data, rather than creating a screen of concepts that conceals this information. Indeed, the distinction between right views and wrong views is commonplace in early Buddhism. As we have already seen, 'right view' is the first aspect of the Eightfold Path. So, though it is true that, according to early Buddhism, one should not become arrogant and proud in holding even right views, this does not mean that the ultimate truth of these views, as statements of 'how things really are', is to be negated.

Perhaps this is correct. Nevertheless, it is also possible that the 'Chapter of the Eights' presents a more genuinely sceptical current in early Buddhism that denies that *any* views, even right views, can apprehend 'things in themselves'. If it is objected that this Buddhist scepticism could surely not deny truth of the three characteristics of existence, it might be replied that, though the Buddhist sceptics would agree that impermanence, suffering and not-self are universal features of experience, this is because experience is always structured by the mind in terms of these concepts, rather than that these features inhere in 'things in themselves'.

The famous unanswered questions of the Buddha might support such a sceptical interpretation of early Buddhism. When asked, at *Majjhima Nikāya* 1, 426–32 (trans. Ñāṇamoli and Bodhi, 1995, pp. 533–6), whether the world is eternal, not eternal, both or neither, whether the *tathāgata* continues to exist after death, does not continue to exist after death both or neither, and whether the life principle is different from the body or the same as it, the Buddha did not answer. The Buddha says that he never claimed that he would answer such questions. Rather, he only claims to teach the Four Noble Truths and he suggests that addressing such questions is not relevant to the elimination of suffering.

Whether the Buddha could have answered these questions, but chose not to, is itself an unanswered question and has been the subject of some debate. However, an interpretation of early Buddhism as a form of scepticism might say that the Buddha does not answer these questions because the person asking the questions wants to know about 'things in themselves' – that is, the true nature of the world, of the Awakened person after death and of the life principle. The Buddha recognizes that the questions employ concepts – such as eternal and not-eternal, continuation, sameness and difference – that are impositions of the mind upon 'things in themselves'. Any answer to the questions would thus be misleading. The Buddha, by contrast, only answers questions that can be answered, namely, inquiries about the world as experienced. And the chief question that he is concerned to answer is how suffering, the fundamental problem of human experience, is to be overcome. To answer this question requires no knowledge of the nature of 'things in themselves', which is fortunate, as such knowledge is not possible. That is to say, the Four Noble Truths are truths about experience. They tell us that experience is structured in terms of craving and suffering and also how experience can be transformed so that craving and suffering are eliminated. That is all that the Buddha claimed to know.

Sue Hamilton's early Buddhism

So, it is possible that Madhyamaka scepticism has a long Buddhist pedigree. Indeed, Sue Hamilton (2000) has argued for what seems to amount to such a sceptical reading of early Buddhism, though she does not use this terminology. Her argument is complex, but let me briefly summarize her basic position as I understand it. She claims that the emphasis in the Theravāda scriptures on conceptual diffusion (*papañca*), or 'conceptions of manifoldness' as she translates this term, indicates that these early Buddhists recognized that the only world that human beings can have access to is the *world of their experience*, which is always mediated by the interpretive structures of their own minds. It is *papañca*, in other words, by which the mind fabricates the manifold world of entities and their interrelations.

Hamilton (2000, p. 78) points to an important passage in the Pāli Canon, *Majjhima Nikāya* 1, 111–12, which shows, according to her, how four of the *khandha*s – form, sensation, apperception and consciousness – function together in the process of constructing experience. These *khandha*s, she says, describe the mechanics of having an experience, that is, the process by which objects become individuated. In Hamilton's translation, the passage reads: 'Seeing occurs where there is contact between an eye and [visible] forms, accompanied by consciousness; this gives rise to sensations, which one then identifies; and what one then identifies one reflects on and makes manifold.' According to Hamilton, the fifth *khandha*, consciousness (*viññāna*), is the basic awareness that is required in order to have any experiences at all. Sensory information comes into contact with the sense organs (*rūpa*) and, given that we are conscious, this creates initial but relatively undeveloped sensations (*vedanā*), such as of pleasure or displeasure or neutrality. Sensations are one's initial, undeveloped awareness of the sensory information. The next and most important stage is *saññā*, which Hamilton translates as 'apperception' but is sometimes rendered by other translators as 'perception' or 'conceptualization', whereby the sensory information is identified or named. Hamilton presumably favours this translation because, according to her, at the level of *saññā* the mind is actively interpreting the received sensory information. *Saññā* is not, according to her, a bare perception which simply and innocently reads off the data presented to it. On the contrary, Hamilton (2000, p. 76) says that, for early Buddhism, what one is actually doing here is 'imposing categories on unclassified data: the experience becomes more and more clearly defined and identifiable'. One comes to have a distinct, well-formed perception of the object. It is here that the 'making manifold' of the world of experience occurs in earnest, which draws the mind further and further away from the 'things in themselves', that is, the sensory information or 'unclassified data'. Although not mentioned in the passage above, the fourth *khandha*, volitional activities (*saṃkhāra*), is essentially one's emotional response to the object of experience – for example, whether one hates it, desires it, is uninterested in it and so forth – which, of course, is a further layer or dimension of the mind's interpreting activity (Hamilton, 2000, pp. 75–80).

So, Hamilton contends that Buddhist truths are teachings about this world of our experience, constructed by the *khandha*s, rather than a world as it exists independently of our minds. The universality of these truths – such as impermanence, not-self and suffering caused by craving – is because human experience is always organized and structured in this way. They are universal features of the fabricated world. The Buddhist knowledge of 'how things really are' is thus in reality knowledge of 'how human experience really is'. As she writes:

> What really matters [for early Buddhism] is understanding one's experience: it is this, no more and no less, that brings liberating insight ... In explaining how the *khandhas* work, he [the Buddha] focuses in particular on the fact that we cannot have access to anything else: *all* our experience is mediated to us by means of them. And our 'world' is simply that. We cannot have access to an 'external' world because we cannot get outside of our experience. Our experience, then, *is* our world. (Hamilton, 2000, pp. 107–8)

This explains, in Hamilton's view, the famous early Buddhist statement, at *Aṅguttara Nikāya* 2, 48–9, that: 'In this fathom-long living body, along with its apperceptions and thoughts, lies the world, the arising of the world, and the cessation of the world.' It is the mind, with its apperceptions and thoughts, that creates, on the basis of undifferentiated sense data, the world of individuated entities which people experience. This world of experience is dependent for its existence on the active, interpreting nature of the cognitive apparatus (Hamilton, 2000, p. 109).

Hamilton argues that this is why all experienced things are referred to as conditioned (*saṃkhata*). They are always conditioned by the conceptualizing mind. She points out that *saṃkhata* can also mean 'constructed' or 'made'. This indicates, according to Hamilton, that all entities of experience are constructed or made when the 'things in themselves' come into contact with the human mind, which is far from a passive recipient of this information. She is here in agreement with Bhikkhu Ñāṇananda (1971, p. 71) who says that: '*Saṅkhata* denotes what is compounded, concocted or put together. In the last analysis, it is the *mind* that does this.' According to early Buddhism, Hamilton (2000, p. 109) says, 'it is we ourselves who construct the world as we know it from the mass of incoming sensory data we continually receive'.

Thus Hamilton's interpretation of early Buddhism includes a very Kantian commitment to unknowable 'things in themselves' (the 'transcendentally existent Reality' as she calls it) which are necessary as the basis stuff or raw material out of which the mind constructs its world of experience:

> We are unable to see Reality as it is in itself because we cannot transcend our cognitive apparatus. But we can only experience the world *at all* because Reality is actually there: what we are experiencing is our *interpretation of* a transcendentally existent Reality. (Hamilton, 2000, p. 188)

So, here we have a clear attempt to interpret early Buddhism in a way that makes it a species of scepticism. This is not, however, a total scepticism because it includes a knowledge claim that there exists an otherwise unknowable mind-independent world, that is, the transcendentally existent Reality. This has the interesting effect that Madhyamaka, if interpreted as I have suggested earlier in the chapter as mitigated scepticism, and early Buddhism can be seen as having essentially the same philosophical message, namely, that the only world we have access to is that of experience and that 'things in themselves' are forever concealed behind the fabricating activity of the human mind. But we can at least have the liberating realization that the experienced world is a fabrication, and we can, furthermore, achieve the understanding that everything in this fabricated world of experience is impermanent, without self, and causes suffering when craved. And the practitioner can also come to know by acquaintance that the Buddhist path leads to the elimination of craving, and hence suffering, from one's experience.

Scepticism about scepticism

Nevertheless, it might be doubted that the divide between 'things in themselves' and the conceptualizing mind is as complete as this Buddhist scepticism maintains. There has, of course, been a perennial debate between sceptics and philosophers who are more optimistic about our prospects for knowledge of the mind-independent world. Such epistemological optimists would suggest that scepticism makes too severe a break between mind-independent things and the ability of one's concepts to apprehend them. The sceptical Buddhists are thus too mistrusting of the ability of concepts to correspond to 'things in themselves'. It is no doubt true that some conceptualization is pernicious, and leads one away from reality and into fantasy. But it is not clear that this is true of all conceptualization. Maybe some conceptualization correctly identifies, and does not distort or falsify, the sensory information. Conceptualization is not necessarily always a barrier to knowledge of the mind-independent world. Might it not be, then, that the sceptics are too pessimistic? For instance, do not the sceptics concede rather too easily that concepts such as time, space and causality are mental constructs, imposed on the 'things in themselves'? Is it not at least as plausible that the mind-independent world is spatial, temporal and has some sort of causal structure?

Indeed, it might be argued that the Buddhist sceptics' notion of 'things in themselves' is difficult to make sense of unless the categories of causality and time *do* apply to it. For surely the unknowable 'things in themselves' are thought by the Buddhist sceptics to *cause*, in conjunction with the conceptual impositions of the mind, the world of experience! And does not the Buddhist sceptics' account imply that these 'things in themselves' exist temporally prior to the world of experience to which, in conjunction with the fabricating activity of the mind, they give rise? Might it not be, then, that time and cause actually inhere in the 'things in themselves' rather than being mind-produced distortions of reality?

The optimist might argue that the epistemological problem that one can never get outside one's experience, so to speak, to observe things as they are independently of our experience does not require us to take the sceptical step of concluding that 'things in themselves' are entirely masked by structures of the mind, which are always at variance with and imposed on 'things in themselves'. Undeniably, it is true that it is difficult to disentangle our interpretations and cognitive contributions from what is actually there mind independently, and thus it is very hard to prove that any of our perceptions do measure up to a mind-independent reality. However, this lack of proof does not in itself entail that the mind-independent world remains entirely hidden from view, that is, as a totally inaccessible basis for our fabrications. Even if we have difficulty demonstrating it, the conceptualizing mind might be capable of using its concepts to apprehend the true nature of things.

It seems uncontentious that our cognitive apparatus and our tendency to interpret what we perceive heavily influence our perceptions of the world. Naive epistemological realism, which says that the mind-independent world exists exactly as we perceive it, is not a defensible position. But the optimists might argue, without falling into naive realism, that 'things in themselves' are known or knowable to us by means of our concepts. This position, a moderate (rather than strong or naive) epistemological realism, would claim that one's apprehension of the 'things in themselves' is always mediated by the mind. However, this mediation does not always and in every way cut one off from mind-independent things. They do not remain entirely concealed from us. On the contrary, it is our only means of access to them. 'Things in themselves' are revealed to us, even if that revelation is often partial and distorted. The Middle Way is here between scepticism and naive epistemological realism, for this position acknowledges both that mind-independent things can be apprehended, that is, there is no unbridgeable gulf between the conceptualizing mind and reality, and that the apprehension of these things is often, but not irrevocably and totally, obscured by the mind and its interpretations.

Indeed, it seems to me that early Buddhist sources could be construed as advocating such moderate epistemological realism. Let us look again at *Majjhima Nikāya* 1, 111–12: 'Seeing occurs where there is contact between an eye and [visible] forms, accompanied by consciousness; this gives rise to sensations, which one then identifies; and what one then identifies one reflects on and makes manifold.' It seems to me that, contrary to Hamilton's interpretation, this passage might mean that conceptualization in the form of *saññā* identifies correctly, without falsification or distortion, the sense data. But the Unawakened mind then reflects on what has been identified and 'makes manifold'. In other words, perhaps the passage is actually distinguishing *saññā*, which remains true to the 'things in themselves', from a further level of conceptualization, *papañca*, in which the Unawakened mind fabricates on the basis of whatever 'things in themselves' *saññā* has identified. Here *saññā* would be benign, and only *papañca* would be malign. Perhaps *saññā* can be equated with a bare perception and conceptualization which identifies correctly what is really there rather than being an already distorted interpretation of the sense data?

In another famous early Buddhist text, *Udāna* 1, 10 (trans. Ireland, 1997, p. 21), the Buddha exhorts his disciple Bāhiya to train himself so that 'in the seen will be merely what is seen; in the heard will be merely what is heard; in the sensed will be merely what is sensed; in the cognized will be merely what is cognized'. In other words, Bāhiya should pay attention to and identify what is actually being apprehended through his five senses and mind. This can be read as a warning to stop the conceptual diffusion or 'making manifold' which is *papañca*. That is, one should desist from fantasies and unwarranted interpretations of whatever sense data one apprehends. Bhikkhu Ñānananda (1971, p. 31) says that Bāhiya is being encouraged to practise 'sense-restraint' which 'consists in "*stopping short*", at the level of sense-data without being led astray by them. He who succeeds in this has truly comprehended the nature of sense-data.' According to Ñānananda, this 'stopping short' normally does not occur, because people become involved in *papañca*. Now, in order to truly comprehend the sense data, to identify them correctly, it seems plausible that *saññā* would be required. It is by means of *saññā* that one discriminates what one is really seeing, hearing and so forth, that is, the 'things in themselves'. Most importantly from a Buddhist spiritual perspective, one identifies that the things one sees, hears and so forth are impermanent. By contrast, it can be suggested, *papañca* takes the mind away from what is really there and thus the mind gets trapped in its web of fantasies and interpretations. The most spiritually harmful of these delusions is that the things one perceives have a stability and permanence that in fact they do not possess. Conceptualization thus both opens up and closes off 'things in themselves'.

I do not here wish to adjudicate between scepticism and this moderate epistemological realism. It is plausible that they are both defensible philosophical stances and are also arguably both possible readings of early Buddhist sources. My point is that a Buddhist who favours moderate epistemological realism might argue that certain of our concepts, such as impermanence, not-self, dependent origination and so forth, do express aspects of 'things in themselves'. They are 'how things really are'. They are not constructs, not even constructs applied by human minds universally. They are not simply truths of experience or of the world as it appears to us. They are truths about 'things in themselves'. That we usually only have at best a partial and often distorted understanding of these 'things in themselves' is the result of the finitude and fallibility of our minds, with their limited cognitive power as well as their tendency to distraction and false conceptualization. But we do nevertheless have some understanding of these mind-independent truths, and maybe this knowledge can be strengthened. Perhaps here we have a viable alternative Buddhist epistemology to the scepticism I have discussed in this chapter.

CHAPTER SEVEN

Mysticism and Ineffability

As we have seen, Buddhist scepticism says that the character of 'things in themselves' is not and cannot be known. The Awakened Buddhists are those people who realize and accept this. They thus let go of the craving for and attachment to such knowledge. However, in this chapter I want to explore the possibility that, by contrast, some Buddhists contend that there is a special, non-conceptual and ineffable knowledge of 'things in themselves' achieved by Awakened people. This is scepticism with a mystical twist. It claims that 'things in themselves' are concealed behind the veil of the mind's fabricating activity but not irrevocably. Awakened people stop the fabricating and thus see the 'things in themselves' in an insight which is not describable, given the falsifying nature of all language.

As we saw in the last chapter, the basic concepts – such as space, time, quantity, cause and effect and so forth – that apply to all experience (mystical sceptics would say all Unawakened experience) are thought by the Buddhist sceptics to be impositions on 'things in themselves'. Now, I would suggest that all words in one way or another function in terms of these basic concepts. Thus, if Awakened Buddhist sceptics were to apprehend 'things in themselves', it would be impossible for them to describe them as large or red, for instance, without assuming the reality of space, for things that have size and colour are necessarily spatial. And it would be impossible to describe 'things in themselves' as permanent or impermanent, for example, without assuming the reality of time. Thus, any knowledge that Awakened Buddhist sceptics might gain of 'things in themselves' would be a sort of wordless wisdom which apprehends a reality that language cannot reach.

Which Buddhists would make the claim that there is such an ineffable gnosis? In this chapter I will argue that it is possible to construe Yogācāra Buddhism as mystical scepticism. Furthermore, some Madhyamaka sources are open to such a reading as well. So, here we have yet another interpretation of Madhyamaka Buddhism! The chapter will also consider the common Buddhist notion of *nirvāṇa*, arguing that it too has often, though not always, been understood as an inexpressible reality somehow beyond or behind the mundane world and which is accessible to Awakened minds alone. For such Buddhists liberating knowledge is thus not simply about apprehending the three characteristics of existence, but also involves seeing this further mysterious reality. Finally, the chapter will establish that the idea of ineffability in Buddhism is a very complex one, and a number of other senses in which Buddhists might hold that reality is inexpressible will be explored.

Ineffability in Yogācāra Buddhism

In Chapter 5, I presented Yogācāra Buddhism as a form of anti-realism that asserts that only the flow of consciousness, that is, the dependent aspect, exists inherently. In other words, Yogācāra anti-realism amounts to ontological idealism, that is, the position that only the mind is real. So-called external objects are products of the mind. The notion that they are 'external' is a delusion of Unawakened people and constitutes the imagined aspect. However, there have been various Western scholars who have argued that Yogācāra is saying that the unfabricated reality is indescribable. Thus, labelling it as 'mind' or 'consciousness' is erroneous. In which case, Yogācāra is not a form of ontological idealism. What are the grounds for this interpretation?

A central theme of the *Tattvārtha* chapter of Asaṅga's *Bodhisattvabhūmi* (see 1966, pp. 26, 32) is the inexpressible inherent nature (*nirabhilāpyasvabhāvatā*) of all *dharma*s which the text equates with suchness (*tathatā*), reality (*tattva*) and emptiness (*śūnyatā*). And in the *Madhyāntavibhāga*, Asaṅga, along with Vasubandhu in the commentary, declares that the signless (*animitta*), as well as suchness (*tathatā*), reality-limit (*bhūtakoṭi*), the ultimate (*paramarthatā*), and the sphere of reality (*dharmadhātu*) are all synonyms for emptiness (*śūnyatā*). That is, emptiness is the signless or inexpressible ultimate reality. Furthermore, in the *Viṃśatikāvṛtti* 10 Vasubandhu says that, though *dharma*s are without self (*nairātmya*) in their imagined aspect, where they are fabricated as dualisms such as subject and object (*grāhaka* and *grāhya*), they nevertheless have an inexpressible (*anabhilāpya*) nature (*ātman*) which is not selfless. I take this to mean that this inexpressible nature is really there, that is, phenomena have an indescribable real essence ('self') that is not a product of fabrication. And the *Saṃdhinirmocanasūtra* (Tibetan text in Powers, 1995, p. 98) says that, unlike the dependent aspect, the imagined aspect 'is established as names and signs'. This would appear to mean that descriptions of the dependent aspect, that is, the unfabricated reality, are falsifying or distorting superimpositions. Thus the *sūtra* proclaims the inexpressible (*brjod med*) nature of reality:

> The conqueror [that is, the Buddha] taught that the profound, inexpressible and non-dual, is not the sphere of fools [that is, the Unawakened] but these fools, confounded by ignorance, delight in verbal diffusion and abide in duality. (Tibetan text in Powers, 1995, p. 20)

Re-thinking *cittamātra*

Furthermore, there are some Yogācāra statements that seem to indicate that consciousness (*citta*), just as much as its objects, is a fabrication. For instance, at *Trisvabhāvanirdeśa* 36 Vasubandhu declares: 'Through the apprehension of *cittamātra* there is non-apprehension of the object to be known. Through the non-apprehension of the object to be known, there should be non-apprehension of consciousness.'

Consciousness itself must be denied as one half of the dualism 'consciousness-object of consciousness'. Object of consciousness and consciousness are correlative notions. Without the object of consciousness, there can be no consciousness. Thus, *Madhyāntavibhāga* 1, 3 says that: 'Its [consciousness's] object does not exist and on account of the non-existence of that [object], it [consciousness] also does not exist.' And Asaṅga, at *Mahāyānasūtrālaṃkāra* 6, 8, declares that:

> Having discerned that [objects which are] different from consciousness do not exist, one thus understands the non-existence of consciousness. Having understood the non-existence of duality, the wise man abides in the sphere of reality (*dharmadhātu*) which is not the domain of that [duality].

The '*dharmadhātu*' here might be the 'things in themselves' which cannot be described either in terms of consciousness or its objects. 'Consciousness' and 'object' are categories that apply only to the Unawakened world of experience. To identify the 'things in themselves' with consciousness would be to endeavour to describe that which is not amenable to expression.

So, perhaps the frequent Yogācāra assertions of consciousness-only (*cittamātra*) and cognition-only (*vijñaptimātra*) are not to be understood as claims that consciousness alone really exists. Rather, they are statements of the Yogācāra position that the world as it is perceived by Unawakened people is a web of mere fabrications superimposed on a completely ineffable reality. That is, the world apprehended by Unawakened beings is *cittamātra* or *vijñaptimātra* in the sense that it is merely imagination. This dualistic world is unreal, a mere product of consciousness. Unawakened people see only the fabricated dualisms. Awakening consists of seeing through them to the underlying ineffable reality. As *Triṃśikā* 29 indicates, Awakened people achieve the supramundane knowledge (*lokottarajñāna*) which sees reality in its true nature, free of superimposition. They are, we can postulate, thus freed from the *cittamātra* or *vijñaptimātra* world which ordinarily conceals the ineffable 'things in themselves'. In support of this interpretation, Ian Harris (1991, p. 83) claims that:

> [Vasubandhu] distinguishes between an unenlightened [that is, Unawakened] state in which one may be justified in saying that mind only [*cittamātra*] or

> representation only [*vijñaptimātra*] operates, and an enlightened state which is equivalent to a radical transformation of the mind which has now been freed to see reality as it is. There is no hint of idealism here. For Vasubandhu enlightenment is the realisation that, in the unenlightened state, one has been deluded into taking the representations of consciousness to be real. This is the true interpretation of the term *vijñaptimātratā*.

Other interpreters, such as Janice Willis and Thomas Kochumuttom, agree. In her study of Asaṅga's *Tattvārtha* chapter of the *Bodhisattvabhūmi*, Willis (1979, pp. 132–3) comments that:

> Far from advocating the superiority of thought over objects, Asaṅga's explication of *śūnyatā* and the Middle Path involves the cessation of both subject and object, both apprehender and things apprehended. Only knowledge freed completely of discursive thought knows an object as it really is ... Hence, not idealism, but a state of intimate, inexpressible knowledge of reality is aimed at.

And Kochumuttom (1982, p. 213), in his book about Vasubandhu, remarks that:

> [Vasubandhu's philosophy of *vijñaptimātratā*] is not an ontological theory worthy of the name idealism: It does not say that reality in its ultimate form is in [*sic*] the nature of consciousness. On the contrary, for the most part it is an epistemological theory, which says that one's (empirical) experience of objects is determined by one's psychic dispositions, especially the idiosyncrasy for subject-object distinction, and that, therefore, one in the state of *saṃsāra* does not at all come to know the things in their suchness (*tathatā*). Things in their suchness are ineffable, and as such are known only to the enlightened ones (*buddhas*).

Madhyamaka 'mystical' scepticism?

Perhaps the Yogācārins are not alone in their mystical scepticism. In the previous chapter I explained the sceptical interpretation of Madhyamaka, according to which Awakened people realize that the character of 'things in themselves' is unknowable and stop hankering after views about them. However, an alternative reading would be that Mādhyamikas, or some of them or some of their texts at any rate, would accept, like the Yogācārins, that 'things in themselves' are unknowable only for the Unawakened people, who are enmeshed in fabrications. Madhyamaka Buddhism does not necessarily want to say that for the Awakened 'things in themselves' are unknowable. Awakened Mādhyamikas, it might be argued, see the conceptually constructed world for what it is, and thus give up their craving for and attachment to it, and they see the futility of views as expressions of the nature of 'things in themselves'. However, this is not the complete content of their Awakened experience. In addition, no longer caught up in conceptual proliferation, they see the unfabricated 'things in themselves', totally unmediated by the distortions of the Unawakened mind. However, they cannot state the content of their mystical knowledge, for to express it is to enter into the realm of conceptual proliferation once again.

There are Madhyamaka statements that perhaps indicate that for Mādhyamikas there is such an Awakened, ineffable gnosis of 'things in themselves'. For instance, the Buddha is described, at *Lokātītastava* 12, as 'having the eye of knowledge' by means of which he sees the world as 'free from characterized objects and characteristics [and] without expression by words'. *Lokātītastava* 27 refers to a 'signless (*animitta*) consciousness (*vijñāna*)', which results from meditation and is required for liberation. *Acintyastava* 44–5 says that the ultimate (*paramārtha*) is unfabricated, inherently existing, true being and so forth, unlike the fabricated conventional world. And *Madhyamakakārikā* 18, 9 says that reality (*tattva*) is the ultimate beyond conceptual diffusion. Furthermore it says that reality 'is not dependent on another', which, according to *Prasannapadā* 373, means that reality can only be understood by direct personal experience rather than by the instruction of another person. This might mean that it is apprehended by an incommunicable knowledge.

Might it not be that the reality or ultimate referred to here is the inexpressible and unfabricated 'things in themselves' that stand behind and support the conventional world of fabrications? In this case, the knowledge free from characterized objects and characteristics or the signless consciousness is the ineffable apprehension of these 'things in themselves'. These 'things in themselves', and thus the knowledge of them, are beyond conceptual diffusion, that is, no concepts or words are able to express their nature. Thus, arguably the knowledge of 'things in themselves' is 'not dependent on the teaching of another person' in the sense that it is a mystical gnosis the content of which is quite inexpressible, realizable only by direct personal experience.

Furthermore, it is possible to interpret the Madhyamaka claims to have no views, no standpoint and no thesis in accordance with this mystical scepticism. Perhaps the point is that Mādhyamikas, through their use of the *reductio ad absurdum* (*prasaṅga*), refute all philosophical positions because they recognize that 'things in themselves' are inexpressible. It is conceivable that the Mādhyamikas think that by refuting all views about reality, especially if this refutation is combined with meditative practices where the mind becomes absorbed and calm, there can be a wordless realization of 'things as they really are'. The mind, cleared of its theories and dogmas, might be open or receptive to such a mystical insight. This would be akin to the common Zen Buddhist idea that an intuitive knowledge of reality arises when the practitioner has fully understood, often by means of the koan method, the futility of all attempts to verbalize or rationally comprehend the true nature of things.

Yogācāra and Madhyamaka: A syncretic approach

The notion that both Madhyamaka and Yogācāra uphold this mystical scepticism is very attractive to syncretists who envisage that the two philosophies are fundamentally saying the same thing. That is, the syncretists will want to stress that there is no basic disagreement between the Madhyamaka and Yogācāra philosophies. They will argue that the Mādhyamikas and Yogācārins are alike in claiming that 'things in themselves' transcend language and are accessible only to Awakened people's wisdom beyond words.

Such a syncretic view has been advanced, for example, by Stefan Anacker (1998, pp. 184–5) for whom the ineffability of reality 'is the fundamental point of contact between the philosophies of Nāgārjuna and Vasubandhu'. And Ian Harris (1991, pp. 2, 176) writes that, 'the axioms of the *Madhyamaka* and *Yogācāra* are found to be held fundamentally in common' (original italics) and that:

> [For both Madhyamaka and Yogācāra] there is an ontological existence realm that is not amenable to predication. Any attempt to describe it is doomed to failure since, by definition, description is intimately associated with a dichotomised world view based on the abstractive tendencies of a mind infected by ignorance. Since the structure of language itself is so infected it will be impossible to state the precise state of reality.

Some doubts about syncretism

However, the syncretists are confronted by an awkward historical fact. As I mentioned in Chapter 5, a number of Madhyamaka texts from the sixth century onwards offer critiques of the Yogācāra philosophy, attacking what they claim to be the Yogācāra contention that consciousness is the reality (*tattva*) that exists inherently. In other words, the Mādhyamikas here accuse the Yogācārins of advocating ontological idealism and of failing to recognize that consciousness itself is a fabrication. Might this not mean, then, that while the Mādhyamikas were insistent that reality is entirely indescribable, the Yogācārins compromised its ineffability by claiming that, though otherwise inexpressible, it could be accurately described as 'consciousness'? This is surely one possible reading.

So, the syncretists might want to advocate the essential philosophical identity of Madhyamaka and Yogācāra thought, but these Mādhyamikas do not appear to share their view. The syncretists might be accused of ignoring the historical evidence that Mādhyamikas themselves did not claim that their philosophical position was in essence the same as that of the Yogācārins. If the Mādhyamikas themselves thought that they had a philosophical position different from and, in their eyes, superior to that of the Yogācārins, then surely the syncretists are wrong to assert the basic identity of the two systems of thought? They are, according to this powerful objection, guilty of artificially unifying the Madhyamaka and Yogācāra philosophies.

It is true that at *Madhyamakālaṃkāra* 92–3, Śāntarakṣita (725–83 CE) effects a famous synthesis of Yogācāra and Madhyamaka. Is there not here, then, evidence for the syncretic interpretation? I do not think so. For Śāntarakṣita does not assert the identity of the two philosophies, but claims that the Yogācāra with its teaching of consciousness-only is a non-definitive (*neyārtha*) teaching, a skilful means. By contrast, he gives the Madhyamaka philosophy, which asserts the emptiness of even consciousness, the status of the final, definitive (*nītārtha*) teaching.

Some possible responses

The syncretists might reply that the Madhyamaka critiques are based on a misunderstanding of the Yogācāra position. However, does it not seem very unlikely that the Mādhyamikas would make such a fundamental mistake about the philosophical stance of their rivals? In which case the syncretists might argue that the Mādhyamikas are engaged in a wilful misreading of the Yogācāra position. Maybe in an environment of competing schools, the Mādhyamikas were prone to misrepresent, even to caricature, their rivals in order to exaggerate or fabricate differences between themselves and their political opponents, and to cast these opponents in a bad light. One should not expect a disinterested, neutral account by the Mādhyamikas of the doctrines of their adversaries.

Indeed, the Mādhyamikas' attacks sometimes seem rather churlish. As Harris (1991, p. 77) notes, Bhāvaviveka (c. 500–70 CE) throws insults at his Yogācārin opponents. In the *Madhyamakaratnapradīpa* he accuses them of having 'mediocre minds' (trans. Lindtner, 1986a, p. 195), while in the *Madhyamakahṛdayakārikā* he becomes quite vitriolic, saying that the Yogācāra criticisms of Madhyamaka are 'the stench of hatred's putrid meat' and this proves the Yogācārins' 'undigested conceit' (trans. Lindtner, 1986a, p. 252). Candrakīrti, at *Yuktiṣaṣṭikāvṛtti* 40–41, compares the Yogācārins to a wild horse that imitates the behaviour of an ass!

One might surmise that the Madhyamaka critiques are the result of insecurity and may originate from a group that felt threatened and marginalized. Perhaps it was the very ascendancy of Yogācāra thought that led to such sustained and rather bitter attacks on the part of the Mādhyamikas. It is interesting that, despite the various lengthy critiques by the Mādhyamikas of the Yogācāra philosophy, there do not seem to be records of any extensive replies by the Yogācārins. One possible explanation is that the Mādhyamikas, though voluminous writers, were not sufficiently numerous or influential to warrant a serious response.

Maybe, then, what is at issue in the Madhyamaka critiques of Yogācāra is political power, influence and status more than fundamental philosophical differences. As Anacker (1998, p. 3) comments about the Indian controversies between the Mādhyamikas and Yogācārins:

> These are really the disagreements of sixth-century followers of Nāgārjuna and Vasubandhu. They belong to a time when Buddhism had become an academic subject at places such as the University of Nālandā. They may have disagreed because they were academics fighting for posts and recognition.

So, perhaps the Madhyamaka attacks on Yogācāra philosophy are examples of rhetoric used in order to establish authority and legitimacy rather than a genuine philosophical criticism of Yogācāra. The Mādhyamikas attempt to discredit their Yogācāra opponents not because they really think that the Yogācāra philosophy is wrong but because the Yogācāra school is a different and rival group. They are the 'competition', to put the point bluntly. The dispute is one about power masquerading in the form of a disagreement about philosophical positions. A good strategy, surely, in a power struggle with a rival group is to concoct an artificial distinction between the two groups to show that one's own group is actually different from and superior to the group one opposes.

But is this argument entirely convincing? I am quite sure that the Yogācārins and the Mādhyamikas would have been engaged in battles for prestige and so forth and would no doubt have sometimes succumbed to the tactic of misrepresenting one another. But the Mādhyamikas' claims that the Yogācārins' position is that consciousness has inherent existence are very frequent and are making a fundamental point about the Yogācāra philosophy. It might be argued that it is improbable that the Mādhyamikas would consistently misrepresent the Yogācārins so fundamentally and crudely. Such a misrepresentation would surely have been too obvious to be sustainable. Furthermore, as Richard King notes (1999a, p. 21), the Indian tradition of philosophical debate emphasizes the importance of presenting a comprehensive and accurate account of the position of a rival school as the initial position (*pūrvapakṣa*) which is then refuted. Misrepresentation of the opponent's position is discouraged. It is arguably unlikely that the Mādhyamikas would have consistently violated this rule of Indian philosophical etiquette. Is it not more likely that the Mādhyamikas thought that they had a genuine and basic philosophical disagreement with the Yogācārins?

Nevertheless, it is worth noting, with Keith Ward (2002, p. 114), that forms of philosophy or religion 'that are very nearly alike tend to proclaim their differences very loudly, even though the differences are not nearly so apparent to anyone else'. Furthermore, perhaps the syncretists' theory may be saved by an appeal to a pristine Yogācāra teaching, later adulterated or transformed. King (1995, pp. 266–7), inspired by the work of Yoshifumi Ueda (1967), considers the possibility that there are two philosophical traditions within the Yogācāra school. The first and original tradition is that of Asaṅga and Vasubandhu whereas the second and later tradition, which 'differs from the works of the early Yogācārins in upholding the ultimate reality of consciousness', is most fully expressed by Dharmapāla (sixth century CE) in the *Ch'eng wei shin lun* as well as by his disciple Hsüan-tsang, founder of the Chinese Fa Hsiang school. As King (1999a, p. 101) comments, Dharmapāla understood the 'transformation of consciousness' (*vijñānapariṇāma*) to refer to the evolution of the external world out of the mind, making his version of Yogācāra clearly a form of ontological idealism. By contrast, it is possible that Vasubandhu intended *vijñānapariṇāma* as a psychological and experiential term, referring to the various transformations that consciousness undergoes, rather than as denoting that the external world develops out of and is a fabrication by consciousness.

The syncretists may thus argue that the Madhyamaka critiques are to be understood as chastising only the later idealistic Yogācāra tradition. Ian Harris (1991, p. 83), for example, argues that it is likely that the Madhyamaka critiques are of the later, deviant Yogācāra tradition and are thus 'taking issue with a point of view which was never held by exponents of the classical interpretation'. It is also not inconceivable that the Madhyamaka critics of Yogācāra, influenced by their contact with the later idealistic Yogācārins, misread as idealism the earlier non-idealistic Yogācāra tradition. The later Yogācāra tradition, by asserting that reality might be described as 'consciousness', deviates from the classical Yogācāra position, which says that reality is entirely indescribable. The syncretists may conclude, then, that for the classical Yogācārins and the Mādhyamikas alike the unfabricated and inexpressible 'things in themselves' are known by the Awakened mind.

Whether there is such an earlier classical Yogācāra is a debatable point, and I suspect that many passages from early Yogācāra thought might be cited to support both the ineffability thesis and ontological idealism. In Chapter 5, I have already shown how a number of early Yogācāra passages attributed to Asaṅga and Vasubandhu might be construed as advocating ontological idealism. Nevertheless, these are often opaque texts, and more than one reading is sometimes possible. In addition, there is no guarantee that these early Yogācārins were consistent in their philosophical ruminations. We need not expect that the early Yogācāra writings express a single, undeviating outlook on reality. They might have veered towards ontological idealism in some statements but not in others.

A philosophical point

That being said, it is arguable that there is a good philosophical reason for the Yogācārins to assert that reality can be described as 'consciousness'. Perhaps they would be right, after all, to compromise the ineffability of reality in this way. As I have already explained, Yogācārins say that Awakening occurs when a supramundane knowledge occurs by which reality is seen as it actually is, without any dualisms. The question arises, who or what is doing the knowing? Presumably, if all that remains when dualisms have been dispelled is the non-dual reality, then it is *reality itself* that is doing the knowing. Liberating knowledge is, one might say, the knowledge by reality of reality. It has come to full self-knowledge. Thus, it seems irresistible to call reality 'consciousness'. For only conscious entities have the capacity for knowledge. To claim that reality is both capable of self-knowledge and is not describable as 'conscious' would be nonsensical. If reality is not describable as 'conscious', then the Yogācārins must deny that it can know itself. But they clearly want to uphold that non-dual liberating knowledge of 'things in themselves' is possible, and thus their position entails that these 'things in themselves' must in some sense have consciousness.

Granted, for the Yogācārins this consciousness cannot be dualistic in form. It is not a consciousness that apprehends an object. It cannot be consciousness of a reality separate from the apprehending consciousness. The 'consciousness-object of consciousness' duality is, according to Yogācāra thought, a fabrication and at the time of liberating knowledge these fabrications do not occur. Relevant here is the Yogācāra notion of *svasaṃvedana*, the self-luminous, reflexive nature of consciousness. In liberation, consciousness is thought to be aware of itself in a non-intentional manner, that is, without taking itself as an object (see Williams, 1998). If my reasoning is correct, then, it seems that the Yogācārins would be justified in holding a tempered version of the ineffability thesis, in order to be philosophically consistent. They should claim that, though reality is in many respects inexpressible, it nevertheless can be described as non-dual consciousness. Perhaps, then, it is the Mādhyamikas in their critiques of Yogācāra who have gone too far in their uncompromising assertion of the indescribability of 'things in themselves'?

Ineffability and pure change

As we have seen, there are frequent Yogācāra references to 'things as they really are' as the dependent aspect, and the Madhyamaka tradition often equates emptiness with dependent origination. It is tempting, therefore, to think that reality or 'things in themselves' in Yogācāra and Madhyamaka is best construed as a flow of pure change. Perhaps the Mādhyamikas and

Yogācārins might say that this reality is ineffable in the sense that there are no identifiable parts or describable entities within this flow. When conceptual construction occurs, this undifferentiated, entity-free process gets carved up, so to speak, into distinct, nameable things. The manifold world of nameable entities is a superimposition on the basic and unfabricated stream. Thus, 'things as they really are' are not really 'things' at all! Jay Garfield (2002, p. 36) seems to imply such an understanding of Madhyamaka when he writes that: '[For Mādhyamikas] to say of a thing that it is dependently arisen is to say that its identity as a single entity is nothing more than its being the referent of a word. The thing itself, apart from conventions of individuation, is nothing but an arbitrary slice of an indefinite spatio-temporal and causal manifold.' Of course, if for the Yogācārins the temporal and causal manifold is the flow of consciousness, then, unlike the Mādhyamikas, they would not agree that it is in any sense spatial.

Note, however, that this philosophical position is a retreat for the Mādhyamikas from the scepticism which says that the concepts of time, causality and space are mental fabrications and do not inhere in the 'things in themselves'. For this philosophy of 'pure change' admits not only that 'things in themselves' can be described as 'process' and 'change' (and thus the ineffability of reality is not complete) but also that they are a 'spatio-temporal and causal manifold'. In the case of the Yogācārins, even if they are ontological idealists and reject the idea that the flow of pure change is spatial, they would presumably still be accepting that this process is temporal and causal. Indeed, once 'things in themselves' are identified as 'process' and 'change', it seems inconceivable that the concepts of time and causality, at least, would not also apply to them.

Understood in this way, Yogācāra and Madhyamaka would thus resemble the philosophy of the ancient Greek philosopher Heraclitus who famously is reported to have said that one cannot step into the same river twice because the river is continually changing. Everything, according to Heraclitus, is constantly transforming from one moment to the next. Heraclitus would not admit that there are *things* which are changing, and which somehow outlast the changes that occur to them. There is just transformation. The superimposition of labels and concepts on the flow of change, turning it into *a*s or *b*s and *c*s, draws boundaries around and makes into distinct, lasting entities what is actually simply flux (see Hospers, 1997, p. 9).

Is this the point Nāgārjuna is making at *Madhyamakakārikā* 15, 3 when he comments that without inherent or independent existence (*svabhāva*) there cannot be existence dependent upon another (*parabhāva*) because existence dependent upon another entails the independent existence of the entity which is depended on? He argues, of course, that there is not independent existence, and therefore there cannot be existence dependent on another. Here Nāgārjuna might be claiming that the teaching of dependent origination, so central to

Buddhism and to Madhyamaka itself, is misconstrued if it is thought of as one or more discrete (that is, 'independent') entities giving rise to or supporting the existence of another or others. To talk of entities giving rise to or supporting other entities is already to apply labels and carve the world up in a distorting way. Nāgārjuna might be indicating that the teaching of dependent origination has a deeper meaning, namely, that all that really exists is process which, in its pristine state, has not yet been divided into things. There are thus no distinct entities to act as causes or effects.

A text that shows both Madhyamaka and Yogācāra influence and that seems to support this 'Heraclitean' reading is the *Gaṇḍavyūha sūtra*. This text seeks to describe the visionary experience of a Buddha, where all individuated things are seen as magic and fictions, lacking inherent existence. As Paul Williams (1989, p. 123) explains, the universe as seen from the perspective of a Buddha, according to this text, is 'the quick silver universe of the visionary perspective wherein all is empty and therefore is seen as a flow lacking hard edges'. What the Unawakened perceive to be distinct things, the Buddha apparently perceives to be a flow of undifferentiated change, while the 'hard edges' that define distinct entities are imposed on this flow by the mind.

Another example of this 'pure change' ontology is found in the thought of Dignāga, who is often classified as a Yogācārin though his work also shows a clear Sautrāntika influence. He claims that the *dharma*s, 'how things really are', are 'unique particulars' (*svalakṣaṇa*). As unique particulars, they are quite indescribable and any attempt to label them involves the imposition of names (*nāma*) and categories (*jāti*) which distort their true, unique nature (see here *Pramāṇasamuccaya* 1, 3). What is really there is thus a series of momentary events which are not at all amenable to description. Unawakened people apply concepts to this ineffable stream of *dharma*s. The Awakened are able to cut through the conceptual impositions and have the pure, unadulterated perception of the inexpressible reality, the unique particulars, as they actually are. Here, then, all conceptualization is a distortion of the true nature of things (see Hattori, 1968, p. 122). Unique particulars are absolutely momentary, instantaneous, and cease immediately after coming into existence. They have a 'pin-point' duration, for any amount of time, no matter how short, can always be divided into smaller moments. On this idea, Paul Williams (2000, p. 120) comments that:

> We are here stretching the bounds of language. The existence of a *dharma* is so short in time that we can no longer speak of it in terms of 'being' at all. Life can best be viewed as an ever-flowing process, and all talk of things, of beings, is merely practical convenience that can easily mislead and engender attachment and consequential suffering.

Whether this position is tenable philosophically is a moot point, however. It might be objected that the idea of 'change' always presupposes *something* that is changing. Change is arguably always a characteristic of an entity. The notion of change without an entity of which it is the change is perhaps incomprehensible. In other words, the idea of an entity-free substratum of change, upon which conceptually constructed entities are imposed, may be incoherent. However, perhaps the Yogācārins and Mādhyamikas might reply that pure change without entities of change only seems incoherent to the dualistic mind, caught still in the web of fabrications, where change and things that change are mutually dependent notions. Language and conceptualization itself is part of the dualistic trap, so that it is not surprising that attempts to conceptualize pure change apart from things which change run into difficulties. One needs to step outside of this ordinary way of seeing things in order to understand the reality which is pure process. Thinking in terms of things which change is simply a conventional way of speaking, and what is actually there is more akin to a constantly moving undifferentiated energy than classifiable entities.

Furthermore, they might contend that it is not surprising that such an insight said to be only fully available to the Awakened in an ineffable gnosis might be hard to understand for the Unawakened mind. Short of Awakening, the mind is unable to perceive the pure flow, and is trapped within distorting conceptual categories which cannot construe change as happening except to discrete things. Of course, the Mādhyamika and Yogācārins' attitude here, based on a claim to privileged experience, would have the effect of ending the discussion, because we are here told that we have no hope of properly understanding this matter short of attaining the liberating knowledge for ourselves. The corollary of this claim is, however, that, short of attaining this liberating knowledge, we have no compelling reason to believe the Yogācāra and Madhyamaka account of reality. Or so an astute critic might claim.

Nirvāṇa and ineffability

It also seems possible that the Yogācārins and Mādhyamikas, or some of them, might reject the 'pure change' account of reality that I have just given and attributed to them. They might make the claim that 'things in themselves' cannot be described as 'pure change', because such a description favours one side of the duality 'change-stasis' and also assumes the unfabricated existence of time and cause. 'Things in themselves' are quite beyond such categories. *Tattva* is a 'timeless' reality, so to speak, so that 'permanence', 'impermanence' and so forth, concepts that assume the existence of time, are inappropriate when referring to it. This position would be consistent with a more rigorous application of the principle of ineffability. Furthermore, if the Yogācārin and Mādhyamikas' understanding of *tattva* is construed in this way, it seems to have much in common with earlier notions of *nirvāṇa* as found, for instance, in various passages of the Pāli Canon. Let me explain.

So far in this study, I have treated *nirvāṇa* as the Awakened person's complete eradication of craving and hence suffering. It is also the cessation of all ignorance about 'things as they really are'. As Suzuki Roshi says in the passage I quoted in Chapter 2, *nirvāṇa* is 'finding one's composure in impermanence'. Buddhism usually claims that human beings are capable of eventually totally overcoming their craving and hence suffering. This is the message of the Third Noble Truth, that is, that there is an end to suffering by cutting off craving. This is said to be *nirvāṇa*, sometimes described as an unconditioned (*asaṃskṛta*) domain or sphere (*āyatana*) attained by the liberated person. Here *nirvāṇa* appears to be 'unconditioned' in the sense that it is the sublime state of the liberated person who is irreversibly no longer conditioned by craving and ignorance. As is well known, *nirvāṇa* literally means 'blowing out', and what are blown out are the fires, so to speak, of craving and ignorance. So, *nirvāṇa* is the equanimity of the sage who has cut off all craving and ignorance, and will thus end all propensities to be reborn. So, understood in this way, *nirvāṇa* is the psychological state of the Awakened person.

However, for many Buddhists there appears to be more to *nirvāṇa* than this. As Steven Collins (1998, p. 188) and Paul Williams (2000, pp. 50–52) have noted, *nirvāṇa* is also thought to be an object of consciousness or knowledge. So, *nirvāṇa* is not only the psychological state of the Awakened people, but it is also something that is known by them. What is it that they know? Some texts from the Pāli Canon claim that *nibbāna*, is a 'deathless' (*amata*) reality that transcends the conditioned world of transitory, time-bound entities. It is timeless. It is described metaphorically as a place quite apart from the impermanent world. That is, it is transcendent (*lokuttara*). It is a separate ontological realm, that is, the Unconditioned Reality, which is not subject to dependent origination. Having relinquished all craving and attachment, the liberated person perceives this Unconditioned Reality. As Collins (1998, p. 185) notes, someone who knows *nibbāna* is called a 'knower of the unmade' (*akataññu*). Passages such as *Udāna* 80 seem to refer to such an Unconditioned Reality, quite beyond all possible mundane phenomena and referred to only by means of the negation of these phenomena:

> There is, monks, a domain [*āyatana*] where there is no earth, no water, no fire, no wind, no sphere of infinite consciousness, no sphere of neither awareness nor non-awareness; there is not this world, there is not another world, there is no sun or moon. I do not call this coming or going, nor standing nor dying, nor being reborn; it is without support, without occurrence, without object. Just this is the end of suffering. (trans. in Gethin 1998, pp. 76–7)

This Unconditioned Reality is thought to be indescribable (*na vattabba*) and beyond the reach of reasoning (*atakkavacāra*) (see Collins, 1998, p. 163). Thus it is apprehended only by an ineffable gnosis. Here, then, we seem to have a very strong sense of Buddhist mysticism, akin perhaps to the Yogācārin and Mādhyamikas' ineffable knowledge of *tattva*. What is known, that is, *nirvāṇa*, by the liberated people is of a nature that simply cannot be grasped by words and the rational mind.

The liberated people's realization of this Unconditioned Reality is also said to be blissful. Unlike the impermanent entities of the mundane world, it is considered to be the source of genuine happiness, that is, 'the highest happiness' (*paramaṃ sukhaṃ*) (see Collins, 1998, p. 207). It is a true refuge, because it is not impermanent and unreliable, unlike the objects of the conditioned world. Furthermore, for many Buddhists, particularly of a non-Mahāyāna persuasion, the liberated person passes into it – in some otherwise undefined sense – after death, which is the attainment of the *nibbāna* without a remainder (*anupadhisesanibbāna*). This is why, perhaps, the Buddha did not answer the question about whether the *tathāgata* after death exists, does not exist, both or neither. That is, the *tathāgata*s after death pass into a state that is beyond all predication. They are inconceivable (*acintyā*) (Collins, 1998, p. 205). Perhaps Awakened people do know what happens after their death, for they have perceived the ineffable Unconditioned Reality into which at death they pass, but whatever they might have understood is quite incommunicable. The *tathāgata*'s state of being, if one might call it that, after death is indescribable. At *Sutta Nipāta* 1075–6, this point is expressed succinctly in the Buddha's reply to the monk Upasīva:

> [Upasīva asks:] 'He who has gone out [that is, an Awakened person after death], does he not exist, or does he remain unimpaired for ever?' ... 'There is no measuring of one who has gone out, Upasīva,' said the Blessed One. 'That no longer exists for him by which one might speak of him. When all phenomena have been removed, then all ways of speaking are also removed.' (trans. Norman, 1984, p. 170, slightly modified)

It would seem that for Buddhists who advocate this understanding of *nirvāṇa* there might be a further incentive for relinquishing one's craving for and attachment to mundane, conditioned entities. For, according to these Buddhists, it is not just that in cutting off craving and attachment one will be liberated from suffering, and dwell in a state of tranquil detachment. Furthermore, by cutting off one's craving and attachment, a mystical gnosis is achieved of the Unconditioned and, after death, there is a state of (presumably) permanent blissful union of some sort with it. The conviction that such irrevocable and totally fulfilling happiness is a fruit of the Buddhist path would doubtless give such Buddhists a further rationale for making the effort required to transcend craving and attachment once and for all.

I am far from sure, however, that all Buddhists would accept that *nirvāṇa* is to be understood in this way. For instance, the Sautrāntikas say that *nirvāṇa* is a simple negation (*abhāva*). That is, it is the absence of craving, ignorance, suffering and so forth in the Awakened mind, and it is, an object of knowledge, the absence of permanence and self in all entities. It is not a positive entity. It is not an existent (Williams, 2000, p. 122). And Nāgārjuna at *Yuktiṣaṣṭikā* 6 declares, 'the thorough knowledge of *saṃsāra* is *nirvāṇa*'. On this verse, Candrakīrti comments that the thorough knowledge in question is that *saṃsāra* arises without inherent existence. Furthermore, Nāgārjuna, at *Madhyamakakārikā* 25, 19–20 famously declares that there 'is not the slightest difference between *saṃsāra* and *nirvāṇa*'. This might mean that *nirvāṇa*, understood as an ineffable, Unconditioned Reality, is a fabrication, that is, it is unreal. The only *nirvāṇa* that Nāgārjuna will admit here is, as with the Sautrāntikas, an absence. Psychologically it is the absence of craving and ignorance. Ontologically it is entities' absence of inherent existence. And it is the perception of the ontological *nirvāṇa* which brings about the psychological *nirvāṇa*. Maybe for such Buddhists the ontological *nirvāṇa* is 'unconditioned' in the sense that it is the unwavering, universal truth about entities. For the Sautrāntikas it is always and everywhere the case that entities lack permanence and self. For the Mādhyamikas, it is always and everywhere the case that entities lack inherent existence. That is all.

Nevertheless, even within the Madhyamaka tradition there are claims that suggest an ontologically positive understanding of *nirvāṇa*. I have already pointed to passages from works attributed to Nāgārjuna himself, most notably his 'hymns' (*stava*), which seem to suggest that there is some sphere which is not a fabrication and is beyond all predication. In this case, perhaps *nirvāṇa* or emptiness is not simply the absence of inherent existence of entities. It is an inherently existing domain quite beyond all dualities and unamenable to any conceptualization. *Acintyastava* 37–9 seems to revel in this non-duality of the inexpressible reality:

> That which has gone beyond the duality of existence and non-existence but has not gone beyond to anywhere, is neither [ordinary] knowledge nor an object of [ordinary] knowledge, is neither existing nor non-existing; that which is not one, not many, not both [one and many], and not neither [one or many], is without basis, and is unmanifest, inconceivable and incomparable; that which does not appear and is not concealed, is neither annihilated nor eternal – that, similar to space, is not the domain of words and [ordinary] knowledge.

Finding inspiration in part from Nāgārjuna's hymns, the Tibetan *gzhan stong* interpretation of Madhyamaka, associated especially but not exclusively with the Jo nang pa school, seems to advocate an ineffable Unconditioned Reality which can be called 'emptiness', but not in the sense that it lacks inherent existence (see Williams, 1989, pp. 105–8; Hookham, 1991). Rather, this

Unconditioned Reality is empty in the sense that it is beyond all words, beyond all conceptualization, and empty of all the taints or defilements of the conditioned world. It is quite beyond all categorization, including most fundamentally the concepts of time, space and causality. Emptiness is thus 'Nothing' but this means, not that it is a mere absence, but rather that it is 'no-thing'. That is, it is a reality which, unlike things, cannot be identified or described as *x*, *y* or *z*.

Such an understanding of emptiness need not deny that Madhyamaka teaches that the things of the conditioned, spatio-temporal and causally connected world are one and all empty in the sense that they are mental fabrications. But this mundane sense of emptiness needs to be complemented by the teaching of a further sense of emptiness, which refers to the ineffable Unconditioned reality which lies behind or beyond the conventional world. And this Unconditioned reality is apprehended by the Awakened person's inexpressible knowledge. So, even Madhyamaka Buddhism can, at least on some occasions, be understood as advocating a mystical gnosis of an ineffable, inherently existing reality.

The 'pure consciousness event' versus ineffable knowledge of reality

This common Buddhist notion of knowledge with an ineffable content should, I think, be distinguished from the disputed phenomenon which Robert Forman (1990, p. 28) calls the 'pure consciousness event', defined by him as a wakeful but contentless state of consciousness. Forman claims that, while on a nine-month meditation retreat he experienced a state of wakeful consciousness, lasting an indeterminate amount of time, in which he 'had not been aware of anything in particular'. He says that his mind was 'utterly with content' yet he had not been asleep. It is a moot point whether a pure consciousness event can exist, for, it might be asked, how can one be awake without one's consciousness having some content? The point of contention here is whether consciousness must always be of something. However, what seems clear is that, as the pure consciousness event is defined by Forman as contentless, it would not involve knowledge – effable or ineffable – of anything.

This is not to deny that Buddhism does give support to Forman's theory of the pure consciousness event. On the contrary, as Paul Griffiths (1986) has examined in detail, Buddhist sources refer to states of meditative absorption (*dhyāna*), known as 'the cessation of sensation and conceptualization' (*saṃjñāvedayitanirodha*) and the 'attainment of non-conceptualization' (*asaṃjñisamāpatti*). Buddhist discussion of these meditative absorptions is complex and perhaps open to more than one reading. However, according to many accounts, they seem remarkably similar to what Forman describes. Consciousness persists, but it is without any awareness of anything at all. But such states of trance, where the mind is awake but totally empty, are different from the ineffable knowledge of reality that I am exploring here, where the Buddhists' consciousness is said to have a content, but this content is inexpressible. The Awakened Buddhists understand or apprehend something, their minds are not blank, but what they understand or apprehend is so different from the spatial and temporal mundane objects of this world that no words can describe it.

The paradox of ineffability

It might be objected that Buddhists who posit such an ineffable reality apprehended by an inexpressible gnosis, are caught in a paradox. For they cannot consistently deny that the ineffable reality can be correctly described as ineffable. And yet, if they describe reality as ineffable, then it is not in fact ineffable. That is, if the statement that 'reality is ineffable' is true, then it is false. Thus, it would seem that genuine ineffability is not really possible. Indeed, some Indian philosophers were aware of this paradox of ineffability. For instance, the Indian grammarian Bhartṛhari (fifth century CE) says at *Vākyapadīya* 20 that 'If it were ascertained that what is to be expressed by "inexpressible" is expressible as being inexpressible, then it would be in fact expressible.' However, it seems that the Buddhists need not be defeated by this objection. There are several strategies that they might employ in answering it.

First, they could weaken their claim that reality is totally ineffable. They might say that reality is *almost completely* ineffable. The only exception is that it can be described as ineffable. This would certainly solve the paradox, though admittedly at a price; such an exception to the general rule seems inelegant and leaves one wondering why this one word but not others is able to describe reality. In short, admitting one exception might appear arbitrary. A second possibility would be for the Buddhists to accept the paradox as itself a symptom of the difficulties by which the ordinary mind is defeated when confronted by the notion of an ineffable reality. They might regard the self-contradiction as a challenge to transcend ordinary, dualistic thinking. The paradox does not disprove that there is an ineffable reality. It does prove, however, that ordinary dualistic thinking ties itself in knots when attempting to understand this reality. Indeed, it seems clear that some Buddhists have adopted this type of approach. Most notably, Zen koans are often puzzles that the ordinary, rational mind cannot solve, and appear to be nonsense to it, and which, according to Zen, require a solution that is only available through a non-rational, inexpressible insight. A third option is available for the Buddhists. They might avoid the apparent paradox by arguing that the assertion 'reality is ineffable' is a statement about the inability of language to describe reality, rather than a statement which describes reality. In other words, 'ineffability' is not a predicate of reality, just like my inability to name the capital city of Senegal is not a predicate of Senegal or its capital city. Thus, the apparent paradox in expressing that 'reality is inexpressible' is not really a paradox at all.

Can ineffable knowledge have any content?

But the idea of an ineffable reality, known by an inexpressible knowledge, presents some further philosophical difficulties. Though these Buddhists say that this knowledge has a content – that is, there is something which is known – it might be objected that in fact it cannot have any content. It seems difficult to make sense of a reality the knowledge of which is not convertible into language. How does such a reality differ from mere nothingness, and how is the supposed knowledge of it different from a deep, dreamless sleep?

The Buddhists can reply that, for those who have not had such inexpressible knowledge of an ineffable reality, it does indeed seem incomprehensible. This is because all the mundane knowledge that Unawakened people have access to has a content which is expressible. For instance, the content of my knowledge of the tree, or the house, or my friend Tom is expressible (even if sometimes I may have difficulty in expressing it, because of linguistic incompetence). It is always possible to say and describe what I know, namely, the tree, the house or my friend Tom. So, it is not surprising that Unawakened people, who have not had access to an ineffable gnosis might consider it to be quite contentless.

Doubts that an inexpressible knowledge is possible thus stem, the Buddhists might contend, from the limitations of the Unawakened perspective and experience. It is as though the Awakened Buddhists have developed a sixth sense, the ineffable gnosis, by which they apprehend reality. Given that Unawakened people have not developed this sixth sense, the reality apprehended by it remains inaccessible and a mystery to them. They are thus unable to understand how knowledge of this reality differs from total blankness. The Buddhists might say that trying to describe the content of this gnosis is like attempting to smell a colour or taste a sound.

Perhaps the Awakened Buddhists might use analogies, which indicate that the ineffable reality they have experienced is in some respects and to some degree like something that the Unawakened mind has experienced. Hence the common Buddhist use of metaphors in referring to *nirvāṇa*. It is compared to an island, the further shore, a holy city, ambrosia and so forth (see Sangharakshita, 1987, p. 100). However, if the Buddhists think that the ineffable reality is totally unlike anything experienced by the Unawakened and totally unlike anything that words can describe, then even metaphors will be ineffective for expressing its true nature. At best, perhaps, these metaphors can make the ineffable reality seem appealing and desirable to the Unawakened practitioners, thus providing some incentive to acquire the knowledge of it. They thus play a motivational, poetic role rather than being actual descriptions. In which case, the Awakened Buddhists if seeking to depict the literal content of the ineffable reality can only employ the *via negativa*, declaring only what it is not, and must remain totally silent about its true nature. In the Buddhist tradition, there are plenty of examples of such purely negative or 'apophatic' references to reality. For instance, *nibbāna* in the Pāli Canon is referred to as the inextinguishable (*apalokita*), the indiscernible (*anidassana*), the dispassionate (*virāga*) and so forth (see Sangharakshita, 1987, p. 89). Furthermore, total silence is not an uncommon Buddhist response to questions about the ineffable reality. Most famously there is Vimalakīrti's 'great silence', at *Vimalakīrtinirdeśa* 8, 33 (trans. Lamotte, 1976, pp. 202–3), when Mañjuśrī asks him to explain the doctrine of the entry into non-duality (*advayadharmamukha*). Mañjuśrī praises Vimalakīrti's answer, or non-answer, saying: 'Excellent, excellent, son of good family: this is the entry of the Bodhisattvas into non-duality. In this way, syllables (*akṣara*), sounds (*svara*) and concepts (*vijñapti*) are worthless (*asamudācāra*).'

So, Buddhism seems to recognize both a need to teach Unawakened people about the ineffable reality, that is, to employ attractive imagery to induce them to endeavour to apprehend it, and also that there can be no literal description at all of this reality. As Candrakīrti says at *Prasannapadā* 264: 'What hearing and what teaching can there be of the unutterable truth? And yet, the unutterable [truth] is heard and taught through superimposition (*samāropa*).' Words are superimpositions on the indescribable reality, but they are necessary as pedagogical tools. Thus Nāgārjuna famously proclaims at *Madhyamakārikā* 24, 10, that the teaching of the ultimate truth is dependent upon the correct use of the conventional, the conventional here perhaps being the various words and concepts which point toward the ultimately inexpressible reality. Of course, it remains puzzling how any words can 'point towards' a reality which is not accessible to language and why some words are thought to be more efficacious in this respect than others.

The problem of verification

Furthermore, it is obviously a debatable point whether the supposedly Awakened Buddhists are right to say that they have inexpressible knowledge of an ineffable reality. For, it might be asked, how can it be proven that they do have such knowledge? Of course, these Buddhists will claim that they have the evidence of their experience, perhaps in very concentrated meditation, on their side. For them the experience of the ineffable reality takes the form of authoritative insight. The Buddhists' experience has such weight and power in their minds that they become convinced that they have had a correct apprehension of the Unconditioned or 'things in themselves'. That the Buddhists have realized the ineffable reality in their experience is for them the proof that it exists. Buddhist Awakening is often regarded as a self-verifying experience. The Buddha, for instance, is said not simply to have had an experience of reality. His experience is recorded to have been such that he could not doubt its veracity.

But it can be protested that such an appeal to a self-validating experience will not do. Some people have all sorts of special religious experiences – of God, of themselves as the messiah, of messages from the deceased and so forth. These experiences may be correct or incorrect, but the experience itself cannot be used as proof of its correctness. The object experienced may be a hallucination, perhaps explainable in purely psychological and physiological terms, no matter how strongly the experience is felt to be authentic. There surely has to be some test in order to establish the veracity of the experience. Without any public assessment how can it be known that what the Awakened Buddhist supposedly knows is indeed a case of knowledge rather than a private fantasy? And, given the impossibility of communicating the content of the experience, it is very hard to see how there might be such verification.

The problem of proof is thus acute in the case of the mystical Buddhists' knowledge claim concerning an ineffable reality. However, it would perhaps be overly sceptical to conclude that, even if no proof is forthcoming, these experiences are always and necessarily delusions. Such experiences might be veridical, even if the Buddhists are unable to provide any further justification that establishes the accuracy of their experiences, just like my perception that a bird recently flew by my window might be correct, even if I can now provide no proof for it.

Indeed, there is a strong case for giving the Buddhists the benefit of the doubt here. After all, when people say that they have sense experiences, we generally trust their reports. Many epistemologists, except those who are very sceptical, will say that such experiences are 'innocent until proven guilty'. We trust these experiences, and are right to do so, until evidence to the contrary is provided. They are considered to be usually reliable. If I report that I have had a clear and distinct sense experience of a bird flying past my window, for instance, we would be inclined to consider this to be a veridical experience, unless there was good reason to think otherwise. The experience would be trusted unless it was discovered, for example, that I had recently consumed a large quantity of hallucinogenic drugs, am an inveterate liar or am prone to sensory delusions.

Why not, then, have the same attitude towards the Buddhists' experience of an ineffable reality? Why not accept the report unless there is good reason to doubt it? Suppose that the Buddhists have been observed to be usually reliable in other matters. These Buddhists report their sense experiences accurately and are generally reasonable with regard to the inferences and judgements they make. In other words, these Buddhists are known to be a trustworthy source of information. Given these facts, why not trust that the Buddhists' mystical experience is also likely to be correct? Only if the Buddhists proved to be unreliable, reporting to experience sense objects where there are none or making unreasonable inferences and judgements, might one have good reason to doubt the veracity of their experience of an ineffable reality. To doubt the truth of the Buddhists' experience of the ineffable reality when they are in other cases trustworthy would seem to be unnecessarily sceptical.

Perhaps. But the suspicion might remain that for such important, special experiences, which so few other people seem to have, some extra verification would be highly desirable. The Buddhists are making a claim to exceptional and very important knowledge, and thus it might not be unreasonable to require unusually high levels of proof. However, it is surely still open to the Buddhists, and other religious or spiritual people who claim to have experiences of an ineffable reality, to contend that the doubter is here asking for the sort of evidence (for example, experimental data) which can only be given for things of the material, mundane world. In which case, that such proof of the ineffable reality is not possible demonstrates only that it is distinct from the spatio-temporal world of sensed objects.

Ineffable knowledge and indoctrination

But the doubter might also argue that the Buddhists' experience is not actually an unmediated apprehension of reality. On the contrary, what they experience is a function of the training that they have undergone. Buddhists fully indoctrinated into the view that reality is ineffable might well find that their experiences, cultivated in meditation, confirm their view. This is hardly surprising given that they have been taught to experience reality as ineffable and have perhaps devoted much time and mental discipline to producing such an experience. The experience is thus not actually knowledge of 'things as they really are'. It is simply that the Buddhists' training predisposes them to construct 'reality' in this way. If, by contrast, one were indoctrinated into the view that there is a personal God who can speak to one in one's meditation or prayer, then it is not unlikely that one might start, after intensive meditative concentration on the idea of a personal God, to have experiences of what one takes to be conversations with God. Meditative experiences might be a result of the conceptual system one has adopted, rather than an apprehension of a mind-independent reality.

Indeed, many scholars of mysticism, most notably Steven Katz (1978; 1983), reject the possibility of a pure, unmediated experience. According to them, all experience is mediated by concepts and the mystics' supposedly ineffable experience is no different; it is a product of the socio-religious and cultural context in which it occurs. Thus, the Buddhists might think that their knowledge of reality is ineffable, but their experience of it is actually conditioned by Buddhist presuppositions. Thus, for instance, the Buddhists' experience of reality is influenced and predetermined by Buddhist beliefs that there is more to the world than material things, there is an ultimate reality, it is not a personal God, and it is not the creator of the universe, the ultimate reality can be apprehended by Buddhist spiritual training and so forth. Mystics from other traditions, with different beliefs and presuppositions, have quite different experiences.

It is possible that Katz and other scholars who share his view are right. However, their position does not seem entirely compelling. This is because there is a plausible alternative account. That is, perhaps mystics do have pure, unmediated experiences of reality and it is only *afterwards* that they get interpreted in accordance with the doctrines and views of their particular tradition. In which case, the inexpressible reality is experienced directly, and then, after the event, the mystics use the terms and categories with which they are familiar in their culture and religious group in order to express to others what has been experienced and perhaps to make sense of it for themselves. The interpretation comes after the experience, rather than being part of it. This view of mystical experience is favoured by certain scholars, such as Walter Stace (1960) and Ninian Smart (1980), for whom there is a common unmediated experience of an ineffable reality which lies at the core of the various religions, and which gets interpreted differently according to the doctrines and cultural presuppositions of these religions.

Is ineffable knowledge of reality possible?

It is difficult to judge who is correct in this debate. Are human beings really capable of having a pure apprehension of an indescribable reality? Or are the only experiences that are possible ones that are mediated by an imposed conceptual framework? Richard King (1999b, pp. 167–75) has pointed out that Katz's position on mysticism is rooted in recent Western 'constructivist' philosophical theories about the embedded nature of the finite human mind in its cultural and linguistic context. That is, knowledge is thought to be a social creation. Human beings are considered to be always and in every case products of their environments and inevitably to understand the world from their own particular social and historical vantage point with all its prejudices. There can be no transcendence of this situatedness and no 'view from nowhere' or 'God's-eye view'. Of course, the common Buddhist claim, shared by many mystics from other religious traditions, that there can be a direct knowledge of an ineffable reality contradicts this dominant contemporary Western epistemological attitude. For the Buddhists, transcendence of the limited, conditioned nature of the mind is deemed possible, and an impartial, unmediated apprehension of 'things as they really are' can be achieved. The human mind, in mystical states, can see reality in its naked splendour, no longer masked by the distorting filters of language and culture.

As King (1999b, pp. 174–5) has argued, to insist that any such unmediated knowledge or pure experience of reality is an impossibility can be construed as a case of intellectual colonialism and ethnocentrism. It is perhaps an attempt to impose the dominant contemporary Western conception of knowledge and the limitations of the human mind and to assert the intellectual inferiority of other cultures that do not share this epistemological stance. It might be added that the imposition here is not only on other cultures but also on people within Western society itself who are also inclined to accept the possibility of mystical experience and the direct apprehension of an inexpressible reality. Such people are marginalized, silenced and not taken seriously, having 'naive', 'fanciful' and 'unsophisticated' ideas. They become excluded from 'serious' academic debate and investigation as pre-critical adherents to quaint but untenable spiritual ideals.

This imposition might be quite acceptable if the constructivist account had been demonstrated to be definitely correct. But its correctness is precisely what is at issue here, and I am not aware that it has been firmly established. The question is, of course, how can the proponents of this dominant contemporary Western conception of knowledge be so sure that their epistemology is right, especially as it is itself a product of their specific cultural conditioning? Are not the constructivists' views affected by their own historical situatedness? Perhaps their incomprehension of the Buddhists' claim to have an unmediated knowledge of an ineffable reality is simply a result of their own assumption (and it surely is an assumption) that the human mind is always and necessarily constrained by the limitations of its cultural, historical and linguistic boundaries. Might it not be that their view that the Buddhists must have been indoctrinated, and do not really have a direct insight into reality, is itself a case of indoctrination? Indeed, how could Katz and so forth know that there can be no pure, unmediated experiences? They have obviously never had one, but is it not illegitimate to universalize from their own personal experience?

This is not to say that the dominant modern epistemology is necessarily wrong. It is not implausible that there can be no unmediated apprehension of reality and that human minds are always trapped and prejudiced by their particular social, historical and linguistic circumstances. Maybe the constructivists are right to reject the Buddhist idea of a mystical gnosis of an ineffable reality. However, humility and openness to other possibilities is no doubt desirable. That most human knowledge is influenced by the knower's cultural and linguistic location is no doubt an extremely valuable insight. The constructivists are surely right to emphasize this point. However, to assert categorically that there can be no unmediated knowledge seems myopic, arrogant and is itself a far from indubitable knowledge claim. Perhaps some direct insight into the Unconditioned is indeed possible. Have not the constructivists dogmatically closed off a possibility to which a genuine truth-seeker should remain open? Might it not be that their adherence to their particular views about the limitations of human knowledge, themselves a product of modern Western attitudes concerning the finitude and fallibility of the human mind, have blinded them to the possibility that human beings can and occasionally do have undistorted mystical insights? All that seems certain is that there is uncertainty here. It is possible, then, that the Awakened Buddhists' liberating wisdom beyond words, that is, their gnosis of an ineffable reality, is veridical, but, given the challenge of constructivism as well as the difficulties of ever proving the veracity of such a mystical knowledge claim, it would be going too far to claim that we know this to be the case.

Buddhism and mystery

This study began with the examination of the Buddhist claim that knowledge of the three characteristics of existence is a key to liberation from craving and suffering. Such knowledge is really a thorough seeing of the mundane world for what it is – that is, impermanent, without abiding essence and the cause of suffering when craved. No doubt it is possible to construe Buddhist liberation as simply about insight into and emotional acceptance of this mundane reality. Here Buddhism would offer a form of peace and tranquillity in the face of the vicissitudes of life. But this chapter has shown that there can often be a further dimension to the Buddhist understanding of liberation, namely, a mystical realization of an indescribable supramundane truth. For Buddhism understood in this way, the goal is not simply to see and accept the mundane world for what it is, but also to see beyond the spatio-temporal world to a sacred mystery which stands behind or beyond it.

Some more types of ineffability

The mystical impulse in Buddhism is, I think, undeniably strong and there is frequently a commitment to such an ineffable reality. However, I think that there are a number of other senses in which the idea of inexpressibility occurs in Buddhist contexts, all of which might be called 'weak' and 'down to earth' in that they do not entail the existence of such a mysterious ontological realm or a mystical gnosis which apprehends it. In the remainder of this chapter, I want to examine these further 'common sense' varieties of ineffability.

The ineffability of knowledge by acquaintance

Philosophers are fond of making the distinction between words and their referents. But one need not be a philosopher to see that words and their referents are certainly not to be identified. It is common sense that, for instance, the word 'water' is not the water to which the word refers. Hence different words in other languages are used to refer to what English speakers call 'water'. Furthermore, unlike its referent, the word 'water' is unable to get one wet or to quench one's thirst. It seems clear that words describe their referents, rather than being identical with the objects of experience which they depict. How close is the 'fit' between the descriptions provided by words and their referents? How accurately do words, when properly used, depict the objects of experience which they describe? Let me suggest an answer that, I think, might be palatable to some Buddhists and which reveals a way in which knowledge by acquaintance of the three characteristics might be said to be ineffable.

We saw in Chapter 3 that propositional knowledge or knowledge by description is linguistic in nature. That is, if one has propositional knowledge one knows that a statement or proposition *p* is true. For instance, Peter knows that 'the tree in the garden is green', Helen knows that 'the cat is black and white' and so forth. Now, propositions are made up of words and words generalize. They place particular objects in categories, grouping each object with other similar though not identical objects. A particular object is described as of type *x* and as having properties of type *y* and *z* and so forth. The object thus belongs together with other objects of type *x* and together with other objects having properties of type *y* and *z*. If Helen knows, for example, that the cat is black and white, then this propositional knowledge places the known object in the category 'cat' and as having the properties of 'blackness' and 'whiteness'.

Now, in performing this function of categorization, words arguably do not convey the distinctive nature of an object *qua* individual object. Any particular object of type *x* is similar but not identical to other objects of type *x* and its properties *y* and *z* are similar but not identical to properties *y* and *z* possessed by other objects. Arguably each and every object has a particularity that can never be captured by words. An object may be red, but the description 'red' never expresses the distinctive nature of the specific red that the individual object alone has. This is always 'left out' of the description. Even if one describes the object's colour as 'very light red', this object's colour has still been grouped in the category 'very light red', which does not get at the very particular character of the very light red of the specific object, and precisely how it differs from other very light reds. The philosopher Friedrich Nietzsche (1999, p. 185) has expressed this point very well: 'Every concept arises from the equation of unequal things. Just as it is certain that one leaf is never totally the same as another, so it is certain that the concept "leaf" is formed by arbitrarily discarding these individual differences and by forgetting the distinguishing aspects.'

Entities have an individuality that overflows any description that one may attempt. As John Hospers (1997, p. 9) comments, if it is admitted that every entity, indeed, each momentary state, is different from every other, one would require an infinite number of words in order accurately to describe them. Each thing would require its own word to express its individual nature: 'Of course, if we tried to do this, we would soon run out of words. Our language would become infinitely lengthy, and our memory would soon be taxed beyond endurance in trying to recall all those millions of words. In fact, each word would be a proper name for one momentary state.'

By contrast with this knowledge by description, perception seems to give one a pre-linguistic acquaintance with the perceived object. So, it is arguable that knowledge by acquaintance has access to the unique character of the object. One can see, feel, taste, touch and hear an object in its particularity. If one sees the black and white cat, then one sees this particular cat with its particular shade of blackness and whiteness.

A Buddhist version of this theory of perception can be found in the Tibetan dGe lugs pa epistemology. The dGe lugs pas say that perception alone can apprehend the 'specific characteristic' (Sanskrit: *svalakṣaṇa*, Tibetan: *rang mtshan*) of the object. This specific characteristic, for the dGe lugs pas, is the object's unique shade of colour, shape and so forth. By contrast, words function in terms of 'meaning generalities' (Sanskrit: *arthasāmānya*, Tibetan: *don sypi*) – that is, universals or categories – that blur the individuality of objects, failing to express their specificity (see Klein, 1998, pp. 183–205). The words one then uses to describe what one has perceived will describe, if used appropriately, the type of object, and the type of properties of the object, but this description can be no more than a silhouette of the particular object as directly perceived.

This theory of perception gives objects of perception a sort of ineffability. Note, however, that the inexpressibility here is relatively weak. Words do not totally miss their mark. On the contrary, words are accurate as far as they go and can rightly identify similarities between different entities, but they leave out the unique character of each and every specific referent. Thus, it is not that perceived objects are entirely inexpressible; it is just that an entirely accurate, completely adequate description is not possible. Objects are not fully expressible in that their particularity always eludes words. The specificity of an object, rather than the object *per se*, is ineffable.

And this ineffability would presumably apply to perceptions of the three characteristics. So, for instance, Buddhists might say that it is true that 'things are impermanent, without self, and cause suffering when craved'. That is, these words hit their mark and this knowledge by description is legitimate, as far as it goes. However, the limitation of language is that the descriptions cannot convey the uniqueness of any particular thing in its impermanence and so forth. So, the importance of a perception is that, unlike a description, it gives one a vivid and unadulterated experience of the specific object's transitoriness and so forth. This can never be captured by words. Given the common Buddhist emphasis on the perception of the three characteristics as necessary in order to cut off craving, this is an important sense in which liberating knowledge of reality might be said to be inexpressible.

The ineffability of one's inner life

Furthermore, when I perceive an object, such as a tree, mountain, chair and so forth, I have, of course, an experience of the object in question. Now, philosophers sometimes claim that experiences have an inalienably first-person character. In other words, you cannot have my experience and I cannot have your experience. Experiences are not publicly accessible phenomena.

Of course, this raises interesting sceptical issues about how I can ever know that everyone else is not simply an automaton. Perhaps I am the only being who has experiences. Also, even granting that other people do have experiences, how can I ever know that they are having experiences that are similar to my own? Perhaps when they experience what they call 'red' for instance, what they actually see is a colour quite unlike the colour I see and identify as 'red'. Perhaps their sense organs and minds process the data so differently from mine that their experience of objects is radically different from mine. Also, I cannot perceive the emotions of other people, and they cannot perceive my emotions. So, I will never be entirely sure whether the words which I use to describe a particular emotion have the same referent, that is, refer to the same sort of emotion, for other people. When they say that they are 'sad', for instance, how can I know that they are feeling the same emotion as I refer to by that name? How could I ever know, as I cannot have direct access to another person's experiences?

Such sceptical problems have been much discussed by philosophers and they do not have easy solutions. However, let us assume for the sake of argument that we do all have experiences, and that we have similar experiences of external objects and internal states such as emotions. For instance, when I experience 'red' it is similar to your experience of 'red'. When I experience 'sadness' it is similar to the emotional state that you experience and refer to as 'sadness'.

But even making this assumption, it seems probable that my particular sense organs and my individual mind might give my experiences of redness and sadness, for instance, a specific quality that is somewhat different from your experiences, given your particular sense organs and individual mind, of these phenomena. Presumably there are subtle differences between individual minds and sense organs and in the way they process sensory information. Thus, even if I might be able to communicate to you that 'I am having an experience of red' or ' I am having an experience of sadness' perhaps there is always a specificity about my experience, caused by the peculiarities of my sense organs and mental processes, which this description can never express to you (and vice versa). Even if I describe accurately my experience to you, the description will not enable you to know exactly what it is like to have my experience. There is thus arguably an irrevocably incommunicable dimension to one's experience.

This ineffability of one's inner life is, I suppose, a form of inexpressibility that the Buddhists might accept. For instance, might it not be that in experiencing impermanence or suffering, the experience has a specific 'tone', unique to one's own particular mind and sensory apparatus, that is incommunicable to others? One's experience of impermanence or suffering might thus have a quality that is quite private (unless, of course, the Buddhists make the rather extraordinary claim that it is possible to develop a psychic ability in which one actually has another person's experience), just like one's particular experience of red or sadness. Other people might understand when I refer to my experience of impermanence or suffering, and they might confirm that they too have had that type of experience. But precisely what it is like for me to experience impermanence and suffering arguably is not expressible. And, equally, quite how it would feel for me to be liberated might vary somewhat from your experience of liberation and perhaps that very specific, personal difference can never be communicated. In other words, it is ineffable.

Ineffability resulting from lack of linguistic ability

Yet another 'weak' sense of ineffability arises from the fact that everyone has been faced on occasion with the difficulty of being unable to find the right words to express something that one is experiencing. It is quite possible to experience the object to which a word refers without having access to the word that refers to it.

This problem is particularly acute when working in a language with which one is not particularly familiar. It is also an especially noticeable difficulty for children still grappling with increasing their vocabulary, confronted with a world of objects for which they have yet to learn the conventionally acceptable labels. Young children notice objects yet they have still to acquire the ability to describe the objects that they perceive. Most non-human animals are also able to discriminate objects yet, in so far as they do not have language, they never have the capacity to describe what they discriminate. In this case, the objects that they apprehend are permanently inexpressible for them. Furthermore, even quite articulate adults often are unsuccessful when attempting to describe objects. For instance, such people might be unable to find the right words because of lack of concentration, failing memory or insufficiently extensive vocabulary. Sometimes one simply forgets or is too distracted to recall the appropriate word or else one simply does not have knowledge of the particular words required. In addition, one may be unable to describe what one is experiencing because of one's total absorption in the experience in question. When one is overwhelmed by an aesthetic experience, for instance, one is sometimes incapable of doing anything at the time except dwelling in that experience. One is 'lost for words'. Or, faced by a terrible accident, one may be rendered speechless. There is no mental space or distance, as it were, from the experience that would enable one to formulate a description of it.

These are very ordinary and easily recognizable ways in which objects can be inexpressible. What unites them all is that the inexpressibility of the object is a result of a temporary or permanent linguistic inability. The ineffability in this case can in principle be overcome and often is overcome when one acquires or regains the necessary linguistic acumen. In all of the situations I have described, one can in principle learn or remember how to apply the correct words. If one never gains the capacity to describe the objects of experience – as is the case for most non-human animals or humans with intractably poor language skills – then the deficiency lies with one's inability, sometimes due to irreversible biological conditions, to identify and employ correctly the required words.

Now, it seems clear that, from a Buddhist perspective, this ineffability resulting from permanent or temporary lack of linguistic ability might occur in relation to one's knowledge of the three characteristics. Suppose, for instance, that some people, not linguistically very skilled, comprehend impermanence, not-self and suffering. It seems quite possible that they might have this understanding, perhaps even a very thorough knowledge, without having the ability to enunciate it very well or even at all. People with poor language abilities sometimes know much more than they can express. It is certainly possible to be wise but inarticulate!

Furthermore, suppose that normally articulate Buddhists were to have a particularly powerful experience, perhaps in meditation, of impermanence, dependent origination, suffering and so forth. They might temporarily find themselves unable to express, or to formulate in words, the content of their experience, simply because they are so overwhelmed by and absorbed in the experience. In this case, maybe later they become more articulate and can report the content of their experience. So, it is plausible that the Buddhist can admit that 'the way things really are' can sometimes be inexpressible if someone who knows this reality temporarily or permanently lacks the linguistic ability to describe it.

Ineffability and complete description

There is a final 'weak' sense of ineffability that should be considered. This has to do with our inability to give complete descriptions of entities and their interconnectedness with the rest of the world. Let me explain.

Obviously, when one does not have any knowledge of something, it is impossible to describe this object at all. For instance, I might be asked to describe an elephant. Suppose that I have never seen an elephant, nor have I seen pictures of elephants, nor has anyone ever told me anything about elephants and their characteristics. I will in this case be unable to describe the elephant. Here the inability does not result from a failure in language, but rather from a failure in my knowledge of one of language's referents. I certainly possess the vocabulary with which to describe an elephant – for example, as a very large grey-coloured mammal, with a trunk, large ears and tusks. I know all of the required words and what they mean. But I am unable to describe the elephant because, not knowing what an elephant is like, I do not know which words will be appropriate to describe it.

Of course, in that there are plenty of objects of which I do not and never will have any knowledge, there is much in the world that will remain entirely inexpressible for me. However, as with the inexpressibility resulting from linguistic inability, this sort of ineffability can also in principle be overcome. That is, one can conceivably gain familiarity with the object – by direct perception or the reliable reports of others. For example, I might see or be told about the elephant and its characteristics. Having acquired knowledge of the object, it will be possible, assuming one is also skilled enough with language, to apply the words that correctly describe it. Having seen or heard about an elephant, for instance, I can indeed formulate a correct description of the very large grey-coloured beast with large ears and a trunk.

Nevertheless, even when one knows an object, one's ability to give a description of it is usually partial and limited. There is usually much more that could be said about the object in question. This is because the amount of information that is pertinent for a complete description of a particular entity is generally vast. Often one is incapable of giving such a complete description. Sometimes this is partly because of lack of mental energy or time. It is simply not possible nor is it necessary, given the exigencies of daily life, to give complete descriptions of objects. Partial descriptions suffice. In addition, it is often the case that one does not have the vocabulary and/or the comprehensive knowledge of the entity necessary to provide the complete description. Thus, the description stops before everything that could possibly be said has been said. So, for example, I may describe the elephant as a very large, grey mammal with tusks and big ears. But I have failed to say, for instance, that the elephant is an Indian as opposed to an African elephant. And even if I include this information, I might also have described the diet of the elephant, its genetic constitution, its age, the various things that have happened to the elephant since it was born, the relation between the elephant and its environment and so forth. The description could continue, giving more and more details about the elephant and more and more information about the relation of the elephant to its surroundings, its history and so forth. But it is arguable that still the description will be partial and limited by the constraints of time and of one's knowledge, both of language and the object in question. It is a moot point whether a complete description of any object can ever be given. Is it not possible that there is not always more that might be said? Even if we conclude that complete descriptions are theoretically feasible, it is clear that they would usually require considerable time, vast knowledge of the object and a total mastery of the relevant language.

This form of inexpressibility is relevant in relation to the Buddhist liberating knowledge. For instance, suppose that some Buddhist practitioners have an understanding of not-self. They understand that not-self means that things dependently originate and thus have no permanent essence. But, it might be asked, how extensive is their knowledge of dependent origination? It is one thing to know the general principle that things arise in dependence upon causal conditions; it is quite another thing to know the specific workings of this law, that is, which entities rely upon which causal conditions and in which ways. Given the vastness and intricacies of the universe, there are probably infinite numbers of interconnections between and within entities. Surely no finite human being is able to know all of them. Thus, though the Buddhist practitioners will have an expressible knowledge of the general principle of dependent origination, and some expressible knowledge of the specific interrelations between entities, there will be limits to their knowledge and hence limits to what they can say about 'the way things really are'. Indeed, even the limited amount that they do know about the details of the web of interconnectedness is probably too much to express, given the constraints of time.

Of course, as we have seen, many Buddhists would claim that a Buddha is omniscient, and thus does know dependent origination in all its intricate details. However, even in this case, a Buddha would presumably not be able to express verbally all that he knows, because the articulation of an infinite number of interconnections would surely take an infinite amount of time. So, this is certainly an important sense in which the Buddhist vision of 'things as they actually are' can be said to be ineffable.

Expressing the inexpressible

It is a commonplace of many forms of Buddhism that reality is in some sense 'beyond words' and that liberating knowledge of it is somehow indescribable. We should not, however, conclude that this claim has just one meaning. This chapter has shown, I believe, that the Buddhist notion of ineffability has a number of possible senses. Ironically, there is an enormous amount that can be said about inexpressibility in Buddhism!

CHAPTER EIGHT

Compassion, Faith and Human Fallibility

This study has demonstrated that Buddhist liberating knowledge involves a complex web of ideas. It includes a number of variations and interrelated themes. And Buddhist thought is often characterized by a degree of philosophical fluidity that allows for a range of interpretations. Liberating knowledge in Buddhism is thus not a simple matter. In the introductory chapter I raised the possibility that Buddhism is not one entity but rather an 'umbrella concept' for a family of closely connected but distinct phenomena. This book has, I believe, supplied a considerable amount of evidence for this theory. The forms of Buddhism that I have been reflecting on share much in the way of vocabulary and basic assumptions about 'how things really are' – such as the three characteristics of existence, the notion that craving causes suffering and ought to be eradicated and so forth. Furthermore, they generally give knowledge, in the context of the Buddhist path as a whole, a crucial role in bringing about emancipation. But within these parameters there is also considerable divergence.

Thus, the various types of Buddhist anti-realists would say that the teaching of not-self means that most or all entities are fabrications and this is what the liberated practitioner perceives. Buddhists who are more inclined to moderate epistemological realism would beg to differ, claiming that all conditioned things are certainly impermanent and dependently originating, but this does not mean that they are mainly fabrications. Buddhist sceptics might claim, by contrast, that the liberating knowledge of the three characteristics is of things as experienced and not of 'things in themselves'. For such Buddhist sceptics, the acceptance that we cannot know any mind-independent reality is thought to have a liberating effect, enabling the practitioner to 'let go' of attachment to views and craving for such knowledge. And then there is the issue of an inexpressible gnosis of an ineffable reality. For the many Buddhists who have this mystical inclination, liberating knowledge is not simply of the three characteristics but also of a further ontological realm that is beyond predication. So, there is significant diversity in the ways in which Buddhists might envisage the content of liberating knowledge.

Furthermore, this study has shown that Buddhist understandings of liberating knowledge, though certainly profound and provocative, are also often philosophically problematic. I have explained that, in numerous ways, Buddhist teachings about 'how things really are' are far from being self-evident truths. This is perhaps a particularly important point to emphasize because some Buddhists at times seem to have the attitude that Buddhism, at least in its so-called 'purest' form, is unlike other religions with their 'superstitious' beliefs in God, heaven and so forth. It is a purely 'rational' religion that does not make questionable metaphysical or moral claims. Buddhist teachings are sometimes regarded as common sense and easily verifiable. Buddhism sometimes gets presented by 'insiders' as *the* Dharma – that is, *the* Truth – in a way that suggests that its truth claims are straightforward and unchallengeable. This way of thinking, it seems to me, fails to recognize both that *the* Dharma is actually *many* Dharmas, or at least many significant variations on the same Dharma, and also that these Dharmas often rely on debatable metaphysical claims (about the nature of reality) and moral principles (about how one ought to act). No doubt such an uncritical attitude on the part of some Buddhists is due partly to an understandable enthusiasm for what are admittedly fascinating and often weighty ideas that, furthermore, practitioners have often found to have important and beneficial transformative effects on their lives. Be that as it may, I would suggest that many Buddhist teachings are not obviously true. Here I must emphasize again, as I did in Chapter 1, that I am not claiming that Buddhism is definitely wrong, just that it is not always necessarily right. I am simply arguing that there are reasonable doubts about and alternative visions to the Buddhist understanding, or understandings, of liberating knowledge, 'how things really are' and 'the good life'.

And this critical perspective is not necessarily destructive of Buddhism and individuals' commitment to it. Indeed, Buddhists might do well to hold together dedication to their spiritual path with openness to uncertainty and doubts. I am sure that this is precisely what some thoughtful Buddhists do. The Buddha, after all, taught that the Dharma was simply a raft, that is, a means to an end, and he encouraged people to test and scrutinize it, and not to accept it uncritically. Such an undogmatic commitment to Buddhism might well foster greater understanding and appreciation of other religious and non-religious traditions and their alternative conceptions of reality and how one ought to live. Buddhists who have this open attitude would recognize that their own spiritual tradition does not give them indubitable access to the truth, whatever that might turn out to be! The point here might be expressed in quintessentially Buddhist terms. As we have discovered, the Buddhists are encouraged to give up craving, attachment and ignorance. Maybe this should include craving for and attachment *to Buddhism* and the misguided dogmatic belief that it has delivered the incontrovertible truth. Otherwise, Buddhism itself can become a cause of suffering.

Knowledge and compassion

Buddhism is renowned for its emphasis on compassion which is often said to be as important as understanding or wisdom. Indeed, it is sometimes said that Buddhist teachings should always make reference to compassion. Otherwise they are incomplete. Perhaps the present study has been deficient in this respect. Compassion has only been cursorily mentioned! The pertinent question, then, is what exactly is the relation between compassion and liberating knowledge?

We have seen already, in Chapter 4, that the weakening and eventual eradication of craving and attachment, which are essentially appropriative and self-referential, leaves an opening for altruistic emotions and desires. When one is no longer motivated by selfishness, the opportunity arises for genuine concern for others. Thus, in so far as mindfulness of and reflection on the three characteristics removes craving and attachment, it makes possible the development of compassion. But equally, in so far as various Buddhist meditative and ethical practices, such as the four *brahmavihāra* meditations and the practice of generosity (*dāna*), directly cultivate altruistic tendencies, they would presumably reduce selfish desire and hence one's own suffering. One would be thinking of and concerned about others, rather than miserably obsessed with satisfying one's own covetousness. In this way, the cultivation of a compassionate attitude might actually contribute to one's experiential understanding, that is, one's knowledge by acquaintance, that suffering can be stopped by cutting off selfish preoccupation. So, there is a reciprocity here – knowledge can support the development of compassion and vice versa.

Furthermore, in Chapter 3 I discussed the idea, found for instance in the thought of Buddhadāsa Bhikkhu, that insight into dependent origination might provide justification for selfless action. Seeing the interconnectedness of self and others, and that one exists always in relationship and reliance upon others rather than as an autonomous being, might provide the motivation for one to stop craving and become more interested in and compassionate towards other people and sentient beings generally.

There is a further link between compassion and knowledge. It seems clear that genuinely effective compassionate activity requires considerable understanding of what will actually help other people; there is often nothing more harmful than altruistic intentions coupled with lack of knowledge with regard to what people really require. So, an empathetic knowledge of people, a mindfulness of their genuine needs, must surely be required for the successful implementation of compassion. Buddhism clearly values such kindly awareness of others. The Buddha, after all, is seen as the 'Great Physician' and applies different 'medicines' depending on the specific spiritual requirements of his 'patients'. In order to do so, he must know what they actually require. In other words, the effective enactment of compassion requires an ability to see people's temperaments, proclivities and personalities accurately and to know what teaching or advice will be most helpful to them in their individual circumstances. I suggested in Chapter 3 that this is possibly the primary reason why the Buddha is often regarded to be omniscient. That is, his omniscience enables him to help all people appropriately, for he can always see precisely what they require. Whatever one thinks about the idea that someone might achieve omniscience, it is nevertheless true that as an ideal – even if quite unattainable – it highlights the importance of understanding others and their real requirements as a prerequisite for successful altruistic activity. It seems hard to dispute that compassion, in order to be useful, does require the cultivation of such empathetic knowledge. Compassion alone is not enough; in addition, it needs to be intelligent or wise.

Finally, it is important to note that in the Mahāyāna tradition there is a belief that, as the Bodhisattvas traverse the ten stages (*bhūmi*) of the path to complete Buddhahood, their insight into emptiness matures or deepens. It is thought that, in gaining deeper and deeper understanding that things lack inherent existence, these Bodhisattvas gain numerous magic powers, such as the ability to travel great distances quickly, to multiply their bodies, to speak all languages and even eventually to answer the questions of all sentient beings at once! (See Dayal, 1932, p. 80 ff.; Honda, 1968, pp. 224–5.) The point here is that these miraculous abilities can be employed to help other sentient beings more effectively. And it is knowledge of emptiness which gives rise to these powers, because, as the Bodhisattvas come to realize the merely fabricated nature of things, they gain mastery over them, being able to manipulate them like an illusionist at a magic show. Of course, it is a moot point whether such magic is really possible, and many might judge that here we have an example of an untenable pre-scientific belief in mere hocus-pocus. Be that as it may, it is clear that knowledge of emptiness is thought traditionally to give the Bodhisattvas these magic powers and thus increase their ability to enact their compassion effectively.

Knowledge and compassion – a discordant note

So, there are important ways in which knowledge and compassion can be supportive of one another for the Buddhists. However, it seems to me that the relationship is not entirely straightforward and that knowledge of 'things as they really are' is not necessarily always encouraging of altruistic endeavour. In particular, the Buddhist claim that liberating knowledge includes an understanding that there is 'no self' can pose some difficulties. Let me explain.

It might be that the knowledge of not-self means simply that the Awakened person sees that the self is not permanent and exists in dependence upon many conditions. In this case, such an impermanent, dependently originating self could presumably act compassionately towards other impermanent, dependently originating sentient beings. This seems uncontentious. However, Buddhists sometimes – particularly in the Mahāyāna *Prajñapāramitā* literature and Madhyamaka – appear to make the more radical claim that the teaching of not-self means that there is no self whatsoever. The self is an illusion, meaning not just that one has no permanent, autonomous essence but also that one's very personality and individuality are unreal. There is not even an impermanent, changing, dependently arising self. It is entirely a fabrication.

The implication of this position for the Mahāyāna Bodhisattva ideal, according to which the Bodhisattva works tirelessly for the Awakening of all sentient beings, is that the wise Bodhisattva would realize that, in reality, there are no sentient beings to help towards Awakening and, presumably, there is no one to help them! And yet the texts insist that these Bodhisattvas do act with compassion, though they realize that they are illusory and so too are the sentient beings that they aid. The *Prajñapāramitā* texts express this situation in what is surely an intentionally paradoxical manner:

> As many beings as there are in the universe of beings ... all these I must lead to Nirvana ... And yet, although innumerable beings have thus been led to Nirvana, no being at all has been led to Nirvana ... If in a Bodhisattva the notion of a 'being' should take place, he could not be called a 'Bodhi-being'. (trans. Conze 1958, p. 25)

It would appear, then, that for such Buddhists all sentient beings are simply phantasms and the Bodhisattvas are the only ones in this grand illusion who see that they and all other beings are illusions. And yet they continue to help all beings. They are, we can say, self-consciously illusory beings helping illusory beings who do not have this self-consciousness. The puzzle here is that, far from motivating Bodhisattvas to be compassionate, surely the Bodhisattvas' liberating knowledge would be more likely to undermine their compassionate motivation. For why should the Bodhisattvas bother to help beings they know to be illusions? What is the point of assisting beings who are known to be unreal and liberating them from a suffering which is equally illusory? The *Prajñāpāramitā* texts' use of paradox here seems to indicate that they recognize that this is a conundrum. No doubt these Buddhists might say that the Bodhisattvas' compassion is undiminished because they realize that the unreal suffering illusory sentient beings apparently undergo seems to these beings to be real enough! Perhaps. What seems indisputable, however, is that in this case the wise Bodhisattvas are motivated to be compassionate despite rather than because of their liberating knowledge that everything, including all sentient beings, is empty.

Knowledge and faith

Compassion is not the only key Buddhist virtue that has been somewhat neglected in this study. Buddhists generally also place great emphasis on faith (Sanskrit: *śraddha*, Pāli: *saddhā*) as necessary if liberation is to be achieved. It is commonly identified as one of the five spiritual faculties (*indriya*), along with energy (Sanskrit: *vīrya*, Pāli: *viriya*), mindfulness (Sanskrit: *smṛti*, Pāli: *sati*), concentration (*samādhi*) and understanding or wisdom (Sanskrit: *prajñā*, Pāli: *paññā*) which needs to be developed in order to achieve Awakening (see, for example, *Saṃyutta Nikāya* 5, 194–203, trans. Bodhi, 2000, pp. 1668–76).

Here *śraddha* is described as faith in the *tathāgata*, that is, the Buddha. It is best to understand Buddhist faith as 'confidence' or 'trust'. Thus, someone who has faith in the *tathāgata* has confidence in the Awakened person's teachings and also in the fact that he gained Awakening. This faith admits of degrees. That is, one can have great confidence or a trust which is more provisional. In Chapter 4 we have seen briefly why such faith is so important. Practitioners, in order to progress on the Buddhist path, need to have confidence in the way to Awakening taught by the *tathāgata*. This means that they must have faith in the Buddhist teachings and practices as efficacious in bringing about liberation from suffering. And they must also trust that human beings are indeed capable of cutting off their craving and attachment. That is, there needs to be faith both in the possibility of Awakening and that the Buddhist teachings can enable one to achieve it. Without such confidence, the Unawakened Buddhists would be left in the uncomfortable and frustrating position of knowing that craving and attachment cause suffering, but without any conviction that the eradication of craving and hence suffering is actually possible. In other words, the Buddhists must have faith that by making the required effort and undertaking the prescribed training liberation from craving and hence suffering can be achieved. Faith is here the great motivator. It is thus especially important at the beginning stages of the Buddhist path.

Paul Williams (1989, p. 215) has noted that faith is said to have the characteristic of 'leaping forward' and a mind with faith is free from the five hindrances of sense-desire, ill-will, sloth and torpor, excitement and worry, and, finally, doubt. As a state of trust in the Buddhist path and its eventual outcome, faith is able to stimulate, to push forward, practitioners in their endeavours, removing the hindrances that would otherwise sap their motivation. As I suggested in Chapter 4, such confidence would presumably grow as the practitioners' efforts on the Buddhist path bear fruit. (Of course, if the efforts do not bear fruit then faith might be weakened and eventually shattered.) This faith in the Buddhist path and in the human capacity to achieve liberation would, if Buddhism is right, culminate in liberating knowledge, when the practitioner would fully know by acquaintance that the Buddhist path does work and that Awakening is possible.

This account might give the impression that faith plays a preparatory role and is finally transformed into knowledge. In this case, once one has liberating knowledge, one would no longer need faith. Faith in the efficacy of the Path and in the possibility of Awakening is something one has when Awakening has yet to be achieved. It is a means to an end. Indeed, Williams (1989, p. 216) says that faith for Buddhism is preliminary and 'the first step of a process the end of which is wisdom'. He points to Nāgārjuna's statement, at *Ratnāvalī* 1, 5, that: 'Through faith one relies on the practices, through wisdom one truly knows, of these two wisdom is the chief, faith is the prerequisite' (trans. Hopkins, 1975, p. 17). Here it might be that faith is being construed as equivalent to a belief that one has only until knowledge replaces it. That is, one has mere belief in lieu of knowledge, like when I say that I believe that you are telling the truth rather than that I know you are telling the truth. If I come to know that you are telling the truth, the knowledge replaces the mere belief. I might say that I do not simply believe any longer because I now know.

However, at least according to many Buddhist sources, it is actually misleading to identify *śraddha* as a mere precursor to knowledge in this way. It seems more accurate to construe faith as the affective state of confidence or trust which is perfected rather than replaced by liberating knowledge. It is striking in this regard that the passage quoted above from the *Saṃyutta Nikāya* says that the Arahant (the Pāli form of the Sanskrit word 'Arhat'), who has achieved liberating knowledge, is one who has 'completed and fulfilled' the five spiritual faculties, including faith. Just as energy, concentration, mindfulness, and understanding or wisdom are perfected in Awakening, so it is with faith. Faith reaches its pinnacle or culmination with the attainment of liberation. Here confidence in the possibility of Awakening and in the Buddhist path as the way to Awakening becomes total because Awakening by way of the Buddhist training has been actualized and is attested in one's experience. In this case, faith is buttressed by liberating knowledge rather than being supplanted by it. Rupert Gethin (2001, p. 111) expresses this point very succinctly when he criticizes K.N. Jayatilleke's claim that in the Pāli Canon *saddhā* is belief that is eventually replaced by direct personal knowledge (*paññā*). Gethin comments that 'the relationship between *saddhā* and ... *paññā* is in fact more in the nature of that between two different but complementary factors' and, he goes on to say that '*saddhā* is the instigator of a process that culminates in *paññā* which in turn reinforces *saddhā*'. Knowledge and faith go hand in hand.

Knowledge versus devotion

There is, however, a quite different sense in which faith functions in some forms of Buddhism. The account of Buddhism I have given in this book has focused on Buddhism as a path of self-effort, where the practitioner achieves liberating knowledge through diligence, ethical conduct, meditation, constant mindfulness and so forth. Of course, the idea that liberation can be brought about through such self-discipline is an important current within Buddhism, and is clearly present from the earliest times. Nevertheless, as I mentioned in Chapter 1, it is not the whole story, and there are various Buddhist traditions – such as Pureland, Nichiren, Tantra and so forth – that place great emphasis on faith in and devotion to – and the need for the saving grace of – a transcendent Buddha or Bodhisattva who is thought to be still accessible and able to assist the devotee. Here faith is similar to *bhakti*, the loving devotion to a personal deity, that is found so commonly in popular Hinduism and also, known by other names, in other theistic religions.

While my focus in this book has clearly been on the liberating knowledge, and on achieving such knowledge in the context of one's own efforts on the Buddhist path, it is important to acknowledge that there is this very different conception of liberation – perhaps 'salvation' would be more appropriate here – in the Buddhist tradition. Here salvific faith replaces knowledge as the primary means to the overcoming of suffering.

Indeed, it might be wondered whether the Buddhists who stress the path of liberating knowledge have an overly optimistic view of human capacities for self-transformation. Whether human nature is such that the complete eradication of craving and hence suffering is attainable by one's own efforts is a debatable point. Does this vision of spiritual perfection through one's own efforts really take sufficient account of what often appears to be intractable human moral and cognitive imperfection? Is it not too sanguine in its claim that such imperfections can eventually be transcended by one's own endeavours? Is such an optimistic view of human nature and its potential for self-transformation really warranted? Might it not be that the helping hand of a transcendent power – be it a Buddha or God or whatever – is the only hope that human beings really have of finding eventual release from the mire of craving, ignorance and suffering in which we find ourselves? This is certainly the view of many religious traditions, including most forms of Christianity and also some schools of Hinduism such as Rāmānuja's Viśiṣṭādvaita Vedānta. And, as I have indicated, many Buddhists would agree.

The tendency to depend for salvation on the assistance of a transcendent, compassionate Buddha is perhaps especially pronounced in the Japanese Buddhist tradition of Jōdo Shin Shū, founded by Shinran (1173–1262), in which devotion to the eternal Amida Buddha, who has vowed to save all suffering sentient beings, is thought to be the only way to overcome one's suffering. This is because all attempts to gain liberation by one's own power (*jiriki*) are tainted by selfish pride, which is only eliminated by giving oneself up to the other power (*tariki*) of Amida. The devotees overcome their egotism and *hubris* by admitting that they are unable to lift themselves out of the mire of greed, hatred and ignorance because the very effort to do so produces conceit. In short, their devotion to Amida is a sign of and strengthens their humility. They give up the stubborn insistence on self-effort and release themselves into the helping hands of their saviour (see Bloom, 1965).

Liberation and human fallibility

Of course, there is another possibility. It might be that human beings are and will remain imperfect. Maybe self-effort will not achieve the eradication of one's ignorance, craving and suffering but neither is there any transcendent power to offer salvation. Perhaps there are no helping hands to rely on and to deliver one from craving and suffering! In this case, perhaps the best one might do is to acknowledge the reality of one's moral and cognitive imperfections and that they cannot be completely overcome – either by one's own efforts or through the grace of a higher power. We are thus simply trapped in the prison of our finitude with no prospect of escape.

This seems a long way from the Buddhism I have been discussing in this volume, with its emphasis on complete transcendence of ignorance and craving. No doubt some Buddhists might regard the claim that complete perfection is not possible as tantamount to 'giving up' and a recipe for laziness and resignation. But Buddhism has shown itself to be an adaptable and multi-faceted religion. Perhaps, then, some Buddhists might countenance the view that human beings are usually inescapably fallible. Indeed, there is a belief, which became widespread in Buddhist societies, that human beings have become degenerate and live in a time of moral and spiritual decline in which Awakening is no longer achievable. As Jan Nattier (1991) has shown, stories about the decline of the Dharma and the inability of latter-day human beings to follow the Buddhist path successfully have been common and influential in both Mahāyāna and non-Mahāyāna traditions. For instance, this belief manifests in Japanese society as the theory of the last days (*mappō*), that is, that we are in a final historical period in which humans have become inveterately wicked and society so corrupt that the effective practice of the Dharma and the eradication of craving are not realistic aims. Furthermore, there is a common Buddhist belief that Awakening, in the sense of the complete eradication of craving and ignorance, takes numerous lifetimes of sustained effort to achieve. The historical Buddha himself is said to have worked towards Awakening for many lifetimes, as recorded in the *Jātaka*s. And the Mahāyāna Bodhisattva path is often considered to take countless lives to complete.

It is arguable that such beliefs introduce a degree of realism into the Buddhist soteriology. At best, it is an extremely rare phenomenon for any human being to eradicate craving and ignorance. For most people it is not in fact possible (in this lifetime, at any rate) to achieve this liberation. The Buddha's Awakening functions here mainly as a 'regulative ideal', that is, it shows Buddhists which values – such as wisdom and selfless compassion – are important, though they are not expected, given widespread human weakness, to embody perfectly. In this case, a mature, responsible vision of 'the good life' would be one in which people endeavour to come to terms with their limitations and those of others, recognizing that complete perfection is not a realistic human goal.

This might seem a rather pessimistic conclusion, but maybe in its own way it could be a form of liberating knowledge. Knowing that moral and cognitive perfection is probably not achievable for them, individuals might be emancipated from the anxiety of pursuing unattainable ideals. Knowing that other people too are in almost all cases also incapable of such perfection, one might be liberated from judging them too harshly. Nor would one suffer the disappointment born from unrealistic expectations. Such knowledge might make the acceptance of human fallibility easier and also might foster forgiveness, both of oneself and others. Is this not possibly a valuable form of liberation? Maybe such a realization of our inescapable moral and cognitive fallibility is itself a modest form of Awakening, that is, a waking up to our true nature as imperfect beings. And, even if absolute perfection is unattainable, perhaps the Buddhist can still claim that some improvement is possible, and in the process one might make important contributions to society and the world. We are surely not condemned to function at exactly the same intellectual and ethical level throughout our lives. Nor is it the case that degeneration is the only possible change. It seems realistic to suggest that positive transformations, of a modest or even a significant variety, of the personality are possible. We can become better, kinder, wiser people, even if we will always have our foibles and shortcomings.

Does this relatively modest vision of human beings' capacities for self-transformation set its sights too low? And is it perhaps blind to the help that some transcendent source might give us? Or does it actually provide a realistic appraisal of the human situation? These are, of course, the central and existentially pressing questions. They are also questions which, unsurprisingly, this book can only pose and not answer.

Bibliography

Anacker, S. (1998), 2nd edn, *Seven Works of Vasubandhu. The Buddhist Psychological Doctor*, Delhi: Motilal Banarsidass.

Asaṅga (1966), *Bodhisattvabhūmi*, ed. N. Dutt, Patna: K.P. Jayaswal Research Institute.

Asaṅga, Vasubandhu (1998), *Madhyāntavibhāgabhāṣya*, in Anacker, S. (ed. and trans.), *Seven Works of Vasubandhu. The Buddhist Psychological Doctor*, Delhi: Motilal Banarsidass.

Atiśa (1981), *Satyadvayāvatāra*, in Lindtner, C. (ed. and trans.), 'Atiśa's Introduction to the Two Truths, and its Sources', *Journal of Indian Philosophy* 9, 161–214.

Bhartṛhari (1965), *Vākyapadīya*, in Iyer, S.K.A. (ed. and trans.), *The Vākyapaīya of Bhartṛhari and its Vṛtti*, Poona: Deccan College Monograph.

Bloom, A. (1965), *Shinran's Gospel of Pure Grace*, Tucson: University of Arizona Press.

Bodhi, Bhikkhu (2000), *The Connected Discourses of the Buddha. A New Translation of the Saṃyutta Nikāya*, Boston: Wisdom Publications.

Bodhi, Bhikkhu and Nārada, Mahāthera (1993), *A Comprehensive Manual of Abhidhamma. The Abhidhammattha Sangaha of Ācariya Anuruddha*, Kandy: Buddhist Publication Society.

Boord, M. (2001), 'Sacred Space', in Harvey, P. (ed.), *Buddhism*, London: Continuum, pp. 290–315.

Boss, J.A. (2002), 2nd edn, *Analyzing Moral Issues*, Boston: McGraw Hill.

Burton, D. (1999), *Emptiness Appraised. A Critical Study of Nāgārjuna's Philosophy*, Richmond: Curzon Press.

Burton, D. (2000), 'Wisdom Beyond Words? Ineffability in Yogācāra and Madhyamaka Buddhism', *Contemporary Buddhism* 1, 53–76.

Burton, D. (2001), 'Is Madhyamaka Buddhism really the Middle Way? Emptiness and the Problem of Nihilism', *Contemporary Buddhism* 2, 177–90.

Burton, D. (2002), 'Knowledge and Liberation. Philosophical Ruminations on a Buddhist Conundrum', *Philosophy East and West* 52, 326–45.

Cabezón, J.I. (1992), *A Dose of Emptiness. An Annotated Translation of the sTong thun chen mo of mKhas grub dGe legs dpal bzang*, Albany: State University of New York Press.

Cabezón, J.I. (2000), 'Truth in Buddhist Theology', in Jackson, R. and Makransky, J. (eds), *Buddhist Theology. Critical Reflections by Contemporary Buddhist Scholars*, Richmond: Curzon Press.

Candrakīrti (1960), *Prasannapadā*, in Vaidya, P.L. (ed.), *Madhyamakaśāstra of Nāgārjuna with the Commentary: Prasannapadā by Candarakīrti*, Darbhanga: Mithila Institute.

Candrakīrti (1970), *Madhyamakāvatārabhāṣya*, in La Vallée Poussin, L. (ed.), *Madhyamakāvatāra par Candrakīrti*, Osnabruck: Biblio Verlag.

Candrakīrti (1990), *Catuḥśatakaṭīkā, chapters 12 and 13*, in Tillemans, T.J.F. (trans. and ed.), *Materials for the study of Āryadeva, Dharmapāla and Candrakīrti; the Catuhśataka of Āryadeva, chapters XII and XIII, with the commentaries of Dharmapāla and Candrakīrti*, Wien: Arbeitskreis für Tibetishche und Buddhistische Studien.

Candrakīrti (1991), *Yuktiṣaṣṭikāvṛtti*, in Scherrer-Schaub, C.A. (ed. and trans.), *Yuktiṣaṣṭikāvṛtti. Commentaire à la soixantaine sur le raisonnement ou du enseignement de la causalité par le maître indien Candrakīrti*, Bruxelles: Institut Belge Des Hautes Études Chinoises.

Collins, S. (1998), *Nirvana and Other Buddhist Felicities. Utopias of the Pali Imaginaire*, Cambridge: Cambridge University Press.

Conze, E. (1958), *Buddhist Wisdom Books*, London: George Allen and Unwin.

Conze, E. (1973), *The Perfection of Wisdom in Eight Thousand Lines and its Verse Summary*, Bolinas: Four Seasons Foundation.

Cooper, D.E. (1999), *Epistemology. The Classic Readings*, Oxford: Blackwell.

Crosby, K and Skilton, A. (1996), *The Bodhicaryāvatāra*, Oxford: Oxford University Press.

Cutler, J.W.C. and Newland, G. (2000), *The Great Treatise on the Stages of the Path to Enlightenment. Lam Rim Chen Mo. Volume 1*, Ithaca, NY: Snow Lion Publications.

Dayal, H. (1932), *The Bodhisattva Doctrine in Buddhist Sanskrit Literature*, London: Kegan Paul, Trench, Trubner.

De Silva, P. (1991), 2nd edn, *An Introduction to Buddhist Psychology*, Houndmills: Macmillan.

Dignāga (1968), *Pramāṇasamuccaya, Chapter 1*, in Hattori, M. (ed. and trans.), *Dignāga, On Perception: Being the Pratyakṣapariccheda of Dignāga's Pramāṇasamuccaya from the Sanskrit fragments and the Tibetan Versions*, Cambridge, MA: Harvard University Press.

Empiricus, Sextus (1994), *Outlines of Scepticism*, trans. J. Annas and J. Barnes, Cambridge: Cambridge University Press.

Everitt, N. and Fisher, A. (1995), *Modern Epistemology. A New Introduction*, New York: McGraw-Hill.

Finnis, J. (1983), *Fundamentals of Ethics*, Oxford: Clarendon Press.

Foot, P. (1978), *Virtues and Vices and Other Essays in Moral Philosophy*, Oxford: Blackwell.

Forman, R. (1990), *The Problem of Pure Consciousness*, Oxford: Oxford University Press.

Frauwallner, E. (1973), *History of Indian Philosophy*, trans. V.M. Bedekar, Delhi: Motilal Banarsidass.

Gadamer, H.G. (1975), *Truth and Method*, New York: Seabury Press.

Ganeri, J. (1996), 'The Hindu Syllogism: 19th Century Perceptions of Indian Logical Thought', *Philosophy East and West* 46, 1–16.

Garfield, J. (2002), *Empty Words. Buddhist Philosophy and Cross-Cultural Interpretation*, Oxford: Oxford University Press.

Gethin, R. (1998), *The Foundations of Buddhism*, Oxford: Oxford University Press.

Gethin, R.M.L. (2001), *The Buddhist Path to Awakening*, Oxford: One World.

Griffiths, P.J. (1986), *On Being Mindless. Buddhist Meditation and the Mind-Body Problem*, La Salle, IL: Open Court.

Griffiths, P.J. (1994), *On Being Buddha. The Classical Doctrine of Buddhahood*, Albany: State University of New York Press.

Gross, R. (1998), *Soaring and Setting. Buddhist Perspectives on Contemporary Social and Religious Issues*, New York: Continuum.

Guenther, H.V. (2001), *The Jewel Ornament of Liberation by sGam.po.pa*, Boulder, CO: Shambala.

Hamilton, S. (2000), *Early Buddhism: A New Approach. The I of the Beholder*, Richmond: Curzon Press.

Harris, I. (1991), *The Continuity of Madhyamaka and Yogācāra in Indian Mahāyāna Buddhism*, Leiden: Brill.

Harvey, P. (2000), *An Introduction to Buddhist Ethics*, Cambridge: Cambridge University Press.

Hattori, M. (1968), *Dignāga, On Perception: Being the Pratyakṣapariccheda of Dignāga's Pramāṇasamuccaya from the Sanskrit fragments and the Tibetan Versions*, Cambridge, MA: Harvard University Press.

Heidegger, M. (1962), *Being and Time*, trans. J. Macquarrie and E. Robinson, New York: Harper and Row.

Honda, M. (1968), 'Annotated translation of the *Daśabhūmikasūtra*', in Sinor, D. (ed.), *Studies in South, East and Central Asia*, Delhi: Śata-Pitaka Series 74.

Hookham, S.K. (1991), *The Buddha Within. Tathagathagarbha Doctrine According to the Shentong Interpretation of the Ratnagotravibhaga.* Albany: State University of New York Press.

Hopkins, J. (1975), *The Precious Garland and the Song of the Four Mindfulnesses*, London: George Allen and Unwin.

Hopkins, J. (1996), 2nd edn, *Meditation on Emptiness*, London: Wisdom Publications.

Horner, I.B. (1971), *The Book of the Discipline Vol. IV*, London: Luzac.

Horner, I.B. (1990), *Milinda's Questions*, Oxford: Pali Text Society.

Hospers, J. (1997), 4th edn, *An Introduction to Philosophical Analysis*, London: Routledge.

Hsüang-tsang (1973), *Ch'eng wei-shih lun*, trans. Wei Tat, Hong Kong: Ch'eng wei-shih lun Publication Committee.

Ireland, J.D. (1997), *The Udāna and Itivuttaka. Two Classics from the Pāli Canon*, Kandy: Buddhist Publication Society.

Jackson, R. and Makransky, J. (2000), *Buddhist Theology. Critical Reflections by Contemporary Buddhist Scholars*, Richmond: Curzon Press.

Kant, I. (1965), *Critique of Pure Reason*, trans. N.K. Smith, New York: St Martin's Press.

Karunadasa, Y. (1967), *The Buddhist Analysis of Matter*, Colombo: Department of Cultural Affairs.

Katz, S. (1978), *Mysticism and Philosophical Analysis*, Oxford: Oxford University Press.

Katz, S. (1983), *Mysticism and Religious Traditions*, Oxford: Oxford University Press.

Keown, D. (1992), *The Nature of Buddhist Ethics*, Houndmills: Macmillan.

Keown, D. (1996), *Buddhism. A Very Short Introduction*, Oxford: Oxford University Press.

King, R. (1995), *Early Advaita Vedānta and Buddhism*, Albany: State University of New York Press.

King, R. (1999a), *Indian Philosophy. An Introduction to Hindu and Buddhist Thought*, Edinburgh: University of Edinburgh Press.

King, R. (1999b), *Orientalism and Religion. Postcolonial Theory, India and 'The Mystic East'*, London: Routledge.

Klein, A.C. (1998), *Knowledge and Liberation. Tibetan Buddhist Epistemology in Support of Transformative Religious Experience*. Ithaca, NY: Snow Lion.

Kochumuttom, T. (1982), *A Buddhist Doctrine of Experience*, Delhi: Motilal Banarsidass.

Lamotte, É. (1976), *The Teaching of Vimalakīrti (Vimalakīrtinirdeśa) from the French translation with Introduction and Notes (L'Enseignement de Vimalakīrti)*, trans. S. Boin, Oxford: Pali Text Society.

Lindtner, C. (1982), *Nagarjuniana*, Delhi: Motilal Banarsidass.

Lindtner, C. (1986a), 'Bhavya's Critique of Yogācāra in the *Madhyamakaratnapradīpa*, Chapter IV', in Matilal, B. and Evans, R. (eds), *Buddhist Logic and Epistemology*, Dordrecht: D. Riedel, pp. 239–63.

Lindtner, C. (1986b), 'Materials for the Study of Bhavya', in Kahrs, E. (ed.), *Kalyāṇamitrārāgaṇam. Essays in Honour of Nils Simonsson*, Oxford: Oxford University Press, pp. 179–202.

Ludwig, T.M. (2001), 2nd edn, *The Sacred Paths of the West*, Upper Saddle River, NJ: Prentice-Hall.

Matilal, B.K. (1986), *Perception. An Essay on Classical Indian Thought*, Oxford: Oxford University Press.

mKhas grub dGe Legs dpal bzang (1972), *sTong thun chen mo*, in *Mādhyamika Text Series vol. 1*. New Delhi.
Moser, P.K., Mulder, D.H. and Trout, J.D. (1998), *The Theory of Knowledge. A Thematic Introduction*, Oxford: Oxford University Press.
Nāgārjuna (1960), *Madhyamakakārikā*, in Vaidya, P.L. (ed.), *Madhyamakaśāstra of Nāgārjuna with the Commentary: Prasannapadā by Candarakīrti*, Darbhanga: Mithila Institute.
Nāgārjuna (1982), *Ratnāvalī*, in Hahn, M. (ed.), *Nāgārjuna's Ratnāvalī, Volume 1. The Basic Texts*, Bonn: Indica et Tibetica Verlag.
Nāgārjuna (1982), *Acintyastava, Lokātītastava, Yuktiṣaṣṭikā, Śūnyatāsaptati*, in Lindtner, C. (ed. and trans.), *Nagarjuniana*, Delhi: Motilal Banarsidass.
Nāgārjuna (1990), *Vigrahavyāvartanī*, in Bhattacharya, K. (ed. and trans.), *The Dialectical Method of Nāgārjuna*, 3rd edn, Delhi: Motilal Banarsidass.
Ñāṇamoli, Bhikkhu (1992), *The Life of the Buddha: According to the Pāli Canon*, Kandy: Buddhist Publication Society.
Ñāṇamoli, Bhikkhu and Bodhi, Bhikkhu (1995), *The Middle Length Discourses of the Buddha. A New Translation of the Majjhima Nikāya*, Boston: Wisdom.
Ñānananda, Bhikkhu (1971), *Concept and Reality in Early Buddhist Thought*, Kandy: Buddhist Publication Society.
Napper, E. (1987), *Dependent Arising and Emptiness. A Tibetan Buddhist Interpretation of Mādhyamika Philosophy Emphasizing the Compatibility of Emptiness and Conventional Phenomena*, Boston: Wisdom.
Nārada, Thera (1978), 3rd edn, *The Dhammapada. Pāli Text and Translation with Stories in Brief and Notes*, Kuala Lumpur: The Buddhist Missionary Society.
Nattier, J. (1991), *Once Upon a Future Time: Studies in a Buddhist Prophecy of Decline*, Berkeley: Asian Humanities Press.
Newland, G. (1992), *The Two Truths in the Mādhyamika Philosophy of the Ge-luk-ba Order of Tibetan Buddhism*, Ithaca, NY: Snow Lion.
Nhat Hanh, Thich (1987), *The Miracle of Mindfulness. A Manual on Meditation, revised edition*, trans. Mobi Ho, Boston: Beacon Press.
Nietzsche, F. (1999), 'On Truth and Lies in a Nonmoral Sense', in Cooper, D.E. (ed.), *Epistemology. The Classic Readings*, Oxford: Blackwell, pp. 180–95.
Norman, K.R. (1984), *The Rhinoceros Horn and Other Early Buddhist Poems*, London: Pali Text Society.
Norman, K.R. (1997a), *The Word of the Doctrine*, Oxford: Pali Text Society.
Norman, K.R. (1997b), *Poems of Early Buddhist Monks (Theragāthā)*, Oxford: Pali Text Society.
Nyanaponika, Thera and Bodhi, Bhikkhu (1999), *Numerical Discourses of the Buddha. An Anthology of Suttas from the Aṅguttara Nikāya*, Walnut Creek: AltaMira Press.

Powers, J. (1995), *Wisdom of Buddha. The Saṃdhinirmocana Mahāyāna Sūtra*, Berkeley: Dharma Publishing.
Rahula, W. (1959), *What the Buddha Taught*, Oxford: One World.
Saddhatissa, H. (1985), *The Sutta Nipāta*, London: Curzon Press.
Sangharakshita, Bhikkhu (1987), 6th edn, *A Survey of Buddhism. Its Doctrines and Methods through the Ages*, London: Tharpa Publications.
Śāntarakṣita (1992), *Mahāyānasūtrālaṃkāra*, ed. S.V. Limaye, Delhi: Indian Books Centre.
Śāntideva (1990), *Bodhicaryāvatāra*, ed. P. Sharma, New Delhi: Aditya Prakashan.
Shakespeare, W. (1974), *The Riverside Shakespeare*, ed. G. Blakemore Evans, Boston, Houghton Mifflin Company.
Smart, N. (1980), 'Interpretation and Mystical Experience', in Woods, R. (ed.), *Understanding Mysticism*, London: Athlone Press, pp. 78–91.
Spiro, M.E. (1982), 2nd edn, *Buddhism and Society: A Great Tradition and its Burmese Vicissitudes*, Berkeley: University of California Press.
Stace, W. (1960), *Mysticism and Philosophy*, London: Jeremy P. Tarcher Inc.
Suzuki, S. (1970), *Zen Mind, Beginner's Mind: Informal Talks on Zen Meditation*, New York: Weatherhill.
Swearer, D.K. (1997), 'The Hermeneutics of Buddhist Ecology in Contemporary Thailand: Buddhadāsa and Dhammapiṭaka', in Tucker, M.E. and Williams, D.R. (eds), *Buddhism and Ecology*, Cambridge: Harvard University Press, pp. 21–44.
Thompson, D. (1997), *The Mindful Way* (video program), Milton Keynes: Open University.
Tsong kha pa, *Byang chub lam gyi rim pa chen mo*, in *Collected Works* vol. pa. Bodleian Library manuscript.
Tsong kha pa, *Drang nges legs bshad snying po*, in *Collected Works* vol. pha. Bodleian Library manuscript.
Tuck, A.P. (1990), *Comparative Philosophy and the Philosophy of Scholarship. On the Western Interpretation of Nāgārjuna*, Oxford: Oxford University Press.
Ueda, Y. (1967), 'Two Main Streams of Thought in Yogācāra Philosophy', *Philosophy East and West*, 17, 155–65.
Vasubandhu (1970–74, 5 vols), *Abhdiharmakośa(bhāṣya)*, in Shastri, Swami Dwarikadas (ed.), *Abhidharmakośa and Bhāṣya of Acharya Vasubandhu with Sphutārtha Commentary of Acharya Yaśomitra*, Varanaṣi: Bauddha Bharati.
Vasubandhu (1998), *Viṃśatikāvṛtti*, *Triṃśikā*, and *Trisvabhāvanirdeśa*, in Anacker, S. (ed. and trans.), *Seven Works of Vasubandhu. The Buddhist Psychological Doctor*, Delhi: Motilal Banarsidass.
Walshe, M. (1987), *Thus Have I Heard. The Long Discourses of the Buddha*, London: Wisdom Publications.

Ward, K. (2002), *God. A Guide for the Perplexed*, Oxford: Oneworld Publications.

Werner, K. (1997), 'Non-Orthodox Indian Philosophies', in Carrand, B. and Mahalingam, I. (eds), *Companion Encyclopedia of Asian Philosophy*, London: Routledge, pp. 114–31.

Whitehall, J. (2000), 'Buddhism and Virtues', in Keown, D. (ed.), *Contemporary Buddhist Ethics*, Richmond: Curzon.

Williams, P. (1989), *Mahāyāna Buddhism. The Doctrinal Foundations*, London: Routledge.

Williams, P. (1998), *The Reflexive Nature of Awareness. A Tibetan Madhyamaka Defence*, Richmond: Curzon Press.

Williams, P. (2000), *Buddhist Thought. A Complete Introduction to the Indian Tradition*, London: Routledge.

Willis, J.D. (1979), *On Knowing Reality, The Tattvārtha Chapter of Asaṅga's Bodhisattvabhūmi*, New York: Columbia University Press.

Index

DATE DUE
